——Nimrod——

Darkness

in the

Cradle of Civilization

Steven C. Merrill MD

xulon PRESS

Acknowledgments

I would like to thank the following people for their support during the writing of this novel.

My son, Nathan, gave me the idea for the book and helped me in the initial research. He has been an inspiration to me and I hope his writing career will someday far exceed mine.

Shirley, my wife, has been a constant source of exhortation during the two long years it took to complete this work. Many times I considered abandoning the effort, but she encouraged me to persist. I am sincerely grateful to her. My 11 children have had to endure countless hours of time when their father toiled ceaselessly on the computer—time which could easily have been spent with them.

My dearest friend and brother in the Lord, Brian Harbert, reviewed the manuscript on numerous occasions, critiquing both grammar and content. His many suggestions have nearly all been incorporated in this work. I am indebted to him.

The pearls provided by a college professor of English and theater, Warren Robertson, helped to make this work palatable for readers of various backgrounds. His suggestions and encouragement were vital to complete this work. Thank you, Warren, for your assistance.

Ada Ezeokoli, my "adopted" daughter from Nigeria, has significantly helped improve my writing skills from her expertise as a journalist and writer.

Sheila Austin, an English teacher from my community, taught me how to write more like an 'author' and less like a 'Doctor.'

The proof readers, Linda Privette, Stephen Robinette, Nancy Schreiber, and of course, my mother, Shirley, who reread the book countless times till she had the novel nearly memorized. To all of these brothers and sisters in Christ, I am deeply grateful.

Preface

The people and the events portrayed in this novel are historically accurate and well supported by the Bible and extra-Biblical historical records. Some of that research will be highlighted in Part 2 of this book.

Many readers will be surprised to discover the true origin of ancient mythology. They will marvel at the thought that polytheism is not an evolutionary precursor to monotheism. Nimrod and his wife, Semiramis, established ancient mythology. They founded a religion that worshipped Satan and marketed it to people of the New World. Nimrod coerced the unwilling to accept it. The religion spread throughout the ancient world with the dispersion of mankind from Babel. Polytheism did not precede monotheism. It arose from the rebellion of this wicked duo. It grew from seeds of bitterness and bore wicked fruit directed against God and His followers. Their mystery religion deified men, women, and even nephilim from the antediluvian world. It embraced all that was evil in God's sight, including child sacrifice, prostitution, divination, and idol worship.

Many similarities exist between Nimrod's time and this present age. Civilization in the New World likely began in the Middle East—in present day Iraq. A plethora of inventions and technological advances occurred then, as now. Yet, man's achievements have never impressed God. The Bible rarely mentions them, but many Scriptures describe human depravity and wickedness. Pride, immorality, and idol worship never fail to move the wrath of a Holy God. His judgment at the Tower of Babel demonstrated this. Western civilization presently exhibits wickedness and moral corruption equivalent to this ancient civilization—perhaps even worse. An evil man (like Nimrod), motivated by rebellion and empowered by Satan, is about to step onto the stage of modern times. He will oppose God and bitterly persecute His followers. God's judgment will fall once again in the last days of the New World. He will destroy Babylon, the city of man, from the face of the earth in one final judgment of fire (Rev 17-18). Look up—the Lord's coming draws near!

Chapter 1

The Allegiance

The arrow zipped through the thicket, followed immediately by a loud bellow and rustling of leaves. Bushes parted and a huge boar with sharp tusks and bared teeth rushed towards its attacker. An arrow protruded from its left flank, but it did not appear to slow the charge of the angry beast.

Zzzing… another arrow flew towards its target, penetrating its right flank.

"A direct hit!" Nimrod exclaimed.

The boar tumbled and rolled over several times, dazed by the second arrow. It slowly stood on its feet and turned to face its attacker. It hurtled forward again, using its last surge of adrenaline.

Nimrod enjoyed this game of domination. He quickly drew his bow and let the third arrow fly from a vantage-point fifteen feet off the ground on a large tree branch. Zzzing…thud. The arrow found its mark in the back of the boar. Its churning legs stopped instantly, but its momentum hurtled it forward into the base of the tree where Nimrod was perched.

"That will teach you to charge the mighty Nimrod!" he

taunted as the animal took its last few shallow breaths with blood and froth drooling from its mouth. "Now you will suffer the flames of my wrath!"

A sharp bronze dagger made short work of the animal. Nimrod soon had its carcass suspended above the flames of the campfire.

Nimrod enjoyed the solitude of this wilderness near the Euphrates River, twenty miles south of his home city, Kish. Here he could escape unwanted attention from a growing reputation. He was not accustomed to fame at the young age of thirty-one. His father, Cush, was adept at meeting people and administering city affairs. Nimrod was not anxious to inherit that leadership. He preferred to command authority by strength—in the same way he controlled the animal kingdom. Compromise was for the fainthearted.

The leaves began to turn copper in the afternoon sun and cool breezes from the Euphrates fanned the fire. Flames leaped into the air, licking at the carcass as great droplets of fat dribbled onto the bed of coals. Black clouds stealthily smothered a clear blue sky. It seldom rained in the Mesopotamian Valley and Nimrod never recalled seeing dark clouds at such a low altitude. Fog descended from the clouds and engulfed the smoke ascending from the fire. Murky gray mist consumed all landmarks beyond the campfire. The earth shuddered, plunging him forward. The quaking stopped as quickly as it began but the tremor persisted in Nimrod's bones. Suffocating stillness pervaded the campsite and dread filled his soul. Nimrod had never feared terrifying beasts, nor had he cowered before men, but he sensed danger and felt powerless to combat it. The fire flickered twice then died, but rain and wind had not extinguished the flames.

"Lord, I sense your presence." Muted words fell from quivering lips and died in the silence surrounding him. "This day is sinister. I have never experienced such a dreadful sensation."

Silence lasted for what seemed an eternity.

"Nimrod, this world is my playground. I determine the rules and decide the winners and losers." The eerie voice came from nowhere in particular but enveloped him from all sides.

Hair on his neck and forearms stood erect like cactus needles.

"I am god, and you are my servant. Bow before me!"

Nimrod did not even have to will himself into a prostrate position. An inexplicable power pushed him to the ground—he tasted the dirt.

"You have never spoken to me in this manner, my lord. Wha, wha, what have I done?"

"Silence! It is time to claim my possession. The world and its inhabitants belong to me. One day I shall rule on His throne."

Nimrod did not respond. He dared not raise his head as the dark lord continued:

I am the morning star—the son of the dawn.
I will ascend to heaven;
I will raise my throne above the stars of God;
I will sit enthroned on the mount of assembly,
on the utmost heights of the sacred mountain.
I will ascend above the tops of the clouds;
I will make myself like the Most High.[1]
My dominion will prevail over the God of Noah.

Nimrod felt the words vibrating in the ground beneath him—his body absorbed the message.

"I have chosen you and given you my spirit. Together we shall conquer the world of men. They will worship me and submit to my authority."

"Have I not pleased you, my lord? I have always obeyed your commands—especially on hunting excursions."

"I demand your allegiance! You will crawl on the ground to follow me if necessary!"

The dark lord's voice softened—an alluring tone, more familiar to Nimrod.

"You will reap substantial rewards in this world by submitting to me. Your reputation will precede you to faraway lands. People will bow at your feet, and future generations will worship the name of Nimrod. Even the stars will portray your glory!"

"What have I done to deserve this?" asked Nimrod, shaking like a willow in a strong breeze.

"You have accomplished nothing without my empowerment!" roared the dark lord as wind swirled rocks and dust into the air. "My power has sustained you. Ferocious beasts fear my authority within you... as will the people of this world."

"What must I do, lord?" Nimrod inquired, rising from his knees.

"Bow before me—your face on the ground!"

Nimrod lunged into a prostrate position, afraid to move a muscle. He felt dizzy—on the verge of losing consciousness. He vomited but refused to move. The wind died and the chill subsided.

"You may rise to a sitting position, my rebellious one. Your name, Nimrod, is quite appropriate for my purpose," mocked the dark lord. "I am thankful your father gave you this name, for it will reveal your destiny."

Nimrod cautiously rose to a sitting position and observed the dying embers suddenly spark to life. Stiff joints refused to loosen after bowing in that awkward position. Frightening images appeared in the dark smoke rising from hungry flames.

"Follow my thoughts," continued the dark lord. "I rule many gods and they all obey my commands. Each of them is proud and strong. They don't need assistance from men to achieve their goals. Weak mortals of your kind must pacify them. Occasionally they grant men's desires if they are pleased."

Nimrod observed many faces in the black billows. Each face contorted into changing shapes and sizes. These leering faces had no substance as the smoke lifted them slowly heavenward. Nimrod feared them but slowly felt his strength returning. He continued to stare intently at the rising smoke.

"Powerful empires will rise and fall depending on the pleasures of these gods. Your kind must labor to appease them. Do you comprehend, Nimrod?"

Nimrod looked at the ground, "Yes, my lord... I understand."

"I am your lord and father." His soothing voice emanated from a gentle wind. "As I have guided you in your youth, so shall I lead you in manhood. You will hunt the souls of men—this is your purpose in the New World. Many will align with you and obey your commands. Satisfy their needs. Allay their fears. Form large hunting parties and go forth to conquer the world, building a vast Empire in my name. Your foremost enemies follow the God of your great grandfather, Noah. Hunt them and conquer their souls. You are mightier than their God because my power exceeds His. Destroy them if you cannot vanquish their souls. Do you grasp these instructions?"

"I apprehend them clearly, my lord and father."

Nimrod's confidence grew as he saw visions of fortresses, walled cities, and thousands of men armed with spears and shields ascending mountains of smoke—marching heavenward.

"I demand your allegiance!" the earth shuddered with the sound, and the fire died instantly.

Nimrod fell to the ground once again.

"I swear my allegiance. I p.. pl...place my life is in your hands."

A gentle breeze blew through the trees. He looked up to see the fire burning brightly once again. The oppressive black clouds lifted and quickly vanished. The blue sky darkened after a crimson fireball on the western horizon radiated its golden beams skyward. Stars gradually appeared after the sun escaped over the horizon. The boar's carcass finished cooking above the hot coals. Nimrod savored the meal, apprehending visions of gods and their exploits in the heavens above. He ate his fill and left the remainder for vultures to find the next morning. Nimrod did not sleep that night or the next day. He felt extraordinary strength surging through his muscles, and his senses grew keenly attentive to the environment. Nimrod began to formulate plans he would never have imagined several days earlier. Gentle breezes from the Euphrates River cooled the air, and a million pinpoints of light revealed their messages on the black tapestry above. After a second sunset, he finally drifted into a sound sleep. Peace prevailed in a naïve New World but an ominous silence robbed the night of all animal sounds.

* * * * * * * * *

Nimrod yearned to share his plans with his father. Surely, Cush would assume an active role creating the new Empire. Nimrod believed his brothers would also assist.

While washing before a morning meal, he heard a racket and growling near the cave where he slept. He ran to investigate the commotion and found a young leopard had ventured into his trap—apparently following the scent of the boar carcass. Nimrod had fashioned the trap from reeds growing along the riverbank.

"I shall teach you to hunt by my commands," Nimrod gloated. "You will learn to protect your master before feeding your belly."

After five days in the wilderness, he mounted a large black mule and returned home, carrying the caged leopard. He immediately began training it, and within several months the animal's loyalty amazed Nimrod's family.

"This leopard will help me track ferocious beasts and protect me from harm," Nimrod boasted to his brothers.

* * * * * * * * *

"Pray for your wayward brother and his family," Noah directed.

Shem grasped his father's twisted hand and they bowed on their knees with difficulty.

"God, my brother, Ham, and his family need Your guidance. Over two-hundred-forty years have passed since he left for Mesopotamia. We know you orchestrated that move, but Ham and his family took it so personally. They have never returned to visit us. I pray they would relinquish the bitterness that still dwells in their souls. I beseech You to reconcile our relationships after all this time."

Shem gazed at the stately mountain behind their large home then turned to look at his father's nine-hundred-year-old body, which seemed too fragile for the spirit dwelling within. He spoke loudly for Noah's deaf ears.

"Father, my descendants have brought news after traveling to the Mesopotamian Valley to trade their goods. They report Ham is still healthy and his descendants rule the cities of Mesopotamia."

Shem felt the ravages of time on his frail body of 350 years. His once curly black hair was now thin and gray. Knobby joints creaked and popped with every movement. Dark splotches tattooed his arms and legs from years of hard labor. Shem appreciated his mortality. He couldn't imagine how his father must feel, being 500 years older. Shem felt blessed, having spent a lifetime with his father. They shared a home in the mountainous lands, where they had lived since arriving in the New World. Hundreds of miles separated them from his brother's family in Mesopotamia—the land between the rivers.

"These majestic mountains remind me of God's omnipotence in a world of change."

Noah silently nodded.

Shem could see Noah's health had rapidly declined over the past decade. Clouded vision impaired Noah from recognizing his numerous descendants. Bowed knees and a crooked spine forced him to look at the ground as he shuffled along with the assistance of a cane. A long gray beard brushed his chest, and a leathery scalp crowned his head.

"Father, I am concerned about your failing health. Your unsteadiness may cause a dangerous fall someday."

"Crooked bones still manage to move me at a turtle's pace, and God's angels have prevented a serious injury these many years," Noah responded.

Shem assisted Noah into a chair under a large shade tree. They sat quietly, appreciating the snow-capped mountains that surrounded their lush green valley. Shem coveted the hour he spent each day with his ailing father. He hungered for the spiritual wisdom Noah had accumulated over nine-hundred long years. Noah's keen mind had not diminished despite the rapidly decaying body of flesh housing it. His mind stored a vivid tapestry of memories from both the Old and New Worlds. Not one human in the New World could boast the equivalent knowledge and godly wisdom of this man. Shem was amazed that Noah still spoke with clarity and insight despite his years.

"Father, my children inform me that life is much easier in Mesopotamia. Rich soil produces abundant crops, but significant challenges face our brethren there. Fearsome beasts roam the Valley, and the great rivers occasionally flood their banks, destroying crops and extinguishing lives."

"God did not promise an easy task, settling the New World. He only commanded us to populate the earth and have dominion over it," returned Noah.

"It appears Ham and his family have filled the Mesopotamian Valley with their descendants," remarked Shem. "Some of my descendants have even joined them."

"I am concerned our family refuses to move beyond that area. They prefer to dwell in Mesopotamia, living in the security of large numbers. Surely they realize this was not God's intention," declared Noah.

Shem had determined to honor his spiritual inheritance and uphold a godly testimony before men despite the difficulties of the New World. As high priest, he felt responsible to remind people of the importance of obeying God's commands. He clearly remembered the spiritual battle for the Old World. Although God had destroyed it by the Flood, He preserved a small remnant of mankind because of Noah's obedience.

"I understand your concern, Father. My children have also informed me Ham's descendants do not follow the God of our patriarchs. They seek other gods, fashioning idols according to their fantasies. My descendants in Mesopotamia have also lost their passion for God. They do not comprehend God's holiness. Less than three-hundred years have passed since the flood destroyed the Old World. Members of our family have short memories."

Shem admired the home he and his sons had built many years before. They had chiseled large boulders from the area into square and rectangular shapes, fitting them precisely together. This house dwarfed all other dwellings in the community and accommodated many visitors who often stayed with the family. He enjoyed the house and the surrounding mountains but would move in a heartbeat if God instructed him to do so.

Noah furrowed his wrinkled brow, thought awhile, and then responded: "These unfortunate developments grieve our Lord. Do you remember the words God spoke in the Old World as we cut trees for that huge ark? They echo in my memory as if spoken just yesterday:

> He planted a pine, and the rain made it grow.
> It is man's fuel for burning;
> some of it he takes and warms himself,
> he kindles a fire and bakes bread.
> But he also fashions a god and worships it;
> he makes an idol and bows down to it.
> Half of the wood he burns in the fire;
> over it he prepares his meal,
> he roasts his meat and eats his fill.
> He also warms himself and says,
> 'Ah! I am warm; I see the fire.'
> From the rest he makes a god, his idol;
> he bows down to it and worships.
> He prays to it and says, 'Save me; you are my god.'
> They know nothing, they understand nothing;
> their eyes are plastered over so they cannot see,
> and their minds closed so they cannot understand.
> No one stops to think,
> no one has the knowledge or understanding to say,
> 'Half of it I used for fuel;
> I even baked bread over its coals,
> I roasted meat and I ate.
> Shall I make a detestable thing from what is left?
> Shall I bow down to a block of wood?'[2]

My son, this was the condition of people living before the flood. I pray it will not recur in this New World. Our jealous God will not permit the worship of false gods. He promised never again to judge the world with a great flood, but He can judge mankind in many other ways."

Shem quietly pondered the teaching.

Chapter 2

Building the Foundation for Rebellion

N imrod fervently desired to share the wilderness experience with his father. Cush arrived home after a two-week visit to relatives in the city of Uruk, and Nimrod immediately accosted him.

"May I have an audience with you, Father?"

"I am weary from traveling, but we can sit in the first-floor meeting room to discuss our concerns," Cush replied.

Nimrod looked down at his father and felt proud to tower above him. Cush was one of the tallest and darkest men in the city of Kish—a man of high esteem throughout Mesopotamia. Nimrod considered the vast Mesopotamian Valley property of his family—the Hamites—descendants of his grandfather, Ham. They called themselves Sumerians and named the vast southern region of the Valley, Sumeria.

"My hunting adventure was a huge success, Father!"

They walked into the spacious meeting room, well lit by sunlight, then sat in beautifully carved chairs in the corner of the room.

"What dangerous animals have you removed from the

wilderness?" Cush asked, smiling at his son. "Can our citizens rest more safely in their homes?"

"I will not claim I have improved their security, Father. I did kill a boar and a lion with my new bow. I fashioned it from a hardwood tree by the river. It shoots arrows much farther than I can throw a spear. I wounded the lion at a safe distance with stone-tipped arrows that easily penetrated its flesh. Then I killed the beast with my spear. I prefer sharper bronze-tipped arrows. Can our metal smiths forge bronze arrowheads?"

"I am confident they can," Cush assured. "We shall visit them tomorrow."

"Father, astounding things occurred on my excursion! I have mined rich treasures of the gods!" An enthusiastic gleam in Nimrod's eyes revealed more than words could express.

"You talk in riddles. I am weary, and we have not yet had our evening meal. State your thoughts concisely, my son."

"The dark lord terrified me with his presence one night near the Euphrates River. He introduced me to gods who follow his commands. My lord revealed his plan to rule an Empire filled with the people inhabiting this world. He has chosen me to accomplish this vision and promised me the earthly throne of authority over his Empire. I shall lead expeditions of men hunting those who rebel against him, and my lord will protect me."

"Who is this dark lord, Nimrod?"

"He rules the gods and has dominion over this world. He has visited me countless times since early childhood. I never discussed it with you because I feared you would not believe me. At times, I even questioned my own sanity. I refused to reveal this to anyone until now. His appearances have progressively increased in frequency over the years. I could not doubt his extraordinary power—protecting me during dangerous encounters with terrifying beasts. He rescued me from certain death on several occasions. He has never failed me, Father. The dark lord has even revealed his plans to me. I cannot remain silent about him any longer. I am not ashamed to proclaim him to the world."

"Nimrod, I refuse to believe this nonsense. Faith in spirits has never benefited me. I remember when spiritual issues divided our family many years ago. My 'spiritual' grandfather cursed our family. Noah alleged God gave him those words, but I never believed him. He needed to justify granting the family inheritance to my uncle. We should focus upon more important concerns—maintaining our successful city and staying alive in this world. We do not need to look for spirits in trees and under rocks."

"I understand your skepticism, but my lord is real. If I do not follow him, another man will. I have vowed allegiance to him, and I intend to honor my word. We share similar goals, Father. You prefer to accomplish them with human intellect and hard work, but the dark lord will enable us to achieve loftier goals than you have ever imagined!"

"You sound like my grandfather, the preacher," Cush remarked sarcastically. "At least the message is different. Your idea stresses success and conquest of the New World. I like that emphasis, but I prefer to eliminate gods from the message."

"I cannot separate the message from the messenger. Someday you will comprehend this."

He realized his father did not know the dark lord and would never be persuaded by things he could not see or touch.

"Nimrod, do you remember your name means, 'to rebel?' Someday you will lead a revolt against the God of Noah."

"I thought you didn't believe in gods, Father."

"Noah taught me about his God when I was a child. However, if Noah's God exists, He has selected His favorites in the world, and our family does not number among them. I have achieved great works without His assistance. Furthermore, I am convinced we can become gods if we topple Noah's God from His throne in people's hearts. You will accomplish this in your lifetime."

"My lord created the New World, and he will direct me to lead this revolt according to his timetable."

* * * * * * * * * *

"We are a goal-driven family. Like this delicious fish, a goal is something that sits before you. You can smell it and see it, but you will never taste it until you grasp it between your fingers and place it into your mouth," Cush instructed.

Cush sat at the dinner table with his entire family. Across the table, Nimrod studied the faces of his younger siblings. Each of his four brothers and four sisters had mud-colored complexions, but none were as dark as his ebony skin. Several brothers and sisters had young children, and they were doing all in their power to suppress squeals and cries during their father's lecture. Nimrod was amused as they tried to listen politely with glazed eyes. They did not appear interested in 'grasping goals' that night. Nimrod was anxious to discuss topics of mutual interest with his siblings, but no opportunity availed itself.

"Furthermore," Cush continued, "you will never attain a goal by wasting time on things you cannot apprehend with your senses. You must steer clear of Sumerian superstitions. They will consume your time and prevent your advancement in life."

Nimrod knew his father generally refused to discuss spiritual topics in the family setting, despite the religious involvement of his children. Perhaps the revelation of Nimrod's spiritual encounter earlier that day was a fishbone that Cush desired to spit from his mouth. Nimrod remembered many occasions his father had reprimanded him for involvement in "foolish religious activities," but this was different. He had just turned the family time into an opportunity for expressing his own views. The entire family squirmed uncomfortably, listening to him rant on and on. Delicious hot fish and vegetables became unappetizing cold lumps on Cush's plate. Nimrod and the others had finished their meal long before. Nimrod finally interrupted the tirade.

"Father, have you lost your desire to taste the delicious fish our servants have prepared? 'Grasp a delicious morsel and devour it to nourish your hungry soul.'"

Cush ignored the remark and continued preaching. Nimrod had learned to avoid religious disagreements because he invariably received a severe tongue-lashing, but he could not hold his tongue that evening.

"Father, I believe some earlier event shaped your views on religion. You justify opinions with intellectual arguments, but you get angry when one of us offers a spiritual explanation. The gods provide adequate answers for many difficult questions. Why do you close your eyes to these realities?"

"They make no sense, Nimrod. Our hard-working people and their accomplishments demonstrate the greatness of this culture. Men will answer today's questions in several years with wisdom that fills the mind with understanding. We cannot fathom what mankind will achieve in future generations. I fully expect to witness famous men and women become the very gods imagined by people of this city."

"We obviously approach reality from two different perspectives, Father. I suppose we shall never agree on this issue."

"Good people explain reality differently, and disagreements are healthy, my son. I am convinced there is no absolute truth in this matter."

Nimrod let the topic die temporarily until the family left

the table. He then confronted Cush once again.

"Father, why do you detest spiritual topics? I perceive these intellectual arguments merely mask deeper feelings that prick your heart."

"Noah's God has caused nothing but trouble for our people. He destroyed every vestige of human and animal life in the Old World by the horrific flood. Industrious people of the Old World invented many things we simply take for granted.[3]

"They discovered the art of tent making and created musical instruments for entertainment. Our ancestors mined copper and tin, purifying them to make metal implements. They even combined these metals to make bronze, which has enabled us to create sturdy plows and other farm tools. Our ability to farm this land and graze animals came from the ingenuity of our forefathers. Noah's God destroyed them all."

The servants cleared the dishes off the table as Cush continued.

"I have already told you about the curse Noah's God placed on our family. Perhaps He will destroy us like He discarded people of the Old World, as so many pieces of driftwood floating upon the sea. If God even exists, He must explain His destruction of the Old World and the suffering He has caused in this New World."

Nimrod was curious to hear more.

"What other hardships did He create for our people, Father?"

"Noah and his God evicted us from our original home in the northern lands. He forced our large family to leave the cool mountains and move to the hot desert of Mesopotamia. We have suffered tribulation in this land, my son. Many of our children have perished from starvation and strange diseases. As you know, it rarely rains in Mesopotamia, but the Euphrates River often floods its banks on cloudless days without warning. Occasionally these severe floods destroy farmlands and sweep our people and their animals downstream in raging torrents—never to be seen again. These floods caused more damage in earlier years because we did not know they would occur. A 'loving God' never warned us."

Nimrod did not miss the sarcasm, but his father continued his list of grievances.

"We have designed our farmlands repeatedly due to the destruction. Even dikes do not hold back the floodwaters at times. Ravaging sandstorms once destroyed our tents and reed homes in this Valley. Our belongings were strewn across the desert on countless occasions. Only intelligence and willpower enabled us to survive these disasters. Fortunately, we learned to create bricks from abundant deposits of clay along the riverbanks. Brick homes have protected us from the terrible sandstorms. If Noah's God exists, He sent the floods and sandstorms to punish us. I have no desire to pursue a relationship with such a vengeful God."

"What bitter thoughts consumed you to give your first son a name meaning, 'to rebel'?"

"I suppose the contemptible curse of Noah's God influenced me, but I also attribute other unforgivable deeds to Him. He irreparably traumatized my soul at your birth."

Nimrod noticed beads of perspiration on his father's black forehead.

Cush continued without prompting: "You came from my loins, but my present wife did not deliver you. Another woman birthed you, and she would have gladly nurtured you. However, Noah's God extinguished her life, and I will never forgive Him."

Slaves had placed candles to illuminate the room. The family had gone to bed, but Nimrod was wide-awake—captivated by the story of his origin. He listened attentively as shadows danced across the wall.

"Please tell me about my mother."

"I married a beautiful woman and loved her dearly. She conceived shortly after our marriage. By the end of the pregnancy, I felt certain she would deliver two infants—her abdomen grew so large. The day of her labor finally arrived, and it began with regular gripping pains. I requested my mother, Marah, to assist, and she arrived as the labor intensified. While calming your mother, she said 'I eagerly await the birth of these children.'

"Your grandmother also calmed my anxious spirit as the contractions continued. She reassured me the labor progressed normally, but I felt a dark foreboding in the depths of my soul. The labor dragged on and on. Twelve hours later your mother wailed as the severity of her pains increased. I never left her side—not even to eat or drink. Finally, after a day of relentless labor your exhausted mother gave birth to an enormous child. You are large now, Nimrod, but at birth you were the size of three normal infants. Your grandmother held you proudly in the air... and then we awaited the birth of the second child. But that infant never came. Your mother lay limp on her bed."

Cush paused momentarily to wipe a river of tears from his cheeks, and then resumed: "Her labor ceased, but the bleeding continued. I noticed a steady drip from the side of the bed, and the pool of blood grew ever larger. The midwife held cloths against the bleeding tissues but to no avail. I can still see the huge gaping tears and blood flowing profusely until there was no more. It didn't take long. Your mother never awakened to hold her newborn son."

Nimrod had never seen his father so overwhelmed with emotion.

"Your grandmother never smiled after that day, and I could not speak for three days. There were no words to fill the void in my soul. You were right, my son. A root of bitterness expanded into that void which has consumed me ever since. Mother took you to my oldest sister, who had fortunately delivered an infant several days earlier. She nursed you for one year along with her child. I rarely held you because of the painful memories your presence evoked. I refused to share the pain with anyone. In fact, it was several weeks after your birth when I visited my sister and held you for the first time. My parents and other family members were there. As I cradled you, a name suddenly came from the depths of my despairing soul. 'The name of this boy is Nimrod, for he will rebel against the God of Noah,' I said. No one challenged me."

The bitterness of Cush was contagious. Its seed took root in the fertile soil of Nimrod's heart. He acquired a desire for revenge that would eventually blossom into full-fledged mutiny in the New World. He walked around the table and placed a huge arm around Cush's shoulders.

"My lord knows your pain, Father. He will help me avenge these terrible wrongs."

* * * * * * * * *

The next morning Nimrod found his father sitting alone in the large first floor meeting room of their home. Sunlight poured through eastern windows and illuminated the heads of many beasts, displaying a formidable array of teeth and claws. Nimrod had personally supplied these trophies from previous hunting excursions. Cush's pensive countenance contrasted the frozen fury of beastly expressions above him. He was obviously pondering an important issue, Nimrod thought. Perhaps he had more to share following last night's discussion.

"Do you fear dragons, lions, and tigers stalking in the wilderness?" Cush asked.

"They do not frighten me. I defeat them before they can attack. My lord protects me on hunting excursions and grants me authority over these animals."

"I am grateful the dark lord protects you, Nimrod, but you must also shield yourself from danger. You are a man now and it is time to reason like a man. Soon you will find a wife and have children. You will rule many people in the Mesopotamian Valley. You have the power to control your destiny. I shall give you a special item as part of your inheritance."

"What can you offer that my lord has not already provided?"

"Faith in the dark lord will not accomplish everything, Nimrod. I hope it will assist you in some situations, but maybe this article of clothing will confer additional protection and increase your stature among men."

"What is this item, Father?" Nimrod inquired, dubious about the protective ability of clothing.

Nimrod sat on a beautifully carved wooden chair and examined the walls, while Cush left the room to rummage through piles of clothing in an adjacent bedroom.

"Someday my appearance will strike fear in the hearts of people inhabiting this world, and I will not need fangs and claws to accomplish this," Nimrod muttered after studying the fearsome faces.

Cush returned several minutes later.

"Take this garment, my son," he offered, holding the item before Nimrod.

Nimrod had anticipated something much more unique. He carefully examined the vestment then said with a hint of sarcasm, "Father, I have killed a variety of animals and fashioned similar garments with animal skins. Keep this for yourself. I am too large to wear it."

"This unique garment has special properties, Nimrod," Cush replied with a sparkle in his eyes. "I also have its match, which you must keep for your future wife. These are not ordinary garments made from animal skins. Noah's God specially crafted them generations ago for Adam and Eve, after they ate forbidden fruit in the Garden of Eden."

"I cannot believe this superstitious tale, Father—especially from one who denounces such things! Weak men have perpetuated this myth! I recall your father telling the grandchildren this story years ago, but I never accepted it as truth."

"Well, Noah insisted the account is genuine—for what that's worth. God supposedly designed the garments to cover their nakedness. However, Noah maintained they also shielded Adam and Eve from severe weather changes and offered protection from wild animals bent on their destruction. These articles of clothing supposedly saved their lives on many occasions. Noah claimed Enoch wore this identical fleece until God took him alive into heaven. The garments were then passed to Methuselah, who lived longer than any other man in history—969 years! He died the day the Great Flood began, but not before he gave the vestments to Noah. Your great grandfather, Noah, transported them on the ark when God destroyed the Old World."

"What happened to them after that?"

"Your great grandfather wore the garment for special events in the New World. One such occasion occurred several years after the worldwide flood. I remember it well, even though I was only a child. Noah called for a grand celebration following the second bountiful harvest from his vineyard. He organized a wonderful feast, if I do say so myself. The men killed several oxen and goats then prepared tender meat for everyone in our large family. Women baked many loaves of bread from newly harvested grain, and my cousins gathered an abundance of fresh vegetables from the garden. Noah provided aged wine he had distilled from the previous year's grape harvest. He informed us the celebration was an appropriate time to wear the fleece, because we had successfully adjusted to the harsh conditions of the New World. Noah alleged his God had enabled the family to survive, but I knew that assertion was ridiculous!"

Nimrod perceived some cracks in the thick shell encasing his father's emotions. Cush had never discussed events of his early life with Nimrod. Now he seemed anxious to relate those experiences, as if trying to force open the door to a prison that trapped his soul.

"During the celebration Noah drank a large quantity of wine and was soon tripping over his fat tongue. He had not even considered the beverage might be more potent than wine of the Old World. Festivities lasted well beyond sunset, but Noah left the celebration early to lie in his tent. Soon the drunken fool fell into a deep stupor and became oblivious to the commotion. Your grandfather waited patiently until he was certain Noah had fallen asleep. He and your uncle, Canaan, quietly stole into the tent and gingerly removed the fleece. They also took the matching garment and quickly fled the scene. Canaan hid the garments in father's tent, and Ham ran to his brothers to mock the naked drunkard. Ham's disrespect angered Shem and Japheth. They hurried to Noah's tent and covered him with another garment, refusing to gaze at his nakedness."

Cush chuckled a moment then completed the story.

"Noah awoke the next morning, furious someone had stolen the fleece. The befuddled old buzzard deserved to lose the garment! Noah cursed our family even though he caused the whole affair. My father refused to return the garments and later gave them to me as the firstborn of our family. I have no use for them now, as I am getting older. You will live many years and must have adequate protection during the revolt you will someday lead—even more than the dark lord can offer."

"I shall gladly accept this gift, Father! I will consider myself blessed if it increases my authority over men and assists me to build a powerful empire."

"I hope it will assist you to accomplish these worthy goals."

Nimrod took the fleece from Cush and pulled it over his head. The material stretched easily to accommodate his huge frame. Noah's God had obviously made the fleece from several animal hides, but Nimrod could not identify a seam joining them. The vestment covered Nimrod's upper arms and extended to the knees. He walked outdoors into the sunlight, admiring the golden glow radiating from the garment. He thought it gave him a powerful appearance. The outside of the soft fleece seemed new, as if recently made from fresh animal skins. It certainly did not portray its ancient age. Nimrod felt the smooth, pliable inner surface and realized the fleece did not cause him to sweat—despite the hot day. It did not even smell of perspiration from the many men who had previously worn it. In fact, the fleece had a rather pleasing odor, not like any wild animal Nimrod had encountered.

"I shall wear this garment on my next hunting excursion," pledged Nimrod.

* * * * * * * * *

Nimrod planned a dangerous hunt to try out the new garment. The trip took several weeks to organize. Several citizens of Kish had reported a large reptile in the region—a terrifying dragon. People feared the ferocious beast. Rumors had spread that its lair was just up river from Kish. Nimrod and several skilled hunters fashioned massive spears for the hunt, and then they rode mules to its reported location. Nimrod wore the special fleece, providing him supernatural protection.

The mighty hunter easily tracked the beast by its colossal footprints, deeply indenting green grasslands adjacent to the Euphrates River. He located the enormous creature after several days of tracking. Nimrod found its nest filled with eggs— little reptiles would soon hatch to terrorize the community.

This dragon did not eat the flesh of men and animals. It was merely a gigantic plant eater. Its footsteps shook the ground like small earthquakes, and its large tail was the size of a generous tree trunk. The unique garment seemed to provide remarkable strength and courage, Nimrod thought. He fearlessly approached the reptilian giant. The dragon did not attack. In fact, it was a timid creature and tried to escape the frightening intruders. Nimrod carefully chose his positions to avoid being crushed beneath its mammoth feet. His terrified friends refused to join him under the creature's immense body. They watched the terrifying scene, marveling at the courage of this valiant hunter. Nimrod thrust the spear multiple times into its chest and neck.

"Look out Nimrod! The dragon is falling! Run for your life!" yelled his companions.

Nimrod used a spear to catapult himself into an adjacent ravine. The dragon crashed to the ground, uprooting full-grown trees. Its massive tail slammed the earth with such force that Nimrod bounced out of the ravine and into the air like a big black frog. The experience was exhilarating.

They could not haul the monstrous carcass to the city, so Nimrod beheaded the reptile and took one of her eggs as proof of the kill. People traveled miles into the wilderness just to view the slain carcass.

"Father, the garment gave me courage and made my hunt an easy task! The dark lord permits me to wear the fleece in future encounters with formidable beasts."

"I rejoice in your success, Nimrod. Someday your reputation will grow as a mighty hunter of men!"

Chapter 3

The Beginnings of an Empire

Nimrod found Cush cultivating the family garden several weeks later. He felt a strong urge to advance the dark lord's agenda that morning.

"Father, I have grown weary of hunting excursions. Perhaps I can assist you to improve our city."

"I welcome that suggestion, Nimrod."

"I have considered the protection of our people. Wild animals quickly repopulate and I cannot possibly hunt them all. A wall surrounding the city would better protect the residents. Many brick masons reside in Kish who can construct this wall. Apprehensive citizens would support the project if we convince them a high partition will prevent wild animals from entering the city."

Nimrod continued: "The people need additional temples to worship the gods. The temple of our chief god, 'An,' is the only place to worship in Kish. Other gods desire temples. The citizens will gladly serve these gods if we provide the opportunity. No one has taught them about Noah's God, so they have created other gods to address their superstitions. They believe the gods afflict them with diseases and produce mysterious floods that ravage the farmlands. City leaders could allocate land for these gods. Superstitious people believe they must bribe the gods to obtain blessings and ward off calamities. I am convinced residents will farm the land because this would encourage the gods to provide food, health, and security. These projects would employ many people and Kish will reap substantial benefits. Priests could collect taxes from worshippers and apply the revenue to make city improvements."

"I like your ideas, Nimrod. The part about the gods disturbs me, but it would not concern the elders. They are superstitious men like the people they govern."

Nimrod and his father met with the city elders that week. Nimrod was encouraged they adopted the new proposals, as Cush had predicted. They hired brick masons and work promptly began. Temples of worship were given foremost priority, and it took nearly ten years to construct them. Brick masons erected the temples near the city center, and they towered above homes and other buildings. The renovated Temple of An dwarfed the palace of Cush. A wall surrounding the rectangular city took six additional years to erect. Nimrod was impressed with the imposing wall and thankful it provided security for the people. Six strong gates made from northern hardwood trees were spaced at regular intervals around the city. A large road proceeded from each gate to the city center, where all major roads terminated.

Priests assigned temple worshipers to cultivate land for the gods. Farmlands extended for miles in every direction beyond the city wall. Fields of wheat and barley produced bountiful harvests. Grasslands grazed by sheep, goats, and cattle transformed the once dry landscape. Nimrod felt proud to initiate these changes for his people.

* * * * * * * * *

Early one morning, after completion of these projects, Nimrod found his father gathering vegetables and removing pesky weeds in a terraced garden behind their home. Nimrod smiled as Cush glanced up from his work.

"Good morning, Father. I have come to help you collect today's harvest."

He immediately began picking ripe fruit and vegetables. They labored silently until Nimrod felt the urge to speak.

"Father, you have witnessed Kish grow substantially since our masons built additional worship centers. Farmlands designated for the gods have netted huge profits. Priests have required minimal grain for sustenance. The remainder has filled large storehouses. Numerous grain shipments have allowed us to purchase valuable supplies for the city."

"I appreciate your counsel, Nimrod. Neighbors to the north and south are jealous of these achievements. Your fame and reputation have spread throughout the Mesopotamian Valley. Other cities strive to emulate our accomplishments and are currently constructing worship centers. I am puzzled that each city has different gods."

"People's needs differ from city to city, Father, and each city faces unique dangers. They worship gods who reflect the dangers they confront, but one lord exceeds them all. I know him and obey his commands."

"I am confident the city of Kish exceeds all cities of the New World. However, I am just as certain you have come to discuss other issues today. What are your real concerns, Nimrod?" Cush asked, smiling at his son.

"The dark lord has expanded my vision, Father. He plans wondrous projects to benefit the people of this world. He desires a worship center that surpasses the temples previously built for other gods. This temple will draw crowds from every part of the Mesopotamian Valley. My lord requires this structure in the capital of an empire that controls all cities of the New World. Hopefully, its influence will even extend northward to the land of your uncles' descendants. People will worship the gods in this magnificent temple. Of course, the dark lord will command the preeminent throne of adulation."

"Why do these visions of grandeur continually fill your mind, Nimrod? Kish has more problems than we can effectively manage. We do not have to look elsewhere for work."

"My lord has an agenda, Father. He has blessed my attempts to follow him thus far and has guaranteed me dominion over an empire. He has promised men will bow at my feet, worshipping me as god. My dream extends far beyond this city. You will also benefit by accomplishing this vision."

"Please explain."

"Our citizens have named you 'Bel,' acknowledging you as 'god'—the divine leader of this distinguished city. They proclaim you as their savior. I recommend the capital of the new Empire be named Babel. That name will also refer to me—'the son of god.' My lord created me to receive praise from men. Your relatives in the northern lands will know 'Babel' as the 'gate of god.' Perhaps Shem's followers will think we exalt their God and then join us in this venture. The priests will discretely lead the worship of deities in Babel. I propose we employ laborers and brick masons to build this magnificent city."

"Nimrod, the task of building this city will overwhelm us. I believe these fantasies exceed your sense of reality. Do you remember the wall around this city required a vast number of laborers to construct it? This enormous city of yours would demand thousands of brick masons and laborers. Although Kish has grown to more than thirty-five-thousand people, its population is laughably small for supplying such a workforce. We could not possibly provide the basic needs of this city if thousands of its citizens were assigned to work on this 'dream' of yours."

Nimrod expected resistance from his father, but it did not deter him.

"I have considered these problems, Father, and I realize construction of Babel will require many thousands of workers. I intend to convince leaders of other Sumerian cities to join us in this endeavor. We can incorporate their gods into a new religion. Residents of these cities would surely desire unification under one religion. Can you imagine the power one religious system will confer to a government ruling the Empire? Noah, Shem, and their God would have great difficulty dealing with such a rebellion. Perhaps this will render Noah's God obsolete... and that would be so unfortunate," Nimrod remarked sarcastically.

Nimrod knew he had captured his father's attention.

"Send me as ambassador to forge an agreement with leaders of each city in this Valley. Uruk is a four-day journey from here and its population exceeds Kish. Surely, I can convince its elders the project will reap numerous benefits for them. Other cities would cooperate if our two large cities spoke with one voice. They would provide the labor force necessary to complete this project. I have determined we can easily recruit sixty-thousand laborers. Constructing Babel and its magnificent temple will bring people of the New World together. They will live in harmony under a new religious system and a central government."

"Have you considered the possibility they will not cooperate with this fantasy, my son?"

"I have considered it."

"What have you planned when your vision meets resistance?" probed Cush.

"My lord has given me the power to deal with that eventuality."

"I do not have the time or desire to begin this new venture with you. Vital needs of Kish require constant attention. If this project is important, the burden to complete it must fall squarely upon your shoulders. Do you understand?"

Nimrod paused momentarily then responded: "I understand, Father."

He left the room confident the argument had swayed his father. He would now discuss the specific details with the dark lord. Nimrod felt invincible. Enemies might arise but no mortal flesh could derail this wondrous vision.

Of all cities in the Mesopotamian Valley, Uruk was the most populous, and Nimrod determined to visit its ruling elite. Residents of Uruk worshipped several gods and called them 'nephilim,' meaning 'those who come from heaven to earth.' They believed the nephilim protected them from danger. However, Nimrod knew the power of his god surpassed the nephilim, and he did not fear facing leaders of a city which dwarfed his own. The dark lord had already guaranteed the success of this mission. Nimrod's reputation as a mighty hunter had earned him fame throughout the Mesopotamian Valley. Now he would magnify that reputation as a hunter of men's souls.

* * * * * * * * *

One morning Shem and his family gathered for worship in the large meeting room of Shem's house. His son, Arphaxad, and many grandchildren sat at the feet of Shem. The room had a high vaulted ceiling and was illuminated by sunlight streaming through east-facing windows. Shem appreciated the warm light on that chilly morning.

"Father, have you heard our brothers in the south worship false gods?" asked Arphaxad. "They have erected elaborate temples to commemorate their deities. People call them, 'nephilim.' Does this concern you?"

"Yes, my son, this news should disturb all of us. Your grandfather and I have discussed these ominous developments. Ham's descendants have even fashioned idols to these 'gods.' My heart grieves because of their intentional rebellion against God. Even members of our family worship these nephilim without considering the consequences that will inevitably follow."

"We must end this nonsense!" Arphaxad declared.

Shem hesitated before responding to Arphaxad's impulsive comment.

"Observe the great stones comprising the walls of this room, my son. They are strong and substantial. Our Lord made them and they portray merely a particle of His omnipotence. God will guide us to effectively deal with this problem. He intervenes in the affairs of men according to His timetable."

"These stones just sit and do nothing."

"Ah... but they perform a mighty work in their silence. Imagine the massive structure they support. Dark developments in this New World worry all of us, Arphaxad, and God does not turn His head from these sinful acts. We must patiently trust God until He directs us to respond. He waited quietly for many years before destroying the Old World. God informed Noah of His pending judgment one hundred years before the flood ever occurred. Those hundred years passed very slowly. People mocked our family and close relatives even ridiculed us. God is long-suffering, and He always allows ample time for repentance. Our finite minds desire to intercede in difficult times, but God's agenda does not coincide with ours. We must not execute judgment on our brothers because we are dismayed with the current state of affairs. God's right arm of justice will correct this problem at the appropriate time."

"Is God grieved by what is happening?" asked Arphaxad.

"He mourns continuously over the evil behavior of mankind. My father, Noah, once shared these words God spoke to him in the Old World:

My heart is filled with great pain. I will wipe mankind, whom I have created, from the face of the earth—men and animals, and creatures that move along the ground, and birds of the air—for I am grieved that I have made them.[4]

God saved a remnant of humans for this New World because of your grandfather's faithfulness. We must trust the Lord as Noah did in those days. Our holy God will not let the world continue its present course."

Shem continued his teaching: "Noah transported the Holy Scriptures on the ark to the New World. God directed Adam, Seth, and other patriarchs of the pre-flood world to write the material in these texts. Father and I frequently study them. Ham and Japheth have refused to consult the records despite the fact our father has made them available. I can still remember Ham's remarks several months prior to leaving for Mesopotamia. 'My family will make their own history in the New World. They do not need to know Old World history,' he said. However, I have found a wealth of valuable information in these manuscripts. I vividly recall the wickedness present before the flood. If we do not know the history of our sins, we will repeat them in succeeding generations. Sacred writings from our forefathers give us remarkable insight concerning present world conditions. We must commit these writings to memory. Sinful desires clamor for our attention like in the days of our forefathers. This has not changed.

"I hope my children and grandchildren grasp this wisdom."

"That will depend on you, my son. You must mentor them in the ways of our Lord. If you fail, the evil one will shape their thoughts in the very next generation.

"I would like to read you a brief passage from the ancient text. It suggests the wickedness of the Old World has returned to spoil the innocence of God's New World.

> When men began to increase in number on the earth and daughters were born to them, the sons of God saw that the daughters of men were beautiful, and they married any of them they chose. Then the Lord said: 'My Spirit will not contend with man forever, for he is mortal; his days will be a hundred and twenty years.' The nephilim were on the earth in those days—and also afterward—when the sons of God went to the daughters of men and had children by them. They were the heroes of old, men of renown.[5]

I vividly remember those days. My brothers, Ham and Japheth, remember them also. Nephilim were terrible creatures—gigantic offspring of women and demonic angels. They wielded great power on the earth and followed commands of the evil one. They consolidated control of the world's population under Satan in the years preceding the Flood. Men obeyed them and cowered in their presence. Now we hear testimony our relatives worship these nephilim and the angels who produced them. People bow before them as gods! Our Lord detests this abomination!"

"Can you tell us more about the nephilim, Father?" asked Arphaxad.

"God originally created angels to obey His commands and serve humans in this world. Satan persuaded a third of the angels to follow him, and then God cast them from His heavenly domain. Some of these demonic spirits produced the nephilim who corrupted the Old World. The name nephilim means, 'to be cast down.' God severely judged the nephilim and destroyed them in the floodwaters of His wrath. He bound the demonic angels who produced them with everlasting chains in eternal darkness—a prison called

Tartarus. He will judge them on the great Day of His Wrath—when this world ends."[6]

"Allow God's Spirit to anchor this teaching in your minds," Shem concluded.

They continued to discuss the plight of the New World. Thereafter, they worshipped the One True God and sacrificed an unblemished ram for their sins, according to the custom of Noah and his fathers. Arphaxad slit the ram's throat and poured its blood over a stone altar behind Shem's house. He burned the fat and entrails on the altar. The family sang hymns and asked God's forgiveness for their sins. They petitioned God to convict the wicked souls inhabiting the New World and prayed for their repentance.

* * * * * * * * *

Nimrod traveled four days on a black mule to Uruk. He rode directly to the city center and tied the mule in front of a large brick building used for city administration. He knew the elders met there to discuss city business. Nimrod paused to caress the impressive sculptures of Uruk's gods, sitting outside the entrance.

"So you are the gods who direct the affairs of this city," spoke Nimrod. "My lord also has business here."

The administration building and the temple of the chief god, An, faced each other from opposite sides of the city center. Nimrod ascended several flights of stairs to a large meeting room, where he found the city leaders convened around a carved wooden table. Nimrod strode into the room without an invitation. Morning sunlight streamed through eastern windows, casting long shadows across the room. The leaders were startled by the sudden appearance of this huge black man. Nimrod impaled the floor with a large bronze spear and glared at the elders.

"My friend, why have you rudely interrupted this meeting?" asked one of the elders. "We have an agenda of important topics to discuss."

The elders gazed at the imposing figure who towered several feet above them. They were mesmerized by the golden fleece and the huge shadow that darkened the room.

"I bring a worthy proposal to invigorate this meeting. My intentions are peaceful, if that is your desire. I am Nimrod, son of Cush. I come from the well-known city of Kish, named after my father. Our citizens know him as Bel."

"We are familiar with your famous father," remarked another elder. "In fact, he is closely related to the founders of our distinguished city."

"Your reputation also precedes you, Nimrod," affirmed a third elder, beginning to warm up to the intruder. "The Sumerian people recite your hunting exploits throughout this Valley. What brings you here today?"

"My father and the gods have sent me to extend our vision to this great city. The gods have commissioned me to unify these cities as the beginning of one magnificent Empire."

"What are you talking about?" interrupted the first elder. "Our cities are large and productive. They satisfy the people's needs and the gods' desires. Combining them is not necessary, as you suggest. We are at peace and this Valley offers multiple resources to move in the direction of our choosing."

Nimrod expected this response from leaders of a city that more than rivaled Kish.

"The gods have ordained me to unite these cities, and I intend to obey them. They desire a lofty dwelling where all the people of Mesopotamia can worship them. Small temples in the cities are not sufficient. The gods have blessed us with more than we need to sustain our lives. They now require sacrifices from the people they unselfishly serve. We must demonstrate appreciation for them."

"Who are you to presume the gods' desires?" asked the second elder.

"I am Nimrod—'the powerful and exalted one.' The gods communicate their desires directly to me, and they have given me authority to accomplish their commands."

The city leaders quietly deliberated for several minutes.

"Grant us time to reach a decision," replied the first elder. "We must consider the needs of Uruk before agreeing to this enormous project. You may stay here and return in three days for an answer. You will find the people very accommodating."

Nimrod pondered their request.

"The gods wait impatiently for our obedience. They prefer immediate results to their demands. Nevertheless, I shall return in three days, as you request. Be ready with an answer at that time."

He left the room after scowling at them for several seconds then exited the building into the heat of the morning sun.

Nimrod decided to examine Uruk over the next several days. He explored several areas of the community. The white temple of An initially captured his attention. Its stunning appearance contrasted the brown brick buildings surrounding it. The huge oval-shaped temple sat on an elevated platform of bricks. Several imposing statues of An guarded the entrance. Nimrod bowed before one of the statues.

"I am honored to worship in your temple, my lord. I ask you to bless my activities in this city."

The stone statue did not speak, so Nimrod walked through the temple entrance and noticed a copper-sheathed lintel several feet above him. It was embellished with three-dimensional figures of bulls and lions. Brightly colored clay cones adorned the interior walls. Artisans had plastered them in a mosaic pattern and covered some with bronze sheaths. An imposing altar sat in front of a rectangular sanctuary. Nimrod knew animal and infant sacrifices were regularly

offered to An. Oil lamps and candles illuminated the sanctuary. All wide avenues of Uruk led to this temple—the most
magnificent building of the entire city.

Nimrod had many relatives in Uruk. Several had previously hunted with him. He decided to visit one—a close
friend in adolescence. He finally found the home of his
cousin, Annuki, as the dying embers of a setting sun gave
their last light. A small plot of land surrounded the modest
brick home. Some of it was tilled for spring planting.
Several large fig trees shaded the front yard.

"Annuki, I have not seen you in years!" Nimrod smiled
as he greeted him at the front entrance.

He observed Annuki had grown considerably over the
years, but Nimrod still looked down to meet his brown eyes.
An abundance of black curls bounced upon Annuki's tanned
muscular shoulders.

"I see you are married and have children! Have you for-
saken the exciting adventures of our youth?" Nimrod asked
playfully.

"Yes, I sorely miss those hunting excursions," Annuki
admitted, "but I consider it a serious responsibility to support a wife and four children. I cultivate fields of the gods
and have a small garden here. I hunt small game to feed my
family but lack the courage for hunting large flesh-eating
animals. Only you, my cousin, boldly face the dangerous
beasts, according to the rumors I hear."

"Large animals fall like the smaller ones when using my
new weapons, Annuki. The thrill of the hunt still excites me.
I feel strong as ever and do not fear the huge beasts."

"Please come into my home. Many things have happened over the years, and we have much to share. Can you
stay for several days?"

"I can indeed! I desire to meet your family. Perhaps we
can visit several relatives while I am in Uruk."

They sat at the table for a generous dinner. Annuki's

children also joined them. His wife served bread, steaming vegetables, wild game, and a bowl of figs.

"My four children range from three to twelve years old. The boys are older. Describe these hunting weapons you have created. My sons will enjoy hearing about them."

Nimrod noted the boys' wide eyes fixed on his every move.

"The heavy spears of old are now much lighter. I fashion their tips with bronze instead of stone. I have also created a lightweight, springy bow from a hardwood tree near the Euphrates. I fastened a thin, tightly woven rope to its ends and carved arrows from the same hardwood, capping them with bronze tips. They strike distant targets with deadly precision—after some practice, of course. I don't get dangerously close to the large beasts until the arrows have seriously wounded them. Finishing the work with my spear is then a simple matter. Arrows often kill the beast, rendering the spear unnecessary."

"That sounds exciting! Can you show us how to shoot arrows with the bow?" asked the oldest son.

"I shall teach this skill to you tomorrow morning. We will also invite your father and brother to join this new game with us."

The boys squealed in delight.

"Nimrod, what exploits besides hunting have you undertaken these past few years?" asked Annuki.

Nimrod had hoped for an opportunity to share new revelations from the dark lord.

"Annuki, my hunting adventures pale in comparison to other developments in my life. I have conversed with the gods—even the king of gods!"

"Gods don't bother with mere men! How can you make such claims?"

"The dark lord has communed with me since childhood. How do you suppose I slayed the giant dragons? My strength was inadequate for these remarkable deeds! The dark lord assisted me. In childhood he treated me gently, like a father would handle his son. Recently, however, he has greeted me with a stern countenance—even dreadful at times. He has planned remarkable things for me, Annuki. He claims the New World as his domain and demands total control of its inhabitants."

"Please explain further."

Nimrod was surprised Annuki desired to know the secrets of darkness.

"My lord is the most powerful deity. He claims the throne of the heavens and commands the gods to do his bidding. I have seen the faces of many of them during my encounters with the dark lord. He has unveiled plans for the New World in a series of revelations. He desires the creation of a vast Empire, which will subjugate all humans of this world. He demands his own temple of worship, far exceeding anything we have constructed for the gods. This temple will sit in the capital of the new Empire. We have named the capital, Babel, which means 'the gate of god.' The dark lord instructed me to accomplish this for him."

"I have never heard of Babel."

"Only because it is not yet built," laughed Nimrod. "This glorious project looms before us, my friend. I have envisioned its location between Uruk and Kish. Babel will surpass these two cities in size and magnificence. People from other cities in this Valley will make pilgrimages to the majestic worship center. The laborers required to build Babel will number at least sixty thousand. We must recruit them from each city in Mesopotamia. My lord commands it, Annuki. Will you join me in this noble endeavor?"

"I don't know how to respond to such a question."

The response dismayed Nimrod.

"You must stand with me, or you will oppose me!" retorted Nimrod, intimidating Annuki for the first time.

"Then I shall stand with you, my cousin. How can I assist in this extraordinary project?"

"Help me recruit the people of Uruk for this cause," Nimrod instructed, grateful his friend had a quick change of heart. "I have already spoken to the city elders about the plan. I sense resistance and intend to challenge them if necessary."

"Do the citizens of Kish support you?" Annuki asked dubiously.

"My father endorses the vision. He rules as King of Kish, and the people obey him. I am certain the city leaders will also back him."

Annuki sat quietly, contemplating the information. Nimrod did not interrupt his thoughts.

"I believe we should rally our family in Uruk," offered Annuki. "We have thousands of relatives here. They can assist us to unify the remaining population."

"That is a good plan. We will visit them over the next two days, but I must leave afterwards. You can gather additional support after my departure. I need a good night's rest. We shall begin this project in the morning."

They awoke early and ate the delicious breakfast Annuki's wife had prepared. True to his word, Nimrod taught Annuki and the boys to shoot arrows. Annuki and his older son became quite proficient hitting a target fifty feet away. The target was an old tunic Nimrod had discarded. He painted a square on the tunic and nailed it to a tree.

"When you improve your accuracy we will go hunting," Nimrod promised.

He knew the boys enjoyed this new sport. Nimrod gave the bow and arrows to Annuki's oldest son.

"I will allow you ample time to practice before we hunt the dangerous prey," he teased.

* * * * * * * * *

Nimrod and Annuki left the house to visit influential relatives in the city. Most were religious and supported Nimrod's vision.

"I think you might find strong support among the religious people of this community," suggested Nimrod after meeting with several of them.

"I agree, and I will arrange to meet with many of them after you leave Uruk."

They strolled through wealthy neighborhoods of the city. Nimrod was enamored with many impressive buildings occupying the center of Uruk—especially the government buildings and spacious dwellings for city officials. All had flat roofs and walls constructed with brown bricks. Unique architectural features embellished each of them.

"There must be thousands of brick structures in Uruk. Where does the clay originate to build all of these structures?"

"Abundant clay reserves near the Euphrates River have provided the material for these buildings," Annuki replied.

"The architecture fascinates me and I will remember it when commencing the construction of Babel."

Nimrod observed donkeys pulling carts loaded with produce on the main thoroughfares of Uruk.

"These carts glide upon round pieces of wood!" Nimrod exclaimed. "I have never seen this invention."

"Two pieces of wood, rounded into semicircular patterns, form the wheels. Leather straps fasten them securely around the ends of a wooden axle. Two long axles rotate beneath each cart. The invention is actually very simple," Annuki remarked.

"Sumerians have used mathematics to create circular wheels," he continued. "Are you familiar with the potters' wheel? It has revolutionized Sumerian culture and provided high quality pottery for the common people. It was created using the same mathematical concepts."

"I am not familiar with how pottery is made. I suppose I

have taken its existence for granted."

"Mathematicians and astrologers have devised our calendar, which addresses the farming needs of the people. They developed this by studying movements of the stars, moon, and sun. The calendar allows us to calculate the time for planting and harvesting. It has improved the yield of grain and vegetables."

"You talk like a true farmer," laughed Nimrod.

Nimrod proudly considered the accomplishments of his people.

"Descendants of Shem and Japheth cannot claim these accomplishments," he boasted.

They departed from the city center and strayed off the main roads to neighborhoods housing the common people. They lived in small brick dwellings packed together along narrow streets.

"Ugh...this is disgusting," Nimrod muttered. "I cannot believe anyone would live along roads littered with garbage and human excrement. Slaves and worthless people populate these areas. I would live in neighborhoods closer to the city center, where the roads are wide and clean. The gods look favorably upon intelligent individuals dwelling in those areas and have blessed them with large homes, gardens, and spacious courtyards."

"I number among those blessed individuals, and I am thankful," Annuki remarked.

Annuki continued the guided tour of Uruk, pointing out interesting sights.

"Observe the vast stretches of farmland surrounding the city, which are dedicated to the gods. A variety of crops grow on this rich land and peasants busily cultivate the fields."

"I can also see a multitude of sheep, cattle, and goats grazing pastures southeast of here," replied Nimrod. "Indeed, the gods have richly blessed the citizens of Uruk, but I feel more secure in Kish. Despite its impressive size,

Uruk is vulnerable to attack—no wall surrounds this city."

"Do you believe cities need walls around them?" Annuki asked.

Nimrod pondered the conquests of ancient warriors of the Old World. People of the New World had never experienced war.

"I remember stories grandfather Ham told me about the remarkable warriors of the Old World. They conquered large cities and ruled many people. Perhaps people of future generations will tell their children stories about our famous victories in the New World."

Annuki did not respond.

* * * * * * * * *

The third day Nimrod left Annuki to meet the city leaders. He arrived at the government building an hour before the elders came. He wore the fleece, which impressively reflected the morning sunlight. When the leaders finally arrived, they eyed him suspiciously. They began the meeting and discussed city business before considering Nimrod's proposal. He grew impatient after sitting several hours. Finally, the presiding elder addressed him.

"We have thoroughly debated the merits of your proposal, Nimrod. We oppose recruiting such a large labor force from Uruk to build this religious center. The risks for this community are not worth the potential benefits. The gods have blessed Uruk, and they have not persuaded us to lead it in another direction at this time. I hope you understand our position."

"I understand your opposition to my proposal. Is that the final answer?"

"Yes, I'm afraid that's the final answer," replied the same elder.

"You have reason to fear!" Nimrod bellowed then spat

on the floor. "We shall see who governs Uruk."

Nimrod turned and exited the room. He walked to Annuki's house and found him cultivating the garden in the late morning hours.

"They humiliated me by conducting the meeting for several hours prior to addressing my concerns," declared Nimrod with disgust. "I sensed resistance before they even acknowledged my presence. They claimed the gods did not lead them to support my vision. These worthless men will now experience the genuine desires of the gods. I shall return in several months, and I will bring company at that time."

* * * * * * * * *

Nimrod decided to spend one more night in Uruk. He had heard of a tavern known for its beer. He knew the residents of Uruk made the best beer in the Mesopotamian Valley.[7] His great grandfather made wine from the fruit of his vineyards, but the Sumerians were famous for their beer. This beverage would taste good after a discouraging meeting with the city leaders. He walked back toward the city center then turned westward, leisurely strolling several blocks down a side street, where he located the tavern. Nearby, people shopped at a busy fish market. A woodshop, specializing in carved idols, sat across the street. Nimrod perused the shop and bought several idols of Sumerian gods for his siblings.

He finally entered the tavern late that afternoon. The three-story tavern was a large rectangular brick building. The first floor dining room overflowed with evening customers. The tavern owner greeted Nimrod at the door, and her beauty immediately captivated him. She gazed into his eyes despite the fact he towered above her.

"You have come to the tavern of Semiramis. May I help you, sir?" she asked politely.

"I...I thought I might purchase a drink of beer...then a room for the night...if you have a vacant one," he managed to say, trying not to rudely stare at her.

"We have the best beer in Sumeria, and we still have several empty rooms. For an extra price I can arrange a pretty woman to attend you this evening."

Nimrod did not realize the tavern was also a brothel.

"I shall take the room and the pretty woman. Make certain she can satisfy a man of my stature. I have traveled many miles from my home."

"Has your wife waited a long time for your return?"

"That is my business!" he answered, irritated by the probing question. He then reconsidered and added, "I have no wife. Life is too busy for a family, and my calling is higher than most men."

"I have the room of the house for a man of 'high calling.' A pan of water sits just outside the dining room. You might want to wash after traveling in this dusty country. When you finish I shall have the cook serve you a hot meal and the special beer you requested."

Nimrod left the room to wash his dirty hands, but he could not remove the vision of this lovely woman from his mind. She was uniquely beautiful among women of the New World. A fair complexion and light brown hair graced her appearance, and eyes as green as a fig leaf seemed to penetrate his heart. Her smile completely disarmed him. She was slender, perfectly shaped, and a very good prize for any man, he thought. He returned to the dining room after washing. The enchanting hostess had disappeared. The cook had prepared a large dinner with vegetables, bread, and fresh river fish. She handed him a large pottery vessel filled with the best beer in Sumeria. The vision of Semiramis pushed all thoughts from his mind.

"Where is the tavern owner who greeted me?" Nimrod asked the cook.

"She left to shop the street market for kitchen provisions," the cook replied. "She requested me to escort you to a room when you finish."

"I appreciate your service."

Nimrod sat by himself at a small table and ate the meal. Ornate candles highlighted the faces of customers sitting at each table. Music from a lute and harp added to the noise of many conversations. Musicians sat in a far corner of the room. Nimrod felt the curious stares of many people. He knew his large stature and dark skin differed considerably from the residents of Uruk. Furthermore, the golden brown fleece was notably unique. He believed that unusual appearance would enable him to command authority over these people. When he finished eating the cook directed him to a room.

"I thoroughly enjoyed the delicious meal," he complemented. "I could not have eaten a bite more than you prepared."

"Thank you, my lord. The mistress asked me to feed you well."

"I commend you for a job well performed."

The cook was tall, dark, and appeared about forty years old. Her timid, respectful demeanor appealed to Nimrod.

She led him up several flights of brick steps to the third floor, and then escorted him to the largest room on the hall.

"Our workers just finished painting this room. As you can see, the shiny white walls expand the room even further. A huge window on the western wall provides an excellent view of the city center. May the gods grant you a good night's rest, my lord."

"Thank you, my lady."

Nimrod peered through the window. He observed priests greeting evening worshippers in front of the temple and several shopkeepers returning home after a long day's work. Fishermen were bringing their day's catch to sell at the market.

"People of Uruk appear friendly enough. Peace reigns for now, but soon I shall shake the security of Uruk at its roots," he murmured.

The sky darkened and the city became silent. Nimrod lit a candle and knelt beside a large wooden bed to commune with the dark lord. Thoughts drifted into deep meditation. The candle flame seemed to grow larger. No evening breezes wafted through the window, but the flame flickered and moved as if blown by a gentle wind.

"My lord," Nimrod muttered under his breath, "I feel your presence. Do you bring me a message this evening?"

Silence prevailed for several minutes, and then a guttural voice seemed to emanate from the flame.

"You have performed well in this city, Nimrod. My spirit has gone before you. Soon Uruk will sit in the palm of my hand. You will find these people eager to serve you, even if you lead them into the sea. However, you must remove several obstacles before consolidating your leadership. Do you know who these are, my rebellious one?"

"I have identified them, and I will plan their elimination. The woman, my lord—what do you intend for her?"

"She is my gift to you. I have a noble plan for her, which will nicely complement your purpose in this Empire."

The eerie voice ended abruptly as the flame flickered and died.

The door to Nimrod's room opened slowly and silently. Through it slipped the most beautiful woman Nimrod had ever laid eyes upon. She was the mistress of the tavern! Her body was draped with a nearly transparent white robe. Glistening brown hair flowed over the back of her robe. Nimrod sat on the bed as she quietly approached him and gazed into his eyes for a long moment.

"I have come to serve you, but you will not receive your desire this night. You must accept only what I can offer. Do you understand? If you do not, I shall leave at once."

"I understand," he replied, dismayed he could not immediately conquer this beautiful woman. She seemed to command authority over him.

"Lie down on this bed and remove your sandals."

She began massaging his muscles. Nimrod enjoyed the new experience. She rubbed scented oil over his body and completed the massage. The temptation was almost unbearable, but he managed to lie still.

"Why have you come to serve me? I thought a lady of the house would provide my needs."

"I am the lady of the house this evening."

"I could not ask for better service. You know something about me. Tell me who you are and where you are from?"

"My name is Semiramis, as I have stated. I live in Uruk and my family also resides in this city."

"Are you married and with children?"

"I am recently married, but we have no children. My husband is an elder of this city. We are wealthy and respected here. The tavern is our family business."

Nimrod could feel the envy. He hoped she did not notice.

"Then I will ask no further service from you at this time."

"I shall honor that request. I do not know your purpose here, Nimrod, but I feel our paths will meet again."

"Indeed they will, my lady."

Nimrod slept well that night, confident in the promises of the dark lord. He awoke the next morning refreshed and ready to return home. He donned the fleece and walked down two flights of stairs to the first floor dining room. Bright sunlight streamed through eastern windows. The obvious absence of the tavern owner discouraged Nimrod. The cook patiently waited for him to devour the delicious breakfast.

"My lady performs her business in Uruk this morning. She bids you farewell." The cook then escorted him from the tavern.

Chapter 4

The Conquest of Uruk

N imrod returned to Kish, passing through a gate in the massive wall surrounding the city. He marveled at the huge gate, made with large tree trunks aligned vertically together. Carpenters had planed the trunks on each side to reveal the beautiful wood grain. Ten bronze rods coursed horizontally through the center of the trunks, fastening them together. Thick bands of copper, eight inches wide, stabilized them from the outside. Twelve of these bands secured the gate, and each was etched with figures of serpents and wild animals. Even larger trunks framed the gate, and they were carved with images of gods believed to protect the city.

"This city is secure and well defended," he muttered after walking through the gate.

People of Kish worked busily that day. Nimrod observed brick masons constructing homes and other buildings within the city limits. Hunters sold their catch in street-side markets. Farmers displayed an abundance of fruit and vegetables. Nimrod couldn't resist purchasing some fruit to allay his ravenous appetite. Shops sporting everything from jewelry to wooden idols conducted a brisk business with customers. Nimrod rode his mule to the city center and tied it before the building of government affairs. It appeared similar to the administration building in Uruk, he thought. It also stretched three stories and was constructed with brown bricks, but it contained more offices for city leaders. Cush had a large office on the second floor. Priests from local temples had offices on the first floor. Canaan, the brother of Cush, also had an office because he functioned as liaison between city elders and temple priests.

Nimrod found his father discussing city business with the elders. They sat at a round wooden table in a third floor room, fully illuminated by sunlight. The windows provided a commanding view of the city. Nimrod patiently waited for them to wrap up business before addressing them.

"My brothers... I have recently returned from Uruk—a huge city with hard working people. Fertile lands surrounding it yield enormous quantities of grain, and a thriving trade exists with people of the north. In fact, Uruk excels this great city in commerce. Many more people reside there than in Kish, and new inventions are common—advanced beyond our achievements. Residents of Uruk carry grain in mule-drawn carts, transporting it to populated areas where the rivers do not reach. Uruk has established many trading partners in this manner."

He paused, not quite sure how to articulate the important issues.

"However, all is not well in Uruk. City leaders rule with authority yet ignore the needs of their population. They acquire riches at the expense of the citizens."

"How does this relate to our city, Nimrod?" an elder demanded, intent to complete the morning business.

Nimrod perceived the elder's impatience.

"Father and I envision the emergence of a vast Empire that will control trade and commerce of the entire New World. A common language unifies people of the world, but cities of Mesopotamia move independently in different directions. Enmity and strife often arise between them. A united Empire will consolidate the culture of this Valley. New gods arise in Sumeria every year due to a variety of superstitions. Spiritual confusion afflicts the growing population. A huge temple of worship in the capital of the Empire will rectify this confusion. Priests will determine spiritual needs of the people and control the emergence of new gods. They will also organize existing gods into an appropriate hierarchy. Political leaders will chart a secular course for the Empire and establish its goals. No obstacle can impede the progress of mankind if inhabitants of this world unite under the authority of an omnipotent Empire. Someday we shall become like the gods we worship!"

"Nimrod, your amazing visions exceed the small agenda for this meeting," interrupted another elder. "How does all this apply to the city of Uruk?"

"Father and I have determined the project will require at least sixty thousand workers. Kish could never support such a labor force. Should the cities of Mesopotamia come together to champion this venture, we could easily amass a work force exceeding this number. My father commissioned me to communicate the vision to cities of the Mesopotamian Valley. Uruk is the largest city, of course. I met with its elders, and they barely gave me time to explain it. Then they dismissed the proposal without consideration, stating they had no desire to expand the vision of Uruk. However, I also met many people from that populous city, who fervently supported the idea. I feel certain the entire population would defend the plan I have humbly presented. Our unity with Uruk is essential to advance this project. The combined population of our cities approaches one hundred thousand. I can easily persuade the remaining cities in this Valley if Uruk and Kish are unified."

"Are you implying the leadership of these two cities must also support this vision to accomplish your plan?"

asked one of the elders.

"Yes, I am."

The elders were silent for several minutes. Nimrod appeared in control of his emotions, but he carefully suppressed the discomfort of tense neck muscles and a cramping stomach. He felt anxious and could not predict the reactions of the city leaders.

Finally, another elder spoke after a long pause.

"What is your plan, Nimrod?"

"I propose we arm a thousand warriors from Kish. I will march them to Uruk and depose the leadership. You will then assume control of that city."

Cush interrupted the ensuing silence to speak for the first time.

"The New World has not known the value of armed conflict. Mighty men of valor in the Old World successfully conquered the masses with this skill. I have thoroughly studied their tactics and feel we can achieve similar success. Without question, Nimrod is the obvious choice to lead an army of warriors against the opposition. He can prepare a thousand men to handle any conflict with his superb hunting skills. We will only need to supply young men and metal to create weaponry. How long will it take you to train an army, my son?"

The direction of the conversation encouraged Nimrod.

"I need three months to equip the warriors and train for battle."

"I am concerned about promoting these aggressive tactics in the New World. This new precedent for armed conflict might result in grave consequences for the future of mankind. I fear this will only be the beginning of military campaigns," remarked a skeptical elder.

"We need not fear if our armed force is mightier than our foes," Nimrod declared, knowing someday he would surely have to depose this leader.

The elders discussed Nimrod's proposal in detail, finally voting to support it with only one abstention. Cush adjourned the meeting and left with Nimrod for the local tavern.

"I thought you and your supporters would accomplish the commands of the dark lord, Nimrod. You have abused our influence with the elders to push this agenda. I fear the consequences of this action you have pursued. You have also taken advantage of me."

"I apologize, Father." A spirit of pride seized Nimrod, like ravenous flames consume a dried twig. "But this adventure will reap substantial rewards. Your authority as governor of Kish will increase in the New World. You will become the noble King of both cities!"

"We shall see about that. Only the gods know the future. Isn't that your understanding, my son?"

"You are correct, Father." Nimrod smiled, encouraged his father had acknowledged the omniscient gods.

* * * * * * * * *

Nimrod did not waste any time gathering men and supplies for the army. He eagerly desired to command the first army of the New World. He recruited one thousand strong men—the best his city could offer. Many were skilled hunters, but Nimrod organized them into an efficient fighting machine. They learned to make weapons and maintain them. Nimrod provided them with wood and bronze from the city surplus. Each warrior fashioned several spears, a shield, and a bow with many arrows. Metal smiths also forged swords and daggers for them. Nimrod exercised each day with the men. They grew strong and confident in their skills. Three months of military training adequately prepared them for the task ahead. All submitted obediently to Nimrod's leadership. Their allegiance was strong, and they would embrace death if Nimrod commanded it.

* * * * * * * * * *

After three months of military preparations Nimrod found Cush in his spacious second floor bedroom.

"Father, I am ready to march the army to Uruk and do battle if necessary."

"I hope warfare is not required, my son. Armed conflict ruins lives and destroys families."

Nimrod perceived his father's misgivings.

"War causes bitterness in those suffering loss. This often spawns retribution in subsequent years," added Cush.

"I have the stomach for such eventualities, but I feel hopeful armed conflict will not be necessary. This is a momentous occasion, Father, and I sense a spirit of glory welling up in my soul! My lord has given me this spirit, and I am certain the people of Uruk will acquire it when their leadership is deposed. They will not mind a small sacrifice to attain a greater glory."

"We shall see, my son. I hope you are thinking beyond Uruk to more complex issues that lie ahead."

"Farewell, Father. I will return soon, crowned in glory!"

Nimrod embraced his father and left the room.

* * * * * * * * * *

Cush heard the front door slam loudly as Nimrod hastily exited the house. Cush looked out the bedroom window to see his son striding purposefully in the direction of the troops on the outskirts of Kish. He knew Nimrod would accomplish his goals at any cost. He felt his son was about to embark on a road to destiny. The great rebellion would soon commence, but Cush could not predict the outcome. He hoped the gods were as powerful as Nimrod claimed.

* * * * * * * * *

The army marched to Uruk in five days. Astonished citizens watched armed men march through the city. Never had they observed such a scene—mighty men carrying frightening weapons. Was this a large hunting party convened to eliminate terrible beasts from the Valley? Talk of the numerous warriors spread rapidly throughout the city. Residents of Uruk would soon learn the hunted were not mere animals.

Nimrod marched at the forefront of the army, appearing magnificent and fearsome. He hailed several distinguished men in the City Square then impaled them with spears. They fell to the ground and died an agonizing death in a growing puddle of blood. Many warriors repeated the same behavior. Within several minutes thirty innocent men suffered in agony, lying helpless on the ground. Death came quickly and without warning to those unfortunate souls.

Nimrod grabbed the tunic of a terrified citizen, whose arms flailed about as he attempted to free himself from the grip of this enormous warrior. Nimrod grasped the man's head and locked his eyes with a steely gaze.

"I order you to find the elders and bring them to me at once! Do you understand this simple command?"

"Yes, my lord, I will g..g..go at once. P...Pl...Please do not hurt me!"

The mighty warrior loosened his hold, and the man quickly ran to the building that housed government officials.

He soon returned with the frightened leaders, who attempted to appear brave before their citizens. Hundreds peered out windows while perching safely beyond reach of Nimrod's troops.

"Why do you terrorize our people?" the foremost elder demanded. "You have no right to enter the city in this manner!"

"I have come to eliminate the poor leadership of this city! Leaders of Uruk have proven themselves inadequate for the task, and the citizens deserve better representation!"

Nimrod leered at the leaders without flinching.

"Now bow before me—on your knees! I am your new leader, and I answer only to King Bel of Kish!"

Several elders dropped to their knees, but one elder hesitated.

"Our priests teach us to bow only before the gods," he timidly explained.

"I stand as a god before you!"

Nimrod angrily pulled a dagger from his belt and grabbed the elder by the hair, lifting him several feet and turning him to face the gathering crowd.

"Your people will cower in my presence! My word is the authority in this city!"

Nimrod sliced through the neck of the young man. Blood spurted several feet and gasps escaped from several in the crowd.

"We have sacrifices for our gods today!" Nimrod proclaimed, throwing the man's carcass to the ground.

The remaining elders bowed prostrate before Nimrod.

"These are lambs for slaughter!"

He thrust them through the back with spears, pinning each to the ground. He left only one elder kneeling before him.

"I have a special punishment for you, Onnes—my friend."

Nimrod summoned Semiramis from the crowd. She obeyed the command but did not cringe before him. He kissed her passionately but fire burned in those green eyes. Nimrod was taken aback at this woman who appeared fearless in the presence of a lion who might devour her. Several warriors pulled the husband of Semiramis to his feet to view the spectacle.

"I will let you see your wife for the last time, and then I

shall personally gouge out your eyes as you surrender her to me. Someday she will reign as Queen of this city!"

The grief-stricken elder did not fear death as much as losing his dear wife. He grabbed the dagger from Nimrod's belt and plunged it deeply into his own chest then fell to the ground, gasping for air. Nimrod looked down and smiled at the helpless man writhing in the dirt.

"You have made my task much easier, Onnes."

Nimrod pulled Semiramis close once again and kissed her before the crowd. He restrained her from stooping to assist her dying husband.

"Greet your new Queen! Legitimate leaders of Uruk will arrive in several days. King Bel of Kish is now the ruler of this city, and I will answer only to him. I command you to bow before me at once!"

The crowd in the City Square bowed quickly, fearing for their lives.

"I expect you to conduct business as usual until new leadership arrives."

Nimrod turned and led the troops out of the city. He took Semiramis to parade her before the people of Kish. She was sullen during the long journey. Semiramis rode a beautiful white mule Nimrod had brought to transport her. He rode beside her on his large black mule. They traveled along the Euphrates River for five days and rested each night. They passed beautiful trees and grasslands, pausing to rest at scenic vistas overlooking the wide river. The troops stopped marching an hour before dusk each day. Crimson sunsets reflected spectacularly on peaceful waters of the Euphrates. Fiery sunbeams extinguished themselves gradually in that huge river. But Semiramis did not delight in beautiful landscapes, nor did she enjoy the company. She declined the services of Nimrod and his warriors, refusing to eat for the entire journey. She only consented to drink meager amounts of water. The Queen of Uruk slept on the ground, far removed from Nimrod and the troops. He could not persuade her to communicate despite repeated pleas and apologies. Finally, Semiramis spoke for the first time as they neared Kish.

"I shall accept the title 'Queen of Uruk,' but I shall also reign as Queen of the Empire. People of Mesopotamia will sing the praises of their Queen as they bow to its conqueror. You will not intimidate me in this matter. My contributions to the Empire will rival yours. My authority shall prevail over the elders, and laborers will obey my commands!"

Blazing green eyes looked upward and locked Nimrod's gaze.

"I shall honor these requests, my lady," Nimrod responded, astonished by this fearless woman who dared to rival his authority.

* * * * * * * * *

Nimrod led the parade of warriors through a large gate in the southern wall, with the beautiful Queen at his side. At mid-morning considerable pedestrian traffic congested the city streets. Warriors marched slowly along the widest avenue of Kish, finally stopping in the City Square. People greeted them with shouts of jubilation, and crowds thronged to the city center to investigate the commotion. Several thousand gathered, converging from all avenues intersecting the city center.

Nimrod stood before the magnificent temple of An—its entrance a backdrop to his enormous body. The semicircular marble frame above the entrance was sculpted with large serpents interspersed with gods of the city. Several of the serpents coiled in a position just above Nimrod's head. They appeared ready to leap from the marble slab onto his outstretched hands, which motioned to quiet the chanting crowd.

"Good citizens of Kish," he began, "I bring joyous news

on this momentous occasion! We have returned from the great city of Uruk. The two largest cities of Mesopotamia have now united under one leadership. The noble King Bel rules both Kish and Uruk! We have witnessed the beginning of an Empire dedicated to the gods. This is the day the gods have made! Let us rejoice and be glad in it!"

Shouts and praises erupted from the crowd: "Praise Bel, our lord and supreme ruler! Long live Nimrod—the mighty warrior and son of Bel!"

"I have more wonderful news. The beautiful woman standing at my side is the Queen of Uruk. She will also rule in the Empire of Babel. The gods have ordained her to be my wife!"

A chorus of cheers echoed through the city. Nimrod and Semiramis descended the steps leading to the temple entrance, and Cush stepped up to address the people.

"My family and friends in the most powerful city of the New World... the gods have blessed us this wonderful day. We are a proud people and have earned the right to revel in this moment. Let the celebration begin!"

Jubilation, dancing, and singing continued long into the night. Many of the people had relatives in Uruk. They welcomed the news their cities had merged under one authority. They praised King Bel and his famous son, Nimrod— mighty hunter before the gods. The stunning beauty of Semiramis impressed them most of all, and they eagerly embraced her as Queen of the Empire.

People sang through the night, "Nimrod conquers the souls of men. The gods have blessed him again and again!"

Nimrod met with Cush and the city leaders in the government building during a wild celebration on the streets below. He introduced Semiramis to the elders.

"I shall soon marry this beautiful woman standing before you, and she will reign as Queen in the Empire of Babel. Only the King and I will have the authority to overrule her commands."

"I made this agreement with the citizens of Uruk," Nimrod explained. "Our marriage will seal it, and residents of both cities will celebrate the wedding!"

He carefully avoided the sordid details about eliminating Uruk's leaders, though he felt someone would probably reveal this information.

"Your authority will expand beyond its present boundaries, my brothers. You will administer both great cities and employ those necessary to accomplish this task."

The dissent Nimrod had expected did not materialize. He figured the elders would be dismayed, having less authority than Semiramis. However, the announcement did not seem to discourage them. They apparently assumed she would merely function as a figurehead—without significant power in managing government affairs.

The meeting adjourned, and Nimrod brought her home to meet his family. The sun's heat was at its peak that afternoon, but the remarkable beauty of Semiramis did not diminish. Her loveliness charmed everyone. They accepted her immediately as one of the family. Young children competed for her attention, and she spent several hours playing with them. Nimrod rejoiced to see Semiramis socializing with the women and childern. He felt comfortable leaving her, so he silently escaped to meet privately with his father. Nimrod and Cush walked to the terraced garden behind the palace and sat between several flowering trees.

"I have brought glory to our family and my lord! I rejoice in this early success, Father. The spoils of victory are sweet."

"I fear the desire for spoils and power will overwhelm you. Lust for power and wealth consumed many men in the Old World. Your grandfather described courageous men of renown who built vast Empires and controlled the lives of thousands. Nothing could satisfy their craving for greatness, and it eventually drove them to destruction. I hope your fate will be different, my son."

"I do the lord's bidding. Personal desires do not drive my decisions. I can adapt to any situation, for it is not I who live but he who lives within me! The dark lord has impressed this clearly in my mind."

"I understand, but I am not convinced you will fare any better than men of the Old World."

"Your mind will change, Father, because you will personally benefit from this adventure!"

"I already have... I cannot deny the truth of that statement. However, we must prepare a wedding that will surpass the marriage ceremony of any mortal in the New World up to this present day. Let us begin planning this momentous event."

Chapter 5

The Eternal Union?

Nimrod was content in those days—like a lion licking his paws after devouring a kill. He knew he had followed the dark lord's commands, and his obedience had reaped substantial rewards. The beginning of a mighty Empire had appeared on the horizon of the New World.

Rumors about the conquest of Uruk and execution of its leaders circulated throughout Mesopotamia. Nimrod's evil reputation spread like wildfire from the great sea in the south to Mount Ararat in the north. Inhabitants of each city feared a military attack, which they could not defend. They did not know the techniques of warfare. How could they battle such a formidable foe? Few valiant men were available to galvanize and train warriors. Nevertheless, each city recruited thousands of young men to fight for local deities. They fashioned spears, axes, and swords then began training for war.

＊ ＊ ＊ ＊ ＊ ＊ ＊ ＊ ＊

Nimrod did not fret about increasing the territory of his Empire. He knew the dark lord had planned for expansion. Flames of romance consumed the lion's thoughts at that moment. He eagerly anticipated the wedding. No woman had ever attracted him like Semiramis... but could he manage this firebrand as a wife? Would she support his vision and stand with him at critical times in the future? Nimrod could not answer these questions, but Semiramis had captured his heart. He would do anything for her aside from forfeiting his exclusive relationship with the dark lord. Nimrod had single-handedly orchestrated her transition to the throne. Semiramis was now the undisputed Queen of Uruk—provided she consummate the marriage with Nimrod.

Priests and city elders convened a meeting to determine the date for the wedding.

"The first day of spring is the most appropriate date for this marriage," proposed the high priest. "Spring planting always begins that day. The gods would surely select it to celebrate the marriage of their chosen Monarchs."

"We teach the creative forces of the gods come together then to enable the birth of new plant and animal life," another priest remarked.

The elders voted to sanction this date as the time for the wedding. King Bel also approved. Nimrod and Semiramis hoped people of future generations would remember the anniversary annually as a time to celebrate the appearance of new life.[8]

* * * * * * * * *

The day of the eternal union finally arrived. City leaders and priests had fully prepared for the event. The wedding would take place in front of the temple of An. Elders had invited citizens of Uruk and Kish to attend. They planned an outside wedding because a huge crowd was anticipated. Residents of Uruk traveled several days to witness the remarkable affair. Temple musicians played lutes and harps as thousands thronged into the City Square. It barely accommodated all the people present that day.

Nimrod dressed in royal apparel. He wore a purple robe bedecked with gold trimmings. A crown of bullhorns embedded with precious jewels sat on his head.[9] For the first time in the New World people witnessed a royal personage wearing a crown. He carried a golden scepter in his right hand, representing authority and power. Artisans had engraved the scepter with Sumerian pictographs, portraying a hunter slaying a terrifying dragon.

Semiramis wore an elegant white linen robe highlighting her voluptuous figure. A delicate veil covered her face. Beautiful brown hair flowed over the white robe and a golden circlet crowned her head.[10] Nimrod thought the Queen grew more beautiful each time he gazed at her. She carried a golden goblet full of red wine.

The high priest from the temple of An conducted the wedding ceremony. Nimrod was surprised by his small size. He wore a long black robe adorned with the bones of various animals. A pyramid-shaped piece of gold embedded with precious stones hung from his neck.

The priest began the ceremony by sacrificing a yearling ram. He collected blood from the spurting neck wound in a shallow bowl then sprinkled it onto a stone altar in front of the temple. He divided the ram into quarters and laid them on the huge altar. Fire quickly consumed the sacrifice. Other priests simultaneously lit smoking bowls of incense, and Nimrod smelled the pungent odors wafting from the temple entrance.

Nimrod escorted Semiramis to the high priest, standing at the altar. Semiramis initially presented the golden goblet to the priest. He held the goblet high and addressed the crowd.

"Our artisans have etched one side of this goblet with a picture of the Queen communing with a serpent under a fruit-laden tree. This symbolizes the mother of the human race speaking with the serpent in the Garden of Eden. The other side of the goblet pictures a dove holding an olive branch in its beak while flying from the outstretched hand of the Queen. This represents the dove that brought Noah an olive branch after our family had floated on the floodwaters for a year.[11] The olive branch proved the waters of the catastrophic flood had receded. The woman who released the dove opened the New World for the settlement of mankind."[12]

Nimrod watched the priest pour the wine on the altar as an offering to An. The priest looked heavenward and announced: "This represents the blood sacrifice our people will make for the Empire."

He took the golden scepter from Nimrod and held it before the couple as they bowed before him. They placed their hands on the scepter.

"I proclaim this eternal union by the authority of the omnipotent god, An. People of this world will celebrate it in future generations. This union marks the beginning of one great Empire of mankind. I dedicate it to the gods. May it count as a pleasing offering to them!" exclaimed the high priest.

"Amen! Amen!" shouted the people.

Nimrod and his new wife rose to face the citizens of Kish and Uruk. Nimrod gently lifted the veil from the face of his bride. It seemed like brushing the dirt from a nugget of gold. He tenderly kissed her, and the crowd applauded. The couple then walked hand in hand through the City Square and mingled with the people.

The crowd dissipated as late afternoon festivities commenced for families of the bride and groom. Personal friends, city officials, and influential citizens were present for the celebration. Nimrod had even invited Annuki and his family to the gathering. He overheard Annuki proudly boasting of his close relationship with the Monarchs.

Slaves of Cush provided food, small delicacies, and wine to all in attendance. The reception was held in an immense rectangular room in the temple of An. Windows did not exist in the sanctuary, but a multitude of candles lit the room.

The bride and groom silently escaped the celebration. The family's servants escorted them beyond the city gates, where they found two mules tied to a tree. Nimrod assisted his bride onto the back of one mule, and then he mounted the other. They rode in silence for several hours, finally arriving at a secluded area adjacent to the Euphrates River— far from human settlements. Large trees surrounded them, and sounds of nocturnal animals echoed eerily in the night. Nimrod helped Semiramis dismount and then escorted her to a large cave he had prepared. He had sworn allegiance to the dark lord in this location many years before. Nimrod could think of no better place to consummate the marriage.

They found a small pile of candles at the entrance to the cave. Nimrod lit one of these and distributed the remainder to multiple spots throughout the cave, fully illuminating it.

"The women of Kish have prepared linens and specially woven blankets to make the cave appear 'civilized.' Several flat-topped boulders sit in various locations, and delicacies of bread and cheese lie on each of them—neatly arranged. Animal skins containing aged wine and drinking vessels sit next to the food," he explained.

Containers of incense burned, dispersing pleasant aromas throughout the cave.

Nimrod desired they remember that night for many years. They nibbled on cheese and savored the aged wine.

"The wine is particularly tasteful, my dear."

"The dainty morsels are also a nice addition to the remote location, Nimrod."

"This unique cave will provide a memorable atmosphere for a wonderful wedding night."

Semiramis nodded her head in agreement.

* * * * * * * * *

Late that night they fell into a restless sleep. Frightful visions and disturbing dreams haunted Semiramis. After several long hours they suddenly awoke from the same horrible nightmare—being pushed from a high precipice. Semiramis felt the ground shaking beneath her, and noticed all but one candle flicker out. A strange stillness pervaded the cave, and the lone flame bent to one side as if blown by a continuous breeze. A terrifying voice came from the blackness surrounding them. Semiramis felt her skin crawling and cold beads of sweat appeared on her forehead. Nimrod dropped to his knees.

"The gods and I are pleased with your marriage. My priest prophesied truthfully of this eternal union. The gods will savor it and people will commemorate it annually for the duration of mankind on the earth. Someday people will worship you as they presently exalt the gods. The stars will even portray your glory."

The voice of the dark lord continued without interruption, but the volume increased until the cave walls shuddered. Stones fell from the ceiling and bounced all around them.

"Your foremost goal is to establish my Empire. I demand obedience! Do not let selfish ambitions interfere with this crucial task. I shall preside over this world as I rule the gods! Do you understand?"

"Yes, lord, we understand," Nimrod responded timidly for both of them. Words would not come to the lips of Semiramis for the first time in her life.

The dark lord's voice suddenly softened and grew more enticing.

"I shall illuminate your path for the remainder of your days. Power and riches lie before you. You will influence kingdoms of mankind in the years ahead. Someday in eternity you will even find greater treasures—beyond your imagination."

Did she hear laughter?

"One day you will join us, and people of this world will worship you!"

Indeed, Semiramis heard laughter. It became louder, echoing through the cave and into the blackness of the night. She detected many voices of laughter that persisted several minutes, and then in an instant... the laughter ceased. A creepy stillness prevailed thereafter. The lone flame flickered and died.

"We have pleased our lord, my love. This memorable occasion should encourage us. His commands will nourish us as bread and wine. We will consider it a privilege to submit to him in the days ahead."

Semiramis remained silent, afraid to utter a word. One word might convict her before the gods. No god had ever spoken directly to her. Semiramis did not desire any more of these encounters. She did not relish the thought of communing with the dark lord, but she would play this game to its conclusion... whatever that might be. She feared the consequences should she not do so. The Queen realized someone invisible in the darkness watched her every move.

Chapter 6

A Struggle for Power

"I will not stay here one more day! I do not have the stomach for another 'spiritual encounter.' Confusion and uncertainty torment my soul," Semiramis confessed.

"I respect your feelings, my lady. I am prepared to depart."

Nimrod knew the short honeymoon was over. He had awakened with a renewed sense of purpose, and he resolved to move forward with the dark lord's program. He eagerly desired to build the Empire of Babel. They mounted the mules and slowly rode toward Kish. Nimrod left the area, confident in the power of Darkness.

"Take me to Uruk—that is my home," she demanded. "I will not live in your city."

"But a huge distance will separate us. Can you at least linger in Kish for several weeks?"

"I shall serve my people in Uruk—that is my responsibility. Take me to the tavern where I will stay for now. I still have duties there. Besides, I have no other home in the city, and I will not rule Uruk from the government building. I feel uncomfortable working under the noses of leaders from your city."

"Do you plan to resume your work as a brothel owner?" asked Nimrod—his question suggesting more than a hint of jealousy. "You know the gods do not permit a married woman to consort with other men."

"I have no qualms about returning to my previous profession. After all, it made me into the woman I am—the one who attracted you. My business is an honorable calling and it provides work for many servants. I have regular customers, and the city needs the tavern."

She paused momentarily, then added: "Nevertheless, I shall honor my commitment to you and the gods."

Nimrod's anger simmered just short of boiling. He determined not to reveal it so soon after the wedding. He did not wish to lose authority in this new relationship.

"The King desires his wife beside him, and the business of the Empire requires it!"

"The Queen will rule her city!" she retorted.

Nimrod noticed green fire blazing in those eyes.

"The Empire requires unification of our cities," she continued. "The gods have commanded it, as you know perfectly well. I can communicate the gods' demands to my people. Citizens of Uruk trust me, and they will accept the changes instituted by their Queen."

Nimrod's anger slowly subsided. He realized he could not control this woman in the same fashion he intended to rule the Empire.

"Very well... I shall take you to Uruk where you can establish your leadership. However, this arrangement is temporary. You must flexibly determine your place of residence when future needs of the Empire beckon! Do you understand?"

He returned her glare with a steely determination.

She did not respond immediately, but looked squarely into Nimrod's eyes.

"Yes, my lord," she finally acknowledged.

"Furthermore, you will restrict your duties as tavern owner. I do not intend to find you servicing rooms with your maids. I am a jealous man and will not spare my cruel wrath if I detect any competition. My wife will not share a bed with another man!"

Nimrod decided to tone down his rhetoric, realizing he truly desired Semiramis to partner with him in future ventures.

"I shall provide laborers for you in Uruk. They will remain at your disposal for projects of your choosing. I suggest you direct them to build a castle as a primary residence. You should have a throne worthy of a Queen in that city. Use discretion with these workers. Perhaps there are other important projects for the community. The Queen will determine these in the future."

Nimrod attempted to build a bridge to his new partner. He liked her bold spirit but hoped she would someday submit to him.

"The Queen will honor the Empire, my lord, and the gods will direct me. Let your mind rest in that fact."

The journey to Uruk took four days. An entourage of servants assisted the move. They retraced the same route they had previously traveled with Nimrod's one thousand elite warriors. They grew weary in the scorching afternoon heat but actually enjoyed travel during the morning hours. The bright blue sky had very few clouds.

"Miles of wheat fields and green grasslands stretch eastward as far as the eye can see." Nimrod gestured. "Herds of domestic animals graze the grasslands. The massive Euphrates River is our companion to the west."

Semiramis appeared to enjoy the scenery on this trip, Nimrod thought. They stopped each night prior to sunset to eat and relax, choosing beautiful scenic vistas along the river. Sunset over the Euphrates was always a magnificent sight. One evening, Nimrod and Semiramis sat with their backs against a boulder, overlooking the river. They ate supper and watched silently as the fiery orb extinguished itself in the opposite side of the river.

"I enjoy these sunsets," she remarked. "Even the meals prepared by the servants taste wonderful."

Nimrod thought he was finally breaking new ground in the relationship. He returned Semiramis to the tavern with many riches.

* * * * * * * * *

The tavern had continued a brisk business in the absence of its owner. The cook had assumed temporary command of the servants, and rooms were regularly filled to capacity. Uruk had resumed its usual commerce and life had not significantly changed.

"I intend to stay with you tonight. I would like to sleep in the third floor suite reserved for special guests. However, customers overflow the inn, filling every room. I shall have to evict several of them."

"I will manage my tavern, Nimrod. I deal tactfully with the customers, and they respond gracefully to my adjustments. They have already observed your ways in this city and will require a long time to accept you."

"I submit to your discretion, my lady."

Nimrod tried to appear calm and agreeable. He ordered his servants to return to Kish.

Semiramis secured the large third floor room for them. Her cook prepared a lavish meal and filled pottery glasses with the best beer of Sumeria. Servants delivered the food and beverage to their room. Nimrod and Semiramis enjoyed the time, conversing more that night than ever before. They planned several projects for the city. Nimrod felt she was growing attracted to him.

"I shall send you a workforce of brick masons from Kish

within several weeks. Use them in projects you deem necessary for this city. I intend to pursue the dark lord's will for the Empire. This work will occupy me for several months—perhaps longer. Summon me if you desire my services. Annuki's sons will know where to find me."

"I appreciate your consideration, my lord, but I also have much work to accomplish. My schedule is full for many weeks, but you may come and go as you wish."

* * * * * * * * *

Semiramis had already occupied herself with the morning business of the tavern. She paused long enough to join Nimrod for a quick breakfast.

"You need not worry about me, Nimrod. The gods have given me a magnificent vision for this city, and I will aggressively pursue it."

"I am also prepared to move forward and fulfill the dark lord's assignments. I shall return soon, my Queen."

Nimrod parted with a long kiss then exited the tavern and entered a new phase of his life.

He decided to meet Annuki before leaving the city. Nimrod found him at home eating breakfast with the family.

"I am happy to find you here, Annuki!"

Nimrod hugged his cousin.

"The embrace of such a large man nearly squeezes out the breath of life!" Annuki joked. "What brings you to my home this morning?"

"I have several matters to discuss," Nimrod replied, as they walked outdoors to the garden behind the house.

They sat down under long drooping branches of a shade tree.

"I have returned the Queen to her tavern. She prefers to live in Uruk for now."

"Semiramis has a strong spirit. She is attached to this

city, but I am sure her affection for you will grow."

Nimrod politely ignored the comment and relayed his concerns.

"I would like you to monitor the activities of the Queen. I do not intend her to have any consorts."

"I will watch her closely."

"Semiramis prefers to continue managing her business, but she has also determined to oversee construction projects in the city—especially the castle."

"Perhaps these projects will occupy her ti.."

"Time will reveal the answers to these questions," Nimrod interrupted, desiring to change this uncomfortable topic of discussion. "I have additional instructions for you. I am planning the next military campaign. Soon we will march to the third most important city in the Mesopotamian Valley, and I need a fully trained army to conquer it. I have assigned you to command the troops from Uruk. What progress have you made?"

"Residents of Uruk have reluctantly complied with the order to recruit eighteen to twenty-five year old men for the new army. The people did not desire a military force and were troubled by the new law after seeing what your troops did to the city. They felt the young men should work the farmlands surrounding Uruk. Nevertheless, they complied with minimal dissent—not willing to incur your wrath."

"Report on the readiness of the troops."

Nimrod paced the floor impatiently.

"Five-thousand young men were conscripted, and military training began immediately. Warriors from Kish have trained them to use spears and swords. They have also taught archery and required physical conditioning exercises. The young recruits have quickly matured into a fearsome fighting force. A formidable enemy will have difficulty defeating them."

"Prepare them for a real battle, Annuki."

"I shall prime them for war, and they will submit obediently to their commander—I assure you."

"I will send word for these troops to join me in Kish, and then we shall advance to the next destination. I must leave for my home city—the gods beckon me. Goodbye, my friend."

Nimrod left as quickly as he had come. He walked to his large black mule, grazing in a pasture of high grass outside the city. He mounted the animal and rode home.

Chapter 7

The Empire Grows

Nimrod intended to make the next campaign more decisive than the last. He had heard rumors of new armies arising in cities of the Mesopotamian Valley. Nimrod knew he must consolidate his Empire quickly. Otherwise, remaining cities in the Valley would have adequate time to prepare for battle. A greater loss of life would result, and he might even fail to achieve his objectives should he delay too long. His troops would meet resistance, but he would overpower it with overwhelming force. He determined to make an example of the next city. Rumors traveled quickly in Mesopotamia, and Nimrod planned to strike fear in the hearts of many people.

He had developed a new weapon for this military campaign. Nimrod remembered the wooden carts carrying grain on the streets of Uruk. Impressed with the wheels transporting those carts, he appointed carpenters to create sturdier wooden wheels designed to carry a smaller wooden box at much faster speeds. Two mules would pull each cart, occupied by two men and their weapons. The carts would precede the foot soldiers and make the initial plunge into enemy ranks. The results would be devastating, he thought. The enemy would surely flee from such a terrible sight.

When Nimrod returned home he inspected the troops. They anxiously anticipated battle.

"Our carpenters have created ten 'chariots' for military purposes, according to your request," a commander declared. "These well-constructed chariots sit low to the ground on four sturdy wheels. Two semicircular pieces of wood tied together with leather strapping comprise each wheel. Leather covers the box to protect the crew. The front of each chariot extends well above the chest of the driver. The carpenters have fashioned it from two round-topped shields with a V in the center, through which passes the reigns. The reigns also glide through a shaft in front of the chariot so the driver can efficiently manipulate them. A second warrior stands behind the driver, armed with spears and stout poles. Each warrior carries daggers and swords. The chariot's low back makes it easy to mount for battle."

"The carpenters have performed an excellent work," Nimrod commended.

"We have trained many men to use the chariots. They are now ready for deployment on the battlefield. Mules pulling them are in excellent shape and obedient to their masters. The warriors have trained them to lunge forward at full speed and stop instantly on command. The chariots travel much faster than a man can run on an open field."

"They will work well to fracture the enemy lines," Nimrod remarked.

Another commander stepped forward.

"We have trained several hundred men from each city as archers, and they have practiced their skill daily for several months. They can now hit moving targets with amazing accuracy, my lord."

A third commander also addressed Nimrod.

"Women from Kish have made uniforms from animal skins to gird the warriors. They have sewn flat pieces of wood and metal into the uniforms, covering vulnerable body parts. Metal workers have fashioned helmets from copper, designed to cover heads and faces. These protective measures will hopefully lessen the casualties in upcoming battles. Each man carries a spear, shield, several daggers, and a curved sword."

"Thanks to your excellent preparations, the warriors are now ready for combat," Nimrod praised. "I will need several days to determine battle strategy, and the troops must learn my battlefield commands. I am nearly ready to lead them to conquer the next city for the Empire."

The anticipation of battle possessed him.

* * * * * * * * *

Nimrod bade farewell to the family, and then paused to speak privately with his father. He located Cush in the courtyard behind the palace.

"I intend to add at least two more cities to the Empire before I return, Father. I am convinced the military is up to the task. They are confident and thoroughly prepared for battle. I enjoy these adventures more than the hunting excursions of my youth!"

"Farewell, my son. I know you will return soon. The gods have given me good omens."

"Have you communed with the gods, Father?" Nimrod asked, surprised by this statement coming from the mouth of his skeptical father. "You have taught the gods are merely a product of superstition."

"So I have, Nimrod." His father grinned. "My attitude changes slowly but definitely leans in a spiritual direction. I credit your faith and good fortune for that!"

"The power of the dark lord is awesome! Greater is he within me than the power of my enemies. I fear nothing."

Nimrod lifted his tunic to reveal the divinely fashioned

garment of animal skins beneath. He smiled as Cush recognized the fleece.

"The god of the winds will bring many blessings. Soon the Empire will expand to the Four Corners of the earth. Someday our Shemitic brethren will beg on their knees to join the Empire!"

Shortly thereafter, Nimrod left the house and walked to a huge tree, where his black mule was tied. He mounted the mule and rode to the outskirts of the city, exiting through a massive timber gate.

Five thousand warriors from Uruk joined Nimrod's army just west of Kish. Nimrod led the procession with Annuki riding beside him.

"Our next destination is the city of Akkad. The territory of Akkad encompasses a large area of northern Mesopotamia. Shemitic people have settled there, and they are scattered sparsely over a vast region. Agriculture produces the major revenue for this area—similar to Kish and Uruk."

"I have heard descendants of Ham and Japheth also live in Akkad," remarked Annuki.

"Yes, but the Shemites vastly outnumber them. Akkad is the third most populous city of the Mesopotamian Valley. The Akkadians' faith in Noah's God has progressively weakened over several generations, but they still refuse to worship Sumerian gods. I view that as an insult to the dark lord. They desire our technology and have assimilated mathematics, astronomy, and writing into their culture. People move between Sumer and Akkad, freely exchanging ideas and discoveries. If they steal our inventions, they must embrace our gods as well."

Nimrod continued: "A loosely organized government rules the Akkadians, but it is not as progressive as the governments of Sumerian cities. Nevertheless, it attends to the needs of its people. My spies have informed me the leaders there have perceived our military threat as an urgent need, and they have ordered the Akkadians to amass several thousand fighting men. Soldiers have armed themselves and are now prepared to defend their city."

One of Nimrod's commanders rode to the front of the procession.

"My men have sighted the enemy on a flat grassy plain sixty miles north of Kish. That is about a mile from here. The plain is midway between the Tigris and Euphrates Rivers, which are only thirty miles apart at this location. A well-traveled road extends northward from the battlefield to the city of Akkad."

"I anticipate resistance from these Akkadians, but we are fully prepared for battle. We shall move forward and engage the enemy in warfare. Instruct the flag bearer of the new Empire to precede the troops."

Shortly thereafter, a colorful flag flapping in the breeze led the procession. It portrayed a huge red serpent preparing to engulf its prey—a man on his knees with head bowed.

Nimrod looked across a vast plain separating the forces and evaluated the defending troops. He noticed they were armed with axes, spears, and swords. Some had helmets, but most wore no protective armor. He estimated the enemy numbered approximately four thousand. They were spread a half-mile across the plain directly facing his troops. Nimrod knew they would not surrender peacefully. He marched his soldiers across the plain, coming within seventy-five yards of the opposing force.

"Stop the advance and spread horizontally across the plain to face the enemy," he ordered. "Alternate archers with spearmen and intersperse the ten chariots at regular intervals."

The warriors obeyed the commands, and then silently gazed across the plain to assess the opposition. Nimrod observed a large man with sandy brown hair and fair skin emerging from the Akkadian ranks, armed only with a spear and sword. He advanced within thirty yards of Nimrod, staring directly at him. He wore no defensive armor.

"Nimrod, son of Cush, we do not welcome your presence among our people! We have not threatened the city of Kish with warfare. We request you return to your homeland and leave us alone."

The mighty warrior stepped forward to size up his opponent and then spat upon the ground.

"I have not come this far to argue with a mere boy. We have marched to this territory to make war—not conversation. My intention is to rule the city of Akkad, and I shall not leave until I accomplish that goal. Step back into your ranks or be smitten where you stand!"

The young man walked back to his comrades, apparently resigned to the fact there would be no negotiations that day. Nimrod perceived some movement among the Akkadian soldiers.

"They are nervous and intimidated by the fearsome appearance of our warriors," he muttered to the commanders.

However, no one fled the battlefield. They seemed intent to hold their ground.

Nimrod raised a hand high in the air, held it momentarily, and then dropped it quickly. Archers stepped forward and began to shoot volley after volley of arrows high in the air. Arrows showered down on the Akkadians like a fierce rain. Deadly volleys eliminated many enemy warriors, for they had no defense against this new weapon and very few even wore helmets.

He then pointed his right arm forward at the enemy lines. Archers obeyed the command by shooting repeated volleys directly into the enemy ranks. Screams of pain and agony carried across the flat plain. Akkadian soldiers fell like ripe wheat in a strong wind. Less than half of them remained standing after the horrific work of the archers.

Nimrod raised a hand once again and dropped it quickly.

Chariots lurched forward. By the time they had raced across the field they were traveling at the full speed of the mules. They crashed into enemy lines inflicting many additional casualties. They advanced another hundred yards beyond enemy ranks and then returned from the other direction—once again at full speed. The chariots repeated these maneuvers over and over again, further shrinking the defense.

Nimrod noticed the Akkadians did not run from the terrible onslaught, but he sensed their fear.

"Have you noticed who controls the events on this battlefield?" he asked the commanders, not expecting an answer.

He lifted his right arm one final time and dropped it quickly. Warriors shouted and charged forward to engage the remaining enemy combatants. For several minutes colliding axes and swords dominated all sounds on the battlefield, but then screams of terror and cries of agony filled the air. The battle did not last long. Nimrod's soldiers slaughtered more than three thousand Akkadians within one hour. Remaining survivors either surrendered or fled to Akkad. The warriors gathered prisoners and brought them before Nimrod.

Nimrod grabbed the large Akkadian who had addressed him prior to the battle.

"Are you willing to retract your words?"

Nimrod pressed his face within inches of the young man, leering at him, and then spat into his face. The young man removed the insult with the back of a hand and stood his ground.

"Bow to the ground before your King!"

The man did not move. A surge of anger stormed through Nimrod's large frame. He let it spew forth in one second, thrusting a sword through the man's abdomen. The man fell to the ground, continuing to gaze into Nimrod's face.

The young man grimaced with terrific pain, but managed

to speak one last time.

"I am your flesh and blood, Nimrod. Noah is the patriarch of both our families. You have sacrificed the blood of your brothers to the evil one. Your vision is dark and clouded. My great, great grandfather Shem hoped I could turn your eyes to the One True God today. I am sorry I did not accomplish his desire. I...I am sorry I also failed you."

The man then looked toward heaven—his spirit not yielding to the cruelty of the wicked man towering over him.

Nimrod's fury barely permitted a response. He saw everything shrouded in red.

"My—god—is—greater—than—yours!!!" Nimrod roared, then plunged his dagger deep into the chest of the Akkadian.

The young man closed his eyes in peace.

None of the warriors spoke a word. Nimrod knew the preceding event had eroded their respect, but an excruciating headache quickly overwhelmed all thoughts. He had never experienced such pain.

"Take the prisoners to the city, and depose the elders from leadership positions. Add them to your prisoners and eliminate all who resist. Have the men secure all temples of worship. I will follow the troops into the city and address the residents of Akkad after sunrise. Leave me alone in the wilderness. I shall rest well in this place."

Nimrod did not desire food or drink. Appetite for battle had also dissipated for the moment. The turbulent spirits would not abate. Nimrod desperately needed privacy.

"Put the wounded warriors out of their misery before you depart. Save our comrades who are salvageable," Nimrod instructed.

After executing the wounded, the men left Nimrod in solitude on the grassy plain and marched into the city.

Nimrod lay on the battlefield all night. He knew he had won a decisive victory and would soon rule Akkad, but he did not feel victorious. His soul did not overflow with the glory he had expected. The agonizing, throbbing headache would not relent, and he vomited repeatedly. Once again, horrific dreams replete with demonic spirits haunted him. They offered no reprieve for an aching head and a tormented soul. Nimrod knew the dark lord would visit that night, and he preferred a quick confrontation. However, the hours passed, prolonging the agony of the mighty hunter.

"Nimrod... why do you persecute yourself?" that familiar voice finally penetrated the stillness of the night.

Nimrod reluctantly pulled himself into a position of respect—on his knees. He could see nothing through the thick blackness enveloping the plain.

"I do not know, my lord. I realize the victory was decisive. We are one step closer to achieving your great Empire. I continue to accomplish your goals, but my spirit torments me and this infirmity overwhelms all thoughts. I have never faced these obstacles and cannot comprehend why I must suffer this misery."

"I understand your troubled soul, my son. You struggle with mortality and do not apprehend the reality of life and the beauty of death. A mortal mind fears eternity instead of embracing it. You have allowed the mere words of a man to influence you and permitted feelings of guilt to enter your soul. Guilt does not exist in the eternal realm."

"Please continue, my lord. I feel the troubling spirits lifting. Your words allay my suffering."

"Guilt is just an emotion humans inflict upon one another. Guilt creates spiritual pain when it becomes impossible to inflict physical pain. Humans are good at such things. You must master the spiritual realm, even as you take authority over the physical realm. The latter has minimal relevance in eternity, but mastering the spiritual realm is extremely important. Do you understand these profound truths, Nimrod?"

"Yes, my lord. I would like to rest and contemplate what you have shared."

"Rest from your labor and lean on me, my son. I will carry your burdens. Save your strength for the tasks of tomorrow." The voice of the dark lord ceased abruptly.

Nimrod fell fast asleep. He awoke the next morning feeling refreshed. His vision had cleared and the headache had vanished. Confusing events of the previous night still clouded his thoughts. He could not comprehend the deep wisdom of darkness but felt reassured he had made no serious mistakes. Nimrod knew the dark lord was proud of his accomplishments. He noticed vultures feasting on many carcasses littering the grassy field. The morning air was thick with the stench of death.

* * * * * * * * *

Nimrod rode his mule into Akkad. The warriors had tied prisoners to hitching posts the previous night and made them stand continuously without rest.

The exhausted appearance of prisoners revealed the torturous ordeal they had endured. Nimrod's men had mercilessly whipped those who fell to the ground. The commanders had deposed the city elders and summarily executed them before the people. Carcasses littered the streets, and families of the deceased were not permitted to remove them. Leaders of Akkad would rot in the streets to demonstrate the consequences of rebelling against Nimrod. He had successfully mentored the art of intimidation.

That morning soldiers of the Empire herded people into the city center to hear the first address from the new leader. Nimrod climbed a hastily built podium and faced the terrified citizens. He wore the divinely crafted fleece, which glistened brilliantly in the early morning sun. Twenty fearsome warriors surrounded the podium.

"Men and women of this important city," Nimrod's booming voice carried easily to the entire crowd, "I bring good tidings and great joy. You now have new leadership worthy of this magnificent city. I have freed you from the oppression of your previous leaders. A wonderful future lies before you. Achievements of men are impressive in this New World. When our vision of a great Empire unifies the people of Mesopotamia, the accomplishments of mankind will advance beyond imagination. The quality of life will improve dramatically, and we will attain our desires. Nothing will limit man's enormous potential when the Empire extends to boundaries of the New World. The gods have richly blessed us, and they demand our worship. They are not interested in lowly men groveling about on the earth. Our gods desire us to reach the sky. I apologize for the pain you experience, but today's pain will produce tomorrow's glory! You will see the fulfillment of these prophetic words."

People initially came with bitterness and anguish, but they now seemed mesmerized by the words and authority of this huge black man. Perhaps they would grant him an opportunity to fulfill these promises. Of course, they had little choice in the matter.

Nimrod continued: "My men will remain to restore order for this unfortunate city. Soon they will select new leaders united with one vision for the future. Join them with enthusiasm to accomplish this vision. The great city of Akkad is unified with Kish and Uruk. Our Empire is rising from the sand of the Mesopotamian Valley! The sky is closer than ever! Look up—the gods beckon you!"

His warriors applauded and shouted praises to the gods. The citizens looked around and joined the applause tentatively at first—then vigorously. Nimrod left the podium and walked to a nearby stone building where his commanders waited. This large, three-story structure had previously housed government officials and functioned as the administrative center of Akkad. It stood prominently above all buildings in the city. Nimrod was dismayed no temple to Sumerian gods sat in the center of Akkad.

Nimrod greeted the commanders. "I congratulate you for successfully restoring order. I must move quickly to the next city designated for assimilation into the Empire. I shall leave today with five-thousand men. I require half the officers. The other half will remain here with two-thousand men. Annuki will command them and direct the reorganization of Akkad. Goals for this city must agree with my aspirations for the Empire. Find good citizens who submit to our demands, and select the best as city leaders. They must understand economic and agricultural needs of the region. Confiscate all weapons from the Akkadians. Execute those who refuse to submit to your authority. Do you understand?"

They nodded in agreement.

"Enslave many from this city. They will soon construct Babel. Hold them here as prisoners and require them to perform works benefiting the community. Transport them to the capital when I send word. They will fulfill their term of slavery there. You may select many young men and women for this group. Do not take more than the city can bear. Farming and commerce must continue unhindered. Do you agree with these terms?"

They nodded affirmatively, once again.

Nimrod left the meeting and hurriedly gathered his troops. He would leave that very day to march to the next destination—the city of Calneh.

* * * * * * * * *

The troops required several days to march southwest to Calneh. They initially confiscated provisions from the grain and vegetable reserves of Akkad. Nimrod intended to feed the troops well to optimize their battle performance. He had two-thousand less warriors than before but felt the experienced military could easily conquer the smaller city of Calneh.

He marched the soldiers to a field within one mile of the city. Rumors of the Akkadian campaign had already traveled to Calneh.

"Men have prepared for battle and convened on the outskirts of the city in a defensive formation," one of the commanders reported.

"I am ready to engage them. I hope they are prepared to face my terrible wrath," Nimrod declared.

Nimrod's warriors advanced within seventy yards of the enemy then paused to size them up. Nimrod noted these men were not Shemites. They were Sumerians—from the family of Ham. All wore helmets and carried shields for defensive purposes. In addition, they were armed with swords, daggers, and spears. Some even had axes. Approximately four thousand troops waited to defend their city against invasion.

"This enemy force will be a worthy opponent," he remarked.

No one stepped forward to challenge Nimrod on this occasion. He thought this a good omen. He let the men stand in battle formation for several minutes, giving them opportunity to evaluate the adversary. Warriors from each side aligned themselves horizontally across a half-mile expanse of a flat plain—similar to the previous battlefield in Akkad. However, this field was brown from recently harvested wheat. Nimrod noticed several ruts that might create problems for the chariots.

Nimrod felt a surge of adrenaline priming him for battle.

"My lord has sent a powerful spirit—a sword of strength and a sign of victory."

He raised his right hand and dropped it quickly. Archers stepped forward and began the usual volleys shot high in the air over opposing troops. Enemy men fell but not as many as before.

"They use helmets and shields effectively," Nimrod commented.

He then pointed his right arm forward. Archers altered the trajectory of the arrows, shooting straight ahead. Many more warriors fell because their shields could not repel all the arrows. Then, following the usual signal, chariots plunged through enemy lines, repeatedly ravaging the ranks. Not one chariot was hijacked, though several careened dangerously on one wheel while rapidly traversing the ruts. Mules and chariots did not swerve to avoid fallen warriors littering the ground. Screams of terror and pain filled the air as chariots mutilated the bodies of many men.

After the final fall of Nimrod's long arm, warriors of the Empire ran forward to engage enemy troops in hand-to-hand combat. Nimrod led the charge—his huge body perfect for battle. The warriors drew confidence from him, as he hacked and speared through scores of enemy combatants. Shouts, screams, gasps, and metallic collisions of weaponry filled the battlefield. Nimrod's men easily slaughtered several thousand enemy soldiers, but his troops also suffered casualties. Nimrod lost four-hundred devoted warriors.

"Execute the wounded on the battlefield. Carrion birds will have a tremendous feast today!" he exclaimed.

Nimrod's men captured one thousand prisoners and confiscated their weapons. His warriors tied their hands and closely supervised them.

"Bring the enemy commanders before me!"

Opposing generals cowered before this huge man, as warriors from both sides looked on.

"You have been a worthy opponent but not strong enough to stand before the mighty Nimrod. Now bow low before me!"

They immediately dropped to the ground, prostrate before this powerful oppressor. Nimrod grabbed a razor-sharp axe, previously wielded by an enemy soldier. The curved axe was mounted on a long wooden handle that fit perfectly in Nimrod's huge hands. He methodically chopped the heads from six commanders—one at a time. He did not rush the execution because he desired all to see and tremble.

"I own the rest of you. You will complete a good work for the Empire."

He took the bloody heads of executed foes and impaled them on spears. He directed six men to move to the front of the procession, holding the heads high for all to see. He marched the troops behind them. Enemy slaves marched last of all with each prisoner's hands bound to the neck of the slave before him. This procession moved slowly through the city of Calneh as horrified citizens watched the gruesome spectacle.

"Bring the leaders of Calneh to the city center," Nimrod ordered.

It took only fifteen minutes to gather the leaders before Nimrod, but he paced the City Square impatiently the entire time.

"On your face before me!" he commanded.

The terrified leaders complied without hesitation.

"Tie their hands behind them, and bind their feet at the ankles."

Nimrod randomly selected six of these men and decapitated each with one stroke of the large axe. Soldiers mounted the heads on long spears driven vertically in the ground at the site of execution.

"Citizens of Calneh will forever know and respect the terrible wrath of Nimrod! The flesh of these men will rot in the City Square. Whoever removes one of the corpses will suffer the same fate. Now bring the warriors, priests, young men and women before me."

The remaining elders lay prostrate before Nimrod for an agonizing period while his men moved through the city gathering slaves for the Empire. They captured thousands of slaves, herding them like cattle into the city center. They left only enough people to work the community farmlands.

"These will be the first to labor in the capital of the new Empire. Babel will soon rise from the sweat and toil of these slaves. Millions of bricks demand tons of clay. Large tracts of land require preparation to construct the capital city. Slaves from Calneh will initiate these formidable tasks. Feed them well, as they must produce a good work. Control them like a flock of sheep, and do not let them disappear from your sight. The gods and I will punish any disobedience!"

Five-hundred soldiers nodded to affirm the instructions and then marched the slaves slowly southward to Babel.

Nimrod's army was still a substantial fighting force—nearly four thousand strong. He marched troops through communities of the Mesopotamian Valley, taking slaves and terrorizing people everywhere. The army met little resistance. He slowly consolidated control over the entire Valley. The very name, Nimrod, struck terror in the hearts of all people in the region. The warriors gathered more than thirty thousand slaves during the campaign in Sumeria. They eliminated all enemy strongholds opposing his rule. Those remaining bowed before Nimrod and submitted to him—though reluctantly at times. The entire campaign took only six months. The dark lord directed Nimrod's exploits during that time.

Chapter 8

Returning Home
from the War

Six months had elapsed since Nimrod had last seen his wife and family. He had not received any news about the Queen while on the battlefront. He thought it an opportune time to return home, and the dark lord did not resist him.

The journey to Uruk took five days. Nimrod had missed the companionship of Semiramis. He would now see if she were worthy of his trust. He arrived at the tavern midday, hoping to surprise the Queen. Her absence dismayed him, but he knew she kept a busy schedule.

The cook appeared to be directing the workers. Nimrod thought she dressed attractively that day. Perhaps Semiramis was allowing her to manage the inn.

"Business seems brisk at the tavern," he addressed the cook. "Occupants have filled the rooms to capacity."

"Why have you left the great battle to visit us, my lord?" the surprised cook inquired.

"I have grown tired of battle," he replied, hoping to fend off probing questions. "Where is my wife? I have missed her these long months and desire her companionship."

"Many projects occupy the Queen. I have not seen her much at the tavern for several months. She comes and goes as she pleases."

"Where must I travel to find her?"

"I believe she is working north of the city today—just outside its boundaries. You can take the main road to that location."

"What is she doing there? That is not a normal place for the Queen to conduct business."

"She prefers to reveal her affairs. I am not at liberty to divulge these details."

"I respect your position. Hopefully I will find her in the area you describe. I shall return for a meal later today."

Nimrod wondered what could possibly occupy a Queen in this remote location. He quickly traveled to the northern boundary of Uruk and located her without difficulty. He was astonished to find her directing the construction of a massive brick wall. The wall already encompassed the northern portion of Uruk. The workers had built it wide enough for several chariots to travel side-by-side on top. A formidable force would find it difficult to breach. Semiramis had designed guard towers along the wall, spaced regularly every one hundred yards. Brick masons worked diligently without complaints. Nimrod could not identify one idle laborer. Semiramis stood in a guard tower directing the whole operation. She could easily observe the project from that vantage point. Several supervisors communicated her instructions to the workers.

Nimrod climbed to the top of the guard tower and silently slipped next to his wife. He had hoped to surprise her, but Semiramis did not appear startled.

She greeted him appropriately, and then spoke, "Are you vacationing from the war, my lord?"

"Constant fighting has made me irritable, and I need a

break from the campaign. I have missed you, my dear."

"Have the gods given you dominion over the cities? Do you bring good tidings?"

Semiramis looked directly into his eyes. Nimrod felt transparent.

"I bring very good news. I control the entire Mesopotamian Valley. Only the northern lands remain for me to conquer. People in the Valley cower in my presence, yet the Queen stands upright before me."

He thought he detected a slight smile parting her lips.

"The gods also guide the Queen, my lord. Even the dark lord converses with me. I have no reason to cower before you or any man."

She smiled—her countenance was radiant. This fearless woman continually amazed Nimrod.

"Standing here with you brings happiness to my soul. However, I cannot accomplish the duties of a brick mason and have not studied the skills of an architect. You must teach me this work someday... sometime." He toyed with her. "Your work is excellent. Perhaps you will construct the capital. Many workers now reside there, and they would consider it an honor to labor for the Queen of the Empire!"

"I intend to finish my projects in Uruk, but I shall consider the request at a later time."

The beauty of Semiramis had not diminished since Nimrod last saw her. On that hot day she wore a lightly colored thin robe, highlighting the curves in her attractive body. He could understand why laborers toiled without complaint for this lovely woman. Her supervisors did not require whips to keep the workers on task.

Nimrod noticed long scaffolds, erected to the top of the wall. Thousands of bricks and large containers of the oily mortar, bitumen, rested on the scaffolds. Masons and scantily clothed servants worked in the hot sun. Prolonged sun exposure had baked the skin of their muscular bodies chocolate brown.

"What other projects have you planned for this city?"

"The wall and towers must surround Uruk. This city will have no less protection than Kish. I intend to oversee construction of my castle and build additional temples of worship. I cannot leave Uruk until these projects are near completion."

They stood silently for several minutes, observing the landscape from the tower. Boats carried goods on the Euphrates River, and rich farmlands extended for miles beyond the city. Nimrod noted fields of wheat, barley, peas, and grass. Groves of fig trees were interspersed between the fields. Irrigation canals carried water from the Euphrates to burgeoning farmlands. He noticed young men harvesting crops and plowing new fields. Boys and girls tended flocks of sheep grazing the grasslands.

Nimrod interrupted the short period of silence: "Doesn't the tavern concern you any longer?"

He hoped for an affirmative answer.

"I continue to oversee the business. I spend some time there. After all, I still have no place to rest my head at night."

The answer did not allay his jealousy.

"The cook is an able administrator. I have given her more responsibility to manage the tavern."

"I agree she is an excellent worker and a responsible manager. Indeed, her devotion to you is obvious."

Semiramis changed the subject: "City elders have much work here, trying to keep farmlands productive and commerce moving via river and over land. They must appease the priests and meet with the people. We should expand the government of Uruk to accommodate these needs. The elders cannot possibly manage the business of two large cities."

"I shall soon travel to Kish and relay your concerns to my father. He will resolve these problems expediently."

"I prefer to focus my efforts on building projects in this city. I do not have time to work with the elders on other issues. However, I realize these matters need attention."

She and Nimrod walked back to the tavern late that afternoon. Customers filled the street markets, purchasing daily supplies of meat, fish, and bread. Nimrod noticed several new taverns had recently opened in the city, and they appeared to have many occupants. Nimrod and Semiramis held hands as they walked past shops displaying the work of local artisans. Nimrod stopped to purchase a beautiful gold ring for his wife. An expensive stone from the northern mountains sat securely on that thick band of gold. Artisans had etched fertility symbols of fruit and flowers on the gold band.

Finally, they arrived at the tavern of Semiramis, where they were greeted with a delicious meal. Servants brought large platters of fish, vegetables, bread, and the fruit of Mesopotamia—olives, figs, dates, and grapes. They also provided pottery vessels filled with beer. Nimrod and Semiramis continued the conversation, sitting at their usual corner table in the dining room. Customers filled the tables to capacity. However, the usual festive atmosphere was subdued that evening. Everyone was acutely aware of a familiar guest in the city, and he still terrified them. Musicians played harps and lutes, providing background music for the dinner. Nimrod felt content, gazing at the face and long brown hair of his lovely wife.

"We will need more workers from Uruk to construct the capital city," Nimrod remarked.

"If you demand workers from here you must also recruit them from Kish. I will not permit my work force to be diminished!"

"I shall honor that request, my lady." Nimrod tried to appear agreeable. "I will make arrangements with the city elders. Farmlands require expansion to feed the growing population of Babel, and farmers need to increase productivity."

"You and the elders must accomplish these tasks. My plate is already full!"

"My plate is empty, but my stomach is quite full!" Nimrod declared loudly for the benefit of the cook. "I hope you can arrange for the evacuation of our special suite tonight, my dear. I will not intervene in the affairs of the tavern."

Nimrod was learning to respect her territory.

"I will handle that problem." Semiramis responded with a smile—her bright green eyes meeting his.

Nimrod truly appreciated this gift from the dark lord. He would attempt to respect the lord's work within her.

The next morning he left the tavern to circulate in the city and make a favorable impression on the people. He realized he could not win their hearts in one short visit, particularly since he required absolute obedience. While walking the streets of Uruk, he grew more impressed with the popularity of Semiramis. Citizens seemed anxious to obey her commands, and some appeared willing to die for her. All spoke favorably of the Queen.

Nimrod stayed in Uruk for several weeks. He mingled with the people, trying to gain acceptance. Each day he walked through different sections of the city, conversing with the residents. Nimrod found this a daunting task, because people feared him after he had terrorized the city several months earlier. Many avoided him like a poisonous viper. Nimrod politely engaged some in conversation and successfully socialized with relatives. The majority of them worked religious or government jobs in the community.

Nimrod worshipped in several ornate temples during the short stay. He thought artisans from Uruk exhibited more talent than those of Kish. The same brown brick temples and government buildings were common to both cities, but a variety of rich colors decorated the temples of Uruk.

Sculptures of animals, serpents, and gods lavishly embellished these buildings. Interior temple walls displayed murals depicting legendary works of the gods.

Nimrod felt he had spent ample time pursuing goals for that visit. He had quickly grown weary of the hypocritical life of a politician.

"I will leave tomorrow to visit my family," Nimrod announced one evening. "I shall spend several days there making arrangements to improve the government of Uruk, according to your requests. Thereafter, I will return to the war. Communities have not yet submitted to my authority, and more people must become citizens of the Empire. I shall resume this work very soon, and it will occupy me for months—perhaps longer. My lord beckons me forward once again."

"Who am I to resist the commands of our lord."

Nimrod sensed Semiramis had grown weary of him. He had slowed her work and negatively impacted business at the tavern.

"Many projects will occupy me, but you are welcome home at any time. Perhaps you can send a messenger to inform me of your next vacation from the battlefront." She smiled coyly.

"I will consider the request."

Nimrod knew she did not enjoy being pulled from a busy schedule, but he would not make any promises. He still did not fully trust her.

* * * * * * * * *

The next morning Nimrod began the return trip to Kish. He traveled day and night, shortening the usual journey to three days. He finally arrived home in the middle of a hot afternoon. A happy heart eased his sleep-deprived body. The family welcomed him with open arms. Initially, he did not discuss the war because he desired to know about the family. Several new nieces and nephews had entered the world since he had departed for the battlefront. Nimrod's siblings had children and grandchildren. He found it difficult to keep up with a rapidly growing family.

Cush embraced Nimrod after arriving home from a long meeting with the city elders. He seemed overjoyed to see his eldest son.

"Join me for a respite in the courtyard behind the house," Cush invited.

"Father, you look tired."

"—the consequence of a long day's work, my son."

Cush summoned the servants to bring a refreshing beverage. They sat together, waiting for the evening meal. Nimrod noticed the pleasant aroma of cooking food, wafting through kitchen windows into the courtyard.

"The city of Kish continues to grow. Several new trade routes have developed overland after we adopted the carts of Uruk. Our carpenters have built larger, sturdier carts. Farmlands outside the city continue to expand as we improve methods for cultivating them. Weights and measures have also improved productivity. The high wall surrounding the city protects the residents from wild beasts," Cush boasted, obviously proud of these achievements.

"One might think I had been gone for years—not months!"

"Unfortunately, the elders are overworked. They have found it difficult to manage both cities."

"Have you considered expanding the government? We will need a larger government as the Empire grows. Good management of resources requires adequate oversight. Citizens should find the leaders accessible and responsive to their needs. Do you agree, Father?"

Cush nodded.

"How is the Queen of Uruk?"

"Semiramis revels in her new responsibilities. Most men will never equal her achievements. She envies our city and intends to oversee substantial improvements for Uruk. She desires to surpass the accomplishments of Kish. The Queen is presently constructing a wall around her city."

"She performs a remarkable work, my son. I fear her goals may one day interfere with yours."

"No problems have arisen thus far. I hope the needs of the Empire will someday unify our visions. Only the gods can determine that, however. I shall submit to the demands of my lord," Nimrod declared, hoping to allay his father's concern.

"I have spoken with the Queen about the growth of the Empire," Nimrod continued. "Many slaves have arrived in Babel, and construction will soon begin. A work-force of thirty thousand will inhabit the city within the month. I feel certain the population will swell to over sixty thousand within a year. Thousands of additional slaves will arrive from the northern lands. They will all labor on this glorious project. Surely you must appreciate the food and shelter requirements for such a large population, Father."

"I cannot even imagine these staggering numbers, Nimrod."

"Do you agree with my suggestions to increase the size of our government?" "I have reached that conclusion and will make these concerns known to the elders in our meeting tomorrow morning. Furthermore, we must supply critical food and shelter for the newcomers in Babel. I know you do not have time to attend to these matters. Therefore, I shall assume that responsibility."

Nimrod knew his father would promptly address these issues. Only Cush could gather enough revenue and provisions to supply the growing population of the capital. Nimrod felt proud of his father's involvement in the creation of Babel. Cush would do all in his power to ensure the success of the Empire.

"The God of the Shemites is losing power. Noah's God could not possibly raise such an Empire from the dust of this Valley. Someday we will boast of our achievement to Noah and his family."

Nimrod continued: "I plan to stay only two more days in Kish. I prefer to spend the majority of that time with the family, and then I shall return to my men in Akkad. My warriors perform a work that would make you proud, but dominion of the Empire must extend to settlements in the northern lands. This territory is filled with followers of Noah's God. I must conquer them soon before they can mount sufficient resistance. I hope you understand the urgency of this matter."

"I understand, my son. Indeed, you have much to accomplish. We will appreciate what little time you can spend with the family."

Nimrod embraced his father and left to converse with the family.

Chapter 9

The Northern Campaign

Nimrod departed after spending only two days with his family. Three weeks had passed since he had left the troops, and he was eager to return. He would initially evaluate the reorganization of Akkad. The journey took only two days, traveling day and night. He traveled without companions and did not stop to enjoy the scenery. He arrived in Akkad late afternoon—just before sunset. After meeting with the commanders he determined reorganization of the city government was proceeding smoothly. Annuki had assigned construction projects to the prisoners. They appeared to labor diligently without complaints, but Nimrod doubted they would remain cooperative in Babel. However, the stable conditions in Akkad pleased him.

"Let me treat you to supper in the largest tavern in Akkad," Annuki encouraged.

They walked several blocks to a plain looking tavern. Nimrod was not impressed. It was much smaller than the Queen's tavern, but he could at least walk through the large entrance without stooping. They strode down a long corridor to a dining area packed with guests. Most of them were Sumerian warriors assigned to keep peace in the city. They sat at a small table and discussed recent events over supper. Nimrod noticed the owner did not provide musicians for entertainment—a customary practice in his wife's tavern. Nevertheless, he enjoyed the meal and Annuki's companionship. They did not deliberate military business that evening. Nimrod preferred to discuss his relationship with Semiramis.

"I am concerned about the activities of my wife outside her responsibilities as Queen. No one in Uruk will provide any information about her private life. I know you rarely visit there, but maybe you can assign other family members to do some snooping."

"I will attempt to honor your request, my lord."

Nimrod sensed the reluctance. Perhaps Annuki feared getting involved in a difficult situation, he thought.

"I am anxious to return to Uruk—at least for a short respite from my work in Akkad," Annuki added.

Nimrod described the major changes occurring in Uruk. He knew the transformation would impress Annuki.

They finished the meal, and Nimrod suddenly felt exhausted.

"I must excuse myself, Annuki. My body craves rest. Let us meet early in the morning at this same table to plan the future of the Empire."

Nimrod retired to a quiet room on the second floor. He had no visitors that night and fell immediately into a restful sleep.

* * * * * * * * *

The next morning Nimrod found Annuki waiting at a table in the dining room. Morning sunlight poured through east-facing windows to illuminate the room. Stonework comprising the walls amazed Nimrod. He wondered how the tavern owners had transported those massive stones from a location far north of Akkad.

Annuki had ordered a large breakfast, and the servants were promptly delivering plates of eggs, bread, and meat. The quick service and tasty food impressed Nimrod.

"I am ready to plan the expansion of the Empire. We have taken many prisoners into custody from the city of Calneh and surrounding communities. In fact, the warriors have captured over thirty thousand slaves for the Empire. Most of them are currently marching to Babel. They will prepare land for construction of the capital and then build living quarters for themselves and the commanders."

Nimrod continued: "I will not send any more slaves to Babel until food and housing are available. I plan to capture thousands of additional slaves during the campaign in the northern territory. Assign the prisoners work here until we can accommodate them elsewhere. Have you found acceptable leaders for Akkad?"

"I have already appointed several citizens to these positions, my lord. We noticed many were impressed with your short inaugural speech. Several of these men volunteered for vacancies in the city government. We have chosen the most capable to serve the community. I have determined descendants of Ham better qualify for leadership positions. They embrace your vision for the Empire. Surprisingly, many Shemites also welcome the changes you have outlined and do not desire to follow Noah's God. Innovations of the Sumerian culture have attracted them to this area."

"I like what I hear, Annuki. Please tell me more."

"A Shemite of high esteem in this community would like to accompany you in the northern lands. He is familiar with city development, but his understanding of military matters is still rather primitive, of course."

"What is his name? Perhaps I have heard of him."

"His name is Asshur, and he claims to be a son of Shem. But he does not seem interested in Shem's God as far as I can determine."

Nimrod decided he would speak to this interesting defector.

"Do you have any bad news to report, Annuki? I always anticipate some disappointments."

Nimrod assumed Annuki would withhold any disturbing information. Annuki paused, appearing ambivalent about answering the question.

"Well… there is one problem I didn't want to bother you with."

"I insist you divulge this information, Annuki."

"We have found other Shemites in Akkad who refuse to bow before our gods, and they do not embrace the Sumerian culture. These Shemites show no enthusiasm for participating in the new Empire."

"I should have suspected as much!" seethed Nimrod. "I will persuade them to support our vision. Bring them to me immediately!"

"But… we have not confined them as prisoners, my lord. I assure you we can locate them, and they will comply with our requests. They desire peace and do not interfere with our activities in this city."

Nimrod knew Annuki had no stomach for confrontations like the one on the Akkadian battlefield.

"Bring them to the City Square at once!" Nimrod shouted—his anger becoming apparent to all in the small dining room. "I shall anxiously wait there."

Annuki and his men left immediately to find the Shemites.

The center of Akkad was smaller than any city in the Empire. The largest building on the perimeter of the square was the three-story government building. However, another structure would soon dominate the landscape. New city leaders had ordered the demolition of four smaller buildings directly opposite the government structure. They had planned to replace them with a large ornate temple dedicated to Sumerian gods. Construction had recently commenced after removing the rubble. As Nimrod waited in the city center, he observed brick masons and slaves working feverishly to lay foundation stones and erect walls of the impressive temple.

Before Nimrod could digest his generous meal, Annuki and the warriors herded the Shemite families into the City Square. Nimrod's face bore greetings of bad omens. The city center filled rapidly with citizens of the community—government officials, business owners, and common people. Brick masons and their Shemitic slaves ceased work to witness the grisly scene about to unfold. All knew something dreadful was imminent.

"The Shemites are gathered before you, my lord." Annuki bowed.

Nimrod noticed beads of perspiration dotting Annuki's pale cheeks and forehead. He scowled at the Shemites, pondering his next move. Thirty-four Shemites stood before him—the majority were children and young women. All appeared terrified. Nimrod initially suppressed his anger as he addressed them.

"My men have informed me some citizens of Akkad refuse to embrace the Sumerian gods. My warriors have brought you before me as those guilty of this offense. What is your plea? Speak up! I am not a patient man."

None of the Shemites spoke, but several children whimpered.

"Since you are at a loss for words, I will make it easy for you to demonstrate loyalty by your actions. I am Nimrod and my god is the dark lord who reigns over all gods. If you bow before me we will forget these accusations and life will return to normal. Now bow on your knees!"

The frightened Shemites stood their ground.

One woman responded meekly: "The One and Only God

demands our full allegiance. He is a jealous God who looks unfavorably on those who worship false gods, and He detests idols created in their image. God is greater than any man in this world. With all due respect, we cannot bow before you or these false gods. God will provide for us in times of danger. If not, He has prepared a better home in eternity."

The woman's response fueled Nimrod's anger. He could not reason with these people and would not permit them to challenge his authority. A sudden impulse rose from deep within his dark soul. He choked back anger and spoke as calmly as possible.

"I like young children. Come here little ones. Children like these please the gods exceedingly."

Nimrod extended his hands to the children. They cowered before him, fearful to pry loose from their mothers' protective hold. Nimrod snatched an infant from his mother in one swift motion. He was the woman's only child.

Nimrod spoke loudly for the benefit of the gathering crowd: "A first born son pleases the dark lord. A young child surpasses the sacrifice of an unblemished ram."

The cruel tyrant brought forth his dagger and slowly beheaded the screaming infant.

"Have the priests sacrifice this carcass on the altar!" Nimrod ordered, after heaving the dead infant beyond the reach of his mother. "Now, do I have any other volunteers?"

Nimrod's warriors restrained the wailing mother.

A young man with deep blue eyes and sandy brown hair stepped forward.

"I will volunteer, sir."

"Are you prepared to bow before me?"

"I request to offer my life as a sacrifice for the others."

The man's wife sobbed uncontrollably as she gazed at her husband in despair. He was clearly in the prime of life, but his resolve did not waver.

"I shall honor your request, my friend."

Nimrod felt he must make an example of the Shemites to intimidate those who opposed his leadership. He turned the young man to face his people. The man's wife looked on in horror, and two teenage sons wrestled to free themselves from the warriors. Nimrod slit the young man's throat with the same sharp dagger, cutting deeply to divide head from body. He held the man's head high before the crowd.

"Those who defy me will forfeit their lives on the altar of the dark lord!"

Nimrod heaved the dead carcass to the side. He did not have the stomach for further blood letting that day.

"Remove these Shemites from my presence! Take them to prison! Soon they will labor as slaves, building the very Empire they refuse to acknowledge—women and children included."

Nimrod's men herded the families from the City Square. They dragged kicking, screaming women in desperate grief. The warriors took them to a small brick building on a narrow street, several blocks away. The Shemites would call this home for the next month. Thick windowless walls made the prison impregnable and prevented sunlight from penetrating the dark interior. The prisoners had virtually no chance of escape.

* * * * * * * * *

Rumors of military campaigns spread as far north as Mount Ararat. All knew Nimrod as a brutal tyrant and killer of innocent women and children. Some called him the dark nephilim. Noah, Shem, and those faithful to the One True God also heard about this evil scourge in the southern lands.

Noah's physical health had deteriorated, and he had become severely depressed. He refused to leave the house and usually stayed in his room, even when summoned for meals. Noah brooded incessantly, refusing to speak unless forced to do so. He lost weight and precious sleep. Nightmares plagued his troubled spirit, reviving memories of evil in the Old World. Noah always awoke from the same dream—forever floating on the water with no land in sight. He grieved continuously because he only saw repetition of sins prevalent in the Old World. Realizing he had fathered the vilest inhabitants of the New World merely worsened the depression. His children were no better than the wicked people living prior to the Flood. He felt some solace in knowing Shem followed the God of his forefathers.

Noah continued to commune with his son and several grandchildren, but he had conferred the spiritual inheritance to Shem several generations earlier. Noah bestowed the spiritual inheritance after Ham had stolen the fleece. Noah encouraged Shem to use his God-given wisdom liberally in a wicked world.

Shem had assumed the responsibility to encourage the family to follow God. He met daily with them to pray and teach God's truth. One morning they met in their usual place of worship—the large meeting room in the house of Noah and Shem. Sunlight streamed through well-placed windows and illuminated two large chairs sitting in the center of the room. Shem and Noah had carved them one hundred years earlier from trees harvested on nearby mountains. They were reserved for these patriarchs. The remaining believers sat on animal skins, spread across the floor. The faithful remnant always began the meetings with praise and singing to the Lord, followed by the fervent prayers of believers. Shem would then teach from the ancient texts, written by patriarchs of the Old World. Noah conspicuously abstained from the meetings in those days because he felt incapable of mentoring the family. He preferred communing with God in the solitude of his room. Arphaxad sat with the family at the feet of Shem. Arphaxad initiated the discussion after the morning prayer.

"Father, we must fight Nimrod and these wicked warriors. They have murdered and humiliated our people!"

Shem studied the appearance of his oldest son, thinking the curly black hair gave him a youthful appearance. However, that gray lock of hair framing a wrinkled forehead hinted at his age of one hundred years. Shem sympathized with his son's frustration but would not capitulate to the impulsive demands.

"I agree these times are difficult, my son, but the Lord does not call us to battle. We cannot coerce the Sumerians into a relationship with God. Even in dangerous times God does not operate that way. He desires the willing submission of each person. We will push them further from the Truth by taking up arms."

"Then what can we do in the midst of an evil that rapidly extinguishes the lights of Truth?" asked Arphaxad.

"God will intervene according to His timetable." Shem spoke with a hope anchored deep within his soul. "God feels intense pain with the loss of each life, but we must not act in His behalf. He has good reasons for delaying His justice. One day is as a thousand years, and a thousand years as one day with our God.[13] I lived in the Old World for one hundred years. No one in the whole world had faith in God by the end of that time except for several members of our family. Sin of all imaginable kinds prevailed on the earth, and God even despaired of creating mankind. The flood annihilated the Old World, but it did not destroy evil in the heart of man. Only God's Spirit can change man's heart. Someday He will do so—at a time of His choosing."

Eber, Shem's great grandson of thirty-three years, asked, "Why does evil continue to multiply in the world, Grandfather? Wickedness appeared destroyed by the great flood, yet it roared right back into the New World within several years."

Shem appreciated Eber's struggle to understand this concept. He knew the human mind preferred to ignore the struggle altogether.

"Evil germinated in this world with the sin of our great father and mother, Adam and Eve—when they disobeyed God by eating the forbidden fruit. But the seed of evil originated even earlier in the mind of Lucifer—God's chief angelic creation. He rebelled in the Kingdom of Heaven and determined to rule on God's throne. Lucifer usurped God's rightful ownership of this world after God cast him from heaven. He became the earth's temporary ruler. We attribute the existence of evil to him. He introduced evil to mankind through trickery and deception. We know him as Satan—the great deceiver and the ancient serpent."

Shem knew he had the children's attention.

"Evil is like a weed. We cut it off at the ground, but it always sprouts back when conditions favor its growth. This is because its deep taproot grows from the rebellious mind of the evil one. The root must be destroyed before evil can be eliminated."

"Who will destroy the root, Grandfather, and when will this occur?" his grandson, Shelah, asked.

Shelah was Arphaxad's son and Eber's father. Shem thought he looked quite young at seventy years—a tall handsome man with an olive-brown complexion. His curly brown hair had no visible streaks of gray. Dark brown eyes portrayed a desire to peer beneath the surface appearance of things.

"Someday God will destroy Satan," Shem replied. "He is the root I have described. Satan's earthly rule will only last for a designated period because God has determined its boundaries. He asks us to live by faith until He destroys the evil one and restores His rightful ownership of the world. God will then free mankind from this curse."

"What can we do now, Father?" asked Arphaxad.

"God asks us to trust Him, and He desires us to model

122

this faith to our children. He has not offered additional instructions, but He will do so in His time. For now He expects us to walk by faith, using what light He has provided. 'His Word is a lamp to our feet, and a light for our path.'[14] His light illuminates the path directly before us, but it does not shine far into the distance. Likewise, He has not promised to reveal our future. If He did, we might not choose to face it. God is holy and He will intervene in the affairs of men once again. Take this truth and share it with your families."

Shem finished his teaching and left the room to spend time with his father.

* * * * * * * * *

Nimrod directed his men to arrange a meeting with Asshur before leaving Akkad. He was curious to learn more about this man. He agreed to meet in Asshur's large stone house, which sat in a grove of trees beyond the populated areas of Akkad—away from the probing eyes of people. Nimrod quickly sized up the man after sitting down with him. Asshur had wrinkled, camel-colored skin with curly gray hair and beard. He appeared short, stout and approximately thirty years older than Nimrod. He nervously drummed his fingers on the side of a chair during the conversation.

"You and I are closely related—my father is your cousin, I believe. Do you live by the same persuasion as the unfortunate Shemites in this community?" asked Nimrod.

"Shem is my father, of course," replied Asshur. "I cannot dispute his good and godly intentions. However, I feel he lives in dreams of the past. He shows no interest in the achievements of men and refuses to embrace the Sumerian culture. I have chosen to move away from him for that reason."

"Please explain further."

"I believe God has granted us intelligence to create

things that improve our lives. I am convinced mankind advances when dwelling in larger communities, such as the Sumerian cities."

Asshur's statements encouraged Nimrod.

"And what spiritual beliefs do you have?" Nimrod asked.

"I suppose I believe in God, but He hasn't spoken to me. I claim to believe in God because my father taught me about Him. However, I do not regard this belief necessary to live in the world. I think man's emphasis on spiritual matters is considerably exaggerated. Superstition and ignorance cause most of this spiritual nonsense."

Nimrod thought Asshur sounded like his father—without the bitterness. Perhaps he could reach the Shemitic people for the Empire. Nimrod determined he could work with this man.

"What role would you prefer in the future of this Empire?"

Asshur pondered the question a moment before responding, silently drumming his fingers on the chair.

"I have repeatedly contemplated this for several weeks. The northern lands do not contain large cities like those of the Mesopotamian Valley. Settlements are scattered sparsely from here all the way to Mount Ararat. I would like to accompany you and assist in developing northern cities for the Empire—if you will have me. I know the Shemitic people and their culture. Perhaps I can encourage them to move into these cities. I also have good relations with most of Japheth's children. They share a similar philosophy, and spiritual concerns do not significantly influence them."

"Then we shall work together—for the Empire, of course!"

Their discussion continued for several hours. They addressed topics of mutual concern. Nimrod liked this intelligent man. Asshur would contribute to the growing Empire,

Nimrod concluded.

"I would like you to meet my father," Nimrod offered. "He shares similar values and is an excellent ruler of Kish."

"I knew Cush many years ago, before his family left the northern lands. He was a talented young man, and I could never defeat him in the games of childhood. I would enjoy renewing the relationship after so many years."

"Then we shall travel to Kish after accomplishing my goals in the northern lands. I will personally facilitate your reunion with my father."

Nimrod warmly embraced Asshur and gave last minute instructions. "Prepare yourself for a long journey north. We shall leave in two days, and I insist you travel at my side. Perhaps we can combine resources to consolidate control over the northern lands."

"I am excited to participate in this venture. I shall be ready and will come when you summon me."

* * * * * * * * *

Nimrod left Akkad with four thousand warriors. Asshur and many Shemitic relatives accompanied him.

"We shall gather the population of this area into four large cities, my friend," Nimrod instructed as they rode their mules northward, leading the troops.

They followed the Tigris River most of the journey. Nimrod felt attracted to this large river with its swift currents and rocky shores, and he enjoyed the cooler northern temperatures.

"March through the country and relocate the people into areas we have designated as new cities. Use all necessary measures to facilitate this movement," Nimrod ordered the commanders.

"I prefer to use diplomacy to reach the people. I will convince them of the benefits of a civilized lifestyle,"

Asshur stated.

"Proceed as you wish but achieve my goals," Nimrod instructed.

Asshur and the Shemites persuaded many to move into the cities, and they even used Nimrod's tactics of intimidation on selected occasions. Asshur reported to his superior one day after six long months.

Nimrod began the conversation: "We have encountered minimal resistance gathering the population into four cities adjacent to the Tigris."

"I cannot persuade the godly Shemites to move," Asshur confessed. "They prefer living in smaller settlements outside the cities."

"Ignore them for now, my friend. I will send warriors to deal with them later. After I secure the boundaries of the Empire I will persecute those who disobey my commands. Appoint elders and encourage them to establish agriculture and commerce in the cities."

"I shall do better than that. I will also hire masons to construct essential buildings in each city."

Months later Nimrod addressed the commanders: "I have spearheaded the formation of the Empire, so I will name the new cities. We will call the southernmost city, Nimrod. People of the north know me as Ninus, 'the son' of the King. I shall name the northernmost city Nineveh—after that name. Future generations will acknowledge me as the founder of these magnificent cities. I will name the other two cities Rehoboth Ir and Resen."

He continued: "Enslave those who refuse to worship our gods and resist settlement in the cities. Send them to construct Babel. I desire sixty thousand slaves to build the capital of the Empire, and I fully intend to achieve that number."

Nimrod and Asshur met regularly with the elders of each city.

"Assign masons to build temples dedicated to Sumerian

gods. Construct roads and government buildings after erecting the temples," Nimrod instructed. "Astrologers will assist you to design the temples and align them with important constellations. Priests will appoint common people to work temple lands. Send fifty percent of the revenue from grain sales to Babel. Use the remainder for local city development."

"I shall oversee the elders and verify they achieve the goals you have established. Furthermore, I will introduce Sumerian culture and religion in each city," Asshur promised.

Asshur worked diligently for several years to fulfill these promises. Nimrod met with him one afternoon after meeting with Nineveh's leaders.

"You have served the Empire well during our tenure in the northern lands, and I am grateful for your assistance, my friend," Nimrod commended.

"I pledged to develop the cities in this territory. I have much work yet to accomplish, but the process is moving in a positive direction."

"We have neglected one important city in the north, however."

"I do not understand, my lord. I thought we effectively administered all these cities," Asshur replied, drumming his fingers nervously on the table.

"We have failed to populate the fifth city of this region. I ordain its location south of the cities we have already developed. People of the New World will know it as the gateway to the northern territory, and they will recognize it by its distinct name—Asshur. Yes, my friend, this city will commemorate the name of its founder."

Nimrod looked down at Asshur, laughing at his astonishment. They rose from their chairs and warmly embraced.

Asshur wasted no time planning the development of his new city.

* * * * * * * * *

Shem heard rumors about Nimrod's growing Empire in the region. His descendants feared for their lives because Nimrod's warriors hunted them like animals and tortured them for their faith. Shem felt the Lord prompting him to confront Nimrod. He decided to obtain Noah's counsel.

"Father, you must leave your room and walk outdoors in the sunlight on this beautiful afternoon. Your body needs exercise."

Noah had spiraled further downward in the whirlpool of depression.

"Walk with me in the woods behind the house. Exercise will help the depression and strengthen your ailing body," Shem encouraged.

Noah did not respond but grudgingly rose from the bed with his son's assistance. They slowly exited the house and walked quietly for twenty minutes, enjoying the wild flowers. Noah's nine-hundred-year-old body had little endurance for mountain walks. Shem frequently slowed the pace, allowing Noah time to catch his breath. They stopped at the shore of a clear mountain lake.

"Do you remember this bench I built many years ago? It invites us to rest, Father."

Time passed as they sat and watched large fish swimming in the deep glacial water. Ducks frolicked and quacked to announce the human intrusion into their domain. After sitting silently for fifteen minutes, Shem initiated the conversation.

"Father, my heart grieves to see the relentless expansion of evil among our descendants. Satan has used Nimrod as his ambassador in the New World. Together they humiliate and annihilate our family, persecuting all believers remaining in this land. Nimrod's warriors have transported many of our descendants to Babel to work as slaves. Messengers have reported they live in miserable conditions and endure horrific persecution under this man's authority. I mourn when I counsel my children to avoid the cities and they end up in the hands of God's enemy."

"I am familiar with Satan's schemes, my son. I wish it were otherwise. The spirit of man is weak, and Satan will easily have his way with our kind. Men cannot possibly withstand him. Only God's grace can protect us."

"Why has God allowed this to happen, Father?"

Shem knew Noah had struggled with this question for years. Noah shrugged his shoulders and looked at the ground.

"I am not privileged to know the mind of God. He has a purpose, kept secret from the beginning of time. God will prevail for the ultimate victory. He will not allow Satan to usurp His throne. Somehow, God will preserve a remnant of believers in this New World. That is His way. He preserved the small remnant of our family from the Old World. He previously informed us His Seed—the Seed of the woman— would crush Satan's head.[15] Someday God's Seed will deliver the mortal blow to Satan. Only then will God free mankind from the power of His enemy and forever eliminate evil from this world."

"Then He will remove the sting of death also," Shem added.

"Indeed, God created us for immortality. He originally intended Adam and Eve to have eternal life in the Garden of Eden. He walked with them daily before they sinned. Their fellowship would have continued forever, but sin and Satan temporarily altered that. However, God will not allow the serpent to thwart His plan. Someday He will restore the eternal relationship with those who embrace Him. Those who refuse are also destined for immortality, but they will not attain a relationship with God. They have chosen to align with Satan and will endure everlasting misery with him. God permits each person to make that choice. One either chooses God as his friend, or he becomes God's enemy. There are no other options. God will not quench the sting of death for His enemies."[16]

Shem interrupted his father to inform him of another related matter.

"Father, I have prayed about the current crisis in this world. The path far ahead is unclear, but in the light where my spirit has discernment, God has directed me to meet with Nimrod."

Noah could not respond for several minutes. Shem knew his father would have difficulty accepting this shocking revelation in his depressed state.

"I fear for your life, my son. I cannot bear to lose you. Please consider the danger."

Shem gazed at his father with compassion, realizing the tremendous burden of suffering this man had endured for many, many years.

"Father, you have just stated God has destined us for immortality with Him. I cannot predict the outcome of this meeting, but I am certain God stands with me, and I will ultimately stand with you regardless of the outcome."

"I am weak, my son, but I won't hinder God's will. My prayers will precede you."

Noah's tears betrayed his weak resolve, but Shem knew his spirit would grow ever stronger by resting in God's will.

Shem slowly walked to the house with his father. The effort was nearly too much for Noah, and he collapsed on the bed when they returned. Shem's family had convened for the daily worship. Shem joined the meeting and immediately addressed the family.

"I will not spend much time with you today, my children. I have come to announce God has spoken to my heart. He has asked me to meet with Nimrod."

Apprehension quickly replaced the joy of fellowship. They could not bear to lose their father and spiritual mentor during this time of crisis.

"Please do not meet with this wicked man, Father,"

Arphaxad pleaded. "He will not listen to your counsel. Furthermore, he will delight in killing a well-known man of God. Nimrod will consider your death a great victory, and this will not advance our cause in the New World."

"I must obey our heavenly Father. He who established this meeting will preserve me, if that is His will. I shall not argue the point any further, my son."

Arphaxad and the rest of the family realized the futility of disputing with their father. Shem left the room to spend time communing with the Lord.

Shem determined he would go alone to meet with Nimrod. He would not endanger the rest of the family. He prayed God would give him the words and strength to stand in the presence of this wicked man. Shem departed before sunrise the next morning, having packed the necessary provisions the night before. He mounted a brown spotted mule and rode toward the Tigris River before his family could make plans to detain him. He had heard a rumor Nimrod was constructing a palace in Nineveh. He would begin his search there.

Chapter 10

The Confrontation

S hem traveled several days before reaching Nineveh. He walked into the city late one morning leading his mule on a short rope. Many stonemasons were busily constructing a defensive wall around the city. Shem noticed scaffolding built to the height of the growing wall. It supported workers and many stones used in the construction. He walked down a wide street where masons toiled to erect buildings of all sizes. The avenue appeared to terminate in the city center. He ventured off the main thoroughfare to traverse smaller roads. Children laughed while playing games on those streets. Small alleys perpendicularly intersected the larger avenues. These narrow alleys were lined with tiny houses packed tightly together. They barely allowed the passage of two carts. Excrement of animals and humans lay in piles interspersed with garbage strewn by residents. Shem was disgusted by this malodorous eyesore and decided to avoid the alleys.

The larger streets were much cleaner. Shem noted they were filled with people and mule-drawn carts, transporting bricks and stones to building sites throughout the city. As Shem approached the city center he observed the construction of much larger buildings. Workers perched atop these growing structures like birds on a tree branch. He presumed several of these buildings were temples dedicated to false deities, and he felt uncomfortable walking by them.

Nearly everyone in the New World was familiar with the godly reputation of Shem. Many in the northern lands had personally met him and they all revered his name.

Shem knew the people recognized him. He noticed some were ashamed to stand before him.

"They prefer to live with the conviction of their guilt—like refusing to remove a large splinter in a fingertip," he muttered.

Shem stopped at a noisy street market, bustling with people. Stands laden with fresh vegetables, fish, and fruit were shaded by animal skin tarps. The wonderful aroma of freshly baked bread tempted him.

He had assessed the spiritual condition of these people. Shem knew God was long-suffering and repeatedly warned His children of impending judgment, but most humans ignored His warnings.

The noise of a busy market abruptly ceased as a multitude recognized the godly man in their midst. Shem decided this was God's time and place to intervene in the affairs of Nineveh.

"Who ordered you to build this city—God or man?" Shem asked the crowd.

A city leader shopping at a fruit stand heard Shem's question and responded after a period of silence.

"Nimrod directed us to build Nineveh for the Empire."

"Why do you live in a city surrounded by walls?" Shem asked.

The same man responded—this time without hesitation: "We follow the counsel of our ruler. He teaches the city protects us and provides for our needs."

"Does God not defend you and supply your needs? Do

you need a city for protection? God commanded you to spread out and populate the New World." [17]

"Nimrod has demonstrated we grow powerful by living in cities. Wild beasts do not bother us, and we are content here," responded another elder.

The crowd remained quiet, preferring not to provoke Shem. They knew he was a man of God.

"You define contentment as dwelling within man-made boundaries? Joy is more precious to the human soul, and you can only find it within the boundaries of God's Will. You dwell in sin when you ignore those boundaries, and joy does not exist in that domain. Do you desire to abide in God's Will? Are His boundaries not sufficient for your children? Do you yearn for joy that only God can provide?"

"We desire security from the dangers of this world," replied the elder.

The people ignored that response. Their ears had focused on Shem's questions. They had previously heard these arguments from Nimrod and the city elders on multiple occasions. Life in Nineveh did not provide joy or contentment, for that matter.

"God will protect you from the dangers of this world, but if you reject Him, He cannot shelter you from Satan's fiery darts. You should fear the ever-present danger of the evil one lurking on the streets of Nineveh, seeking those he can devour."

Shem paused, allowing God's Spirit to anchor these words in hungry hearts.

"I share Truth of the living God. God destroyed every man, woman and child in the Old World except your family for refusing to dwell within His Will. His awesome judgment occurred just three-hundred years ago. Don't you fear the wrath of a Holy God? My dear sons and daughters... our protection comes by obedience to God. Please apprehend this Truth while you still have time."

Their minds began to comprehend the teaching of this godly man, and their souls slowly became receptive to the work of God's Spirit. People continued to congregate in the crowded street market.

* * * * * * * * *

Indeed, Nimrod was present in Nineveh that day. He stood in the city center, directing construction of his magnificent palace. Masons had chiseled stones of the region to fit together and were laboring feverishly to build the edifice. Sounds of busy hammers and chisels filled the air. Workers hoisted large stones into place with the assistance of ropes. Nimrod closely supervised the entire project. The palace sat directly across the City Square from a huge temple to a Sumerian god, simultaneously under construction. Nimrod desired to establish his religion firmly in the hearts of the people, and he intended to command their lives. Therefore, he spent considerable time overseeing construction of these important buildings in the City Square. Nimrod determined to portray the symbol of his authority and the power of his lord prominently in the city center. He entrusted the elders to manage construction of other areas of the city.

Nimrod noticed a warrior running across the City Square like a galloping horse. The man was breathless by the time he reached Nimrod.

"My lord, a commotion occurs in the city! Our enemy, Shem, has arrived, and the people of Nineveh flock to hear him speak!"

"Shem's presence in this city is an abomination to the dark lord! I shall meet the enemy at once and cleanse Nineveh of this terrible stain!" declared Nimrod—his voice rising in excitement.

"I will make an example of him for our people!"

Several hundred warriors accompanied Nimrod each

day. These men policed the palace grounds, protecting Nimrod from harm. They also functioned as his eyes and ears in Nineveh, bringing messages of new developments. Nimrod moved without delay to the crowded market. The warriors quickly surrounded him, and some followed closely behind.

Nimrod arrived to find throngs of people blocking all entrances to the street market. Warriors pushed them aside, clearing a path for their leader. They toppled fruit-stands, but the owners did not seem upset. Their attention was fixed on the strange man in their midst.

The sight astonished Nimrod. A multitude quietly listened to an ordinary looking old man in a long white robe. This frail appearing man had no weapons or defensive armor. He did not incite rebellion among the citizens. Was he the one Nimrod had heard so much about? This was not the enemy Nimrod had anticipated. The mighty warrior prepared to meet his Uncle Shem for the first time. Nimrod was determined to show the people of Nineveh who controlled their city.

Nimrod strode to a point thirty feet from Shem. He flaunted the golden fleece, knowing Shem would immediately recognize it. Warriors surrounded their commander with swords drawn.

"Who is this newcomer—the one sowing rebellion in our streets?" Nimrod demanded.

Shem turned slowly from addressing the people and squarely faced Nimrod. He was a small man in Nimrod's presence but did not appear intimidated. He looked directly into the eyes of his wicked nephew.

"Family reunions are usually joyous events, my nephew. Why do you greet me with such disrespect? Do you need the protection of two hundred men with swords drawn? Does one unarmed man threaten you? I thought your impressive cities protect their inhabitants!"

Nimrod was clearly unprepared to respond to this old man.

"Although I acknowledge you are my relation, I do not tolerate your presence in my city. You are an enemy here. Enemies pose a grave danger to citizens of Nineveh and must be eliminated!"

Shem stared at the ground for several minutes then replied: "I am not your enemy, Nimrod. I am your family. My brother is your grandfather. I have no desire to fight you. You clearly see I bear no arms."

"Then why have you come to Nineveh? What is your purpose bothering me here?" Nimrod demanded.

"I have not come to bother you. God demands your audience, and He requires your repentance."

"My lord already has an audience with me, and he has not asked me to repent. My achievements please the dark lord, and I consistently obey his commands!"

"I am fully aware of that, but you serve God's enemy. Satan is your dark lord, and he has commanded you to kill thousands of our relatives—your family! He has required you to enslave tens of thousands. He is not interested in you, Nimrod. He only covets God's throne!"

"My lord is god, and he reigns over all other gods. He controls our lives and showers us with gifts!" Nimrod countered.

"Your dark lord is not god at all. There are no gods but One, and He created this world and all the people who dwell here. He even fashioned you, but He did not create you as His enemy."

"HE is my enemy, because He is the enemy of the dark lord! He is the enemy of my family and the human race! Your God has no authority over me, and He has no power to alter the course of this great Empire!"

Shem would not permit that insult to stand unchallenged.

"God has destroyed this world for such insolence as you

have just shown, Nimrod. You know this, yet you choose to ignore the Truth that speaks to your heart." Shem turned to the people of the city and addressed them with a word from the Lord.

> The Lord Almighty has a day in store for all the
> proud and lofty,
> for all that is exalted. And they will be humbled....
> The arrogance of man will be brought low
> and the pride of men humbled;
> the Lord alone will be exalted in that day,
> and the idols will totally disappear.[18]
> Stop trusting in man,
> who has but a breath in his nostrils.
> Of what account is he?[19]

Nimrod attempted to speak, but strangely... his lips could not form words. He had never experienced this.

Shem continued:

"The One God declares to you,

> Woe to those who call evil good, and good evil;
> who put darkness for light and light for darkness;
> who put bitter for sweet and sweet for bitter.
> Woe to those who are wise
> in their own eyes and clever
> in their own sight![20]
> This is what the Lord says—your Redeemer,
> who formed you in the womb:
> I am the Lord, who has made all things,
> who alone stretched out the heavens,
> who spread out the earth by myself,
> who foils the signs of false prophets
> and makes fools of diviners,
> Who overthrows the learning of the wise

and turns it into nonsense,
Who carries out the words of His servants
and fulfills the predictions of His messengers."[21]

That terrible headache was returning once again. Nimrod felt the flushing of his face. Even the warriors noticed a reddish hue in the whites of his eyes. His heart pounded in both ears. The headache was exquisitely painful... unrelenting. Nimrod was furious but found no words to respond.

Everyone seemed spellbound by Shem's words, and they continued to flow.

"When you cry out for help,
let your collection of idols save you!
The wind will carry all of them off;
a mere breath will blow them away.
But the man who makes Me his refuge
will inherit the land
and possess My Holy Mountain."[22]

Nimrod felt an overwhelming surge of anger escape from deep within his soul. He screamed loudly to divert the crowd's attention.

"I will not tolerate the lies of an enemy! The Empire has no room for traitors! I will not allow my people to hear these blasphemies. Men, draw your swords! Make short work of him! We will sacrifice his carcass on the altar of our god!"

Shem turned and locked eyes with the dark giant—his vision penetrating deeply into Nimrod's soul. The warriors did not move at their leader's command, enabling the frail old man to address the mighty hunter.

"Why do you fear me, Nimrod? I have no weapons to threaten you. I do not command an army of men. I am merely an old man desiring to speak God's Truth to these people."

"You are an enemy of the Empire, and I intend to destroy you!" roared Nimrod.

He marched toward Shem, intending his warriors to follow. For once, they refused to support their commander. Their feet did not budge. After three steps Nimrod also found his feet stuck firmly to the ground. He glared at the old man, who now appeared larger than life. Thousands of warriors surrounded him—their drawn swords burning with white fire. The very presence of these heavenly warriors dared the approach of such an enemy of God. Nimrod's head pounded like a stone receiving the blows of a mason's hammer. He thought he was hallucinating. Once again, he could find no words for the tip of his venomous tongue. He fell to the ground, clutching his head and moaning in agony.

Shem smiled at Nimrod. He was a rather ordinary old man, but to the people of Nineveh, his stature towered well above the dark nephilim.

"You look ill today, my nephew. Perhaps you should consider seeking God's help for the disease that plagues your soul."

Nimrod could only look up defiantly from the ground. The warriors behind Shem had disappeared. Shem stood alone staring into the darkness of Nimrod's soul. The confrontation amazed the people. Shem turned and walked from the market. He had come alone, but he left Nineveh with many followers. Nimrod could not lay a finger on any of them.

* * * * * * * * *

"Bring me a large blanket—tightly woven," one of Nimrod's commanders ordered a shop owner.

The man hastily complied, and then ten stout warriors carried Nimrod from the street market on the blanket. Earth and sky rotated in a swirl of colors, and he vomited with each movement. The troops transported him to the palace, laying him on a cot in a room open to the sky. The entire palace had a dirt floor. Stonemasons would not lay the marble until builders completed the roof.

His temporary cot was a narrow wooden structure designed to barely accommodate his large frame. Nimrod feared aggravating the vertigo that overwhelmed him so he refused to move. He became feverish and babbled incoherently. Two- hundred warriors dismissed the entire staff of workers then secured the palace grounds from unwelcome guests. Twenty men stayed faithfully at his bedside while Nimrod's unstable condition persisted for hours. He regained consciousness after nightfall and issued orders.

"Go to your quarters. I will be fine when you return in the morning."

The warriors obeyed, leaving him alone in the unfinished palace. They left in small groups to find an evening meal before retiring. Many of them discussed the strange confrontation between Shem and their leader. Some questioned whether Nimrod's god could overpower the mighty God of Shem. Several had actually seen the angelic army protecting Shem, and they had no confidence to engage these warriors in battle.

As Nimrod lay helpless, his gods harassed him with repeated visitations. They mocked him mercilessly.

"Where is the great strength of Nimrod?" they ridiculed. "An old man in a white robe has humiliated the mighty hunter."

Their taunts aggravated his depression, but Nimrod could not respond.

Finally silence and darkness prevailed. A dense black cloud obscured the full moon, and the sounds of nocturnal insects abruptly ceased. Nimrod knew the dark lord had arrived...

"My son, why do you persecute yourself? You have

become humble in the sight of your peers. You show weakness and make yourself vulnerable to mere men." The dark lord's accusations pierced Nimrod's soul.

"I could not control the events of this day. Where was the help from my lord?" implored Nimrod.

"You did not ask for assistance. I stood by with the gods, waiting for your request. We were prepared to strike at your beckoning. You chose to rely on your strength to fight the battle. Do you not comprehend your mortal weakness?"

"Indeed, I am weak. I wish I could command mountains to fall on our enemies, but I cannot even stand on my feet," Nimrod acknowledged.

The mighty hunter wept like a child consumed with self-pity.

"What can I do, my lord? My sense of direction has departed, and confusion overwhelms me."

"Small bumps always occur on a wide road to glory, my son. This is merely a temporary setback, which will actually strengthen you. I use tribulation to sharpen my swords. You are my sword, Nimrod, and you require sharpening. A dull sword cannot conquer my enemies. You must remember my hand wields the sword. If the sword says to its master: 'I will fight the battle,' then it flails aimlessly in the wind. Only a sword in the master's hand can vanquish the enemy."

Nimrod finally fell into a deep sleep. The dark lord left him alone for the remainder of the night.

A bright blue sky greeted Nimrod's cloudy head the next morning. He awoke without the headache but could barely stand due to weakness and persistent vertigo. The warriors arrived shortly after sunrise, bringing bread and milk. He sat with them on the palace lawn, contemplating what to do next. After consuming the nourishment he addressed them.

"I have led this northern campaign for several years. The battle for the Empire has exacted a heavy toll from me. I feel weak and emotionally drained. For long hours I pondered this last night, and I now believe it is time to return to my wife and family. I need assistance to walk to the government building where I can announce my plans to the elders."

Six warriors escorted him across the City Square to the government building. They helped him ascend two flights of stairs to a room where he found the elders discussing city business. Seeing Nimrod enter the room, they ceased their conversation and patiently waited for him to speak.

"I will only take a moment to address this distinguished group," Nimrod began. "I have labored in the northern territory for several years and have spent much of that time in Nineveh. I have grown weary and need rest from these duties. I must restore relations with the Queen and oversee the construction of Babel. Business of the Empire bids me leave Nineveh, and I intend to do so this very day. Competent warriors oversee the security of this city. You may recruit more from nearby cities if trouble arises. I shall transfer command of the northern territory to Asshur until I return. You are familiar with my goals for the Empire. Much work still remains here, and I expect to see it accomplished when I return. Disobedience will provoke swift punishment, I assure you."

Nimrod left the meeting after the elders verbalized their support. The warriors packed supplies on his black mule and escorted him from the city. A weakened condition prevented Nimrod from traveling his usual pace. The city of Asshur was approximately one hundred miles south of Nineveh. He traveled in solitude, resting each night. He paused to enjoy scenery along the Tigris River. On one occasion Nimrod sat for hours beneath a shade tree overlooking the Tigris, observing the spray created by bubbling rapids hitting huge boulders. Boats navigated the currents of the huge river. Nimrod noted the oarsmen worked much harder than those paddling similar vessels on the Euphrates.

Nimrod awoke each morning to watch the rising sun

burn its way upward through the Tigris River into the blue morning sky. He felt invigorated after experiencing the beautiful sunrises. His strength returned by the time he neared Asshur, five days later. One more night in the wilderness would further strengthen his soul, he reasoned. The next morning he would seek Asshur in the city of his namesake. Nimrod was thankful Asshur had not witnessed the humiliation. Nimrod now understood why Asshur still respected his father. He would avoid discussing the encounter and deal with more important issues.

* * * * * * * * *

The next morning Nimrod found Asshur meeting with the elders, planning further city development. Sunlight highlighted the details of clay models fashioned by architects to illustrate the city layout. They had hoped to obtain final approval for the design with Asshur and the elders. Asshur presided in a beautifully carved wooden chair at the end of a long table.

Nimrod strode unannounced into the room, rudely halting the discussion.

"I am sorry to interrupt this important meeting, but I must request a private audience with Asshur, which will only last several minutes."

The elders looked at one another in dismay, knowing this unwelcome intrusion would delay the meeting. However, they carefully concealed their emotions to avoid provoking the wrath of this powerful man. Asshur nervously drummed his fingers on the table.

"Please excuse me, gentlemen. I shall return shortly to finish this business," Asshur requested, and then left the room with Nimrod.

They walked down a long corridor to a stone stairway, descending to the first floor exit then left the building and walked across its landscaped grounds. Asshur located a wooden bench in the midst of some colorful flowers, where they sat to discuss Nimrod's urgent concerns.

"What brings you here, Nimrod? I thought you were consolidating your strength in Nineveh."

"I bring good tidings from all the northern cities, including Nineveh. Thousands have settled in each city. Masons have completed important building projects. The elders have established new markets for produce and opened trade routes to various regions of the world. Residents in the cities enjoy their newfound security and material blessings. Temple worshippers increase monthly, and priests regularly send large profits from grain sales to Babel."

"Then why have you summoned me from an important discussion regarding the destiny of our city?" inquired Asshur, anxiously fidgeting on the bench.

Nimrod perceived the frustration in his friend's response.

"I have come to inform you I am leaving the northern lands to return home for awhile. I desperately need a break. I miss my wife and desire to see Babel arise from the sand of the Mesopotamian Valley. I intend to leave this city today and begin the long journey to Kish. Will you assume command of the northern cities? They are still vulnerable to outside influences."

"I understand your concern, and I shall continue to instruct the people they can only attain security within the city walls. I shall perform an honorable work in your absence. I hope you will leave warriors to crush any dissension that might occur."

Nimrod felt Asshur's initial irritation had subsided.

"I intend to leave all the warriors with you. I have divided them equally among the northern cities. I have also informed them you will assume command in my absence. I hope to return in several years. Please make sure the slaves and revenue continue to flow south from these cities, my friend."

"I will miss you, Nimrod. You are like a brother to me. I shall work with the elders of these cities to accomplish your goals for the Empire."

With that assurance Asshur embraced Nimrod then returned to the meeting.

Nimrod left Asshur and traveled south to Akkad. The journey along the beautiful Tigris River took five days. Nimrod slept under a canopy of stars each night and hunted wild game for nourishment. He had not hunted for several years and had forgotten the satisfaction he derived from this sport.

"Animals are much easier to conquer than the fickle minds of men," Nimrod muttered. "Negotiation and compromise inevitably arise when dealing with humans. These problems never exist with animals. I totally control my encounters with them—especially when I wear this remarkable fleece. I know my lord desires me to achieve the same undisputed authority over the people of this world."

Nimrod noticed dramatic changes in Akkad since he had left several years before. A large population of goats, cattle, and sheep grazed grassy hillsides north of Akkad. Many laborers toiled in fields of wheat and vegetables covering the plains. An impressive wall surrounded the city. He passed through a large wooden gate guarded by four armed warriors.

Nimrod rode his mule down an avenue leading to the center of Akkad. People walked the streets and children played freely. Brick masons labored on scaffolding atop many buildings nearing completion. Mule drawn carts carried bricks, grain, and other items on the streets of Akkad. Nimrod rode to the city center and dismounted before a three-story building containing the offices of government officials. He tied the mule to a hitching post about midday.

Nimrod calculated Annuki would be finishing morning meetings and preparing to break for lunch. He identified Annuki and several elders emerging from the entrance, just as he had predicted. Annuki wore a purple robe to signify his royal position.

"I request an appointment with the honorable governor of Akkad."

Nimrod smiled, and Annuki stared at him in disbelief.

"More than two years have passed since I last saw you in Akkad, my lord! I consider it an honor to dine with you today. Please join me for a delicious meal at the local tavern."

Annuki embraced his large cousin then led the way to the stone tavern where Nimrod had stayed several years earlier.

Nimrod noticed the tavern had been expanded to accommodate the increased business of Akkad. Many famished laborers had ceased work long enough to devour a cooked meal. They filled a much larger dining room, illuminated by huge windows facing the city center. Nimrod enjoyed a view of an impressive stone temple of the gods, presently under construction. Nimrod and Annuki sat together at a small corner table. Annuki isolated the table so no one could overhear the conversation.

"How is life in Akkad, my friend?" Nimrod began.

"No problems exist here, my lord. The people have readily adopted the Sumerian culture. I am sure you have seen many fields of grain surrounding the city. Oxen pulling bronze plows now cultivate those fields. Even harvesters wield sickles of bronze—similar to Uruk. We record business transactions on clay tablets using the cuneiform letters of the Sumerians.[23] Our citizens have dedicated new temples to the gods. A wall nearly surrounds the city, and the residents are happy and secure. We have deported the Shemite prisoners to work as slaves in Babel. Since that time the Shemites have not bothered us with their religion. I have even moved my wife and children to Akkad, and they have grown accustomed to their new surroundings. My oldest son has joined the warriors protecting the city. He is an excellent archer, and you are still his hero, Nimrod!"

Nimrod could not believe the good news. Indeed, the dark lord had prospered the growing Empire. Surely nothing could stand in the way of forward progress.

"I desire to take your son on a hunting excursion some-day. I fear his archery skills have already surpassed mine. If he beats me I will no longer be his hero." Nimrod smiled. "I have complete confidence in your work, my friend, and I have no qualms about leaving you in charge. I am leaving Akkad and the northern lands to spend time with my family and rejoin my wife. Have you gathered any information about her? Has she left the tavern for the worthy responsibilities of a Queen?"

Annuki responded evasively: "I have heard she has built several temples in Uruk and has nearly completed the palace. She is a talented architect, and people extol her abilities. Informants have told me she still runs the tavern but has hired more employees to perform her work."

"Does she marvel at the King's accomplishments for the Empire?" asked Nimrod, hoping for an affirmative answer.

"I cannot say with certainty, my cousin, but you know the Queen. She has never freely bestowed compliments. According to my understanding this tradition continues."

Nimrod continued eating as he quietly pondered the achievements of the Queen. He suspected Annuki might be withholding additional information but decided not to pursue his suspicions.

"Why did you leave the northern lands, my lord?" Annuki asked.

"I am weary of war and the religion of the Shemites. My heart longs for my wife and family. I desire to oversee construction of the capital. A vast number of slaves now live there, and I intend to work them hard on this grand project. I yearn to witness Babel excel all cities of the Empire."

The men finished their last few bites, then Nimrod continued: "I left command of the northern cities to Asshur. He has proven his abilities as a leader and will serve the Empire well. Four thousand warriors and their commanders are spread equally among the five northern cities. The warriors respect the commanders and obey them without dispute. My troops should not have any difficulty keeping order in the northern cities. I do not believe the Shemites will challenge them with warfare. These religious zealots prefer living in isolated settlements. When I return I shall force them to submit to my rule or exterminate them altogether."

"It appears development of the northern cities will proceed smoothly—even in your absence. I suppose your presence is more important in Babel at this time."

"My thoughts exactly," Nimrod concurred.

They rose from their seats and paid the innkeeper for the meal. Nimrod embraced Annuki and bade him farewell.

"Petition the gods for my marriage and for the Empire."

"I shall do so, my lord," Annuki replied with a warm smile parting his lips.

Nimrod left Akkad without delay, desiring to hurry home. However, he still did not know the condition of the Queen. Three burning questions occupied his mind for the entire trip: "Was she faithful? Had his absence caused her heart to desire him? Could they rule together in the Empire?"

Chapter 11

The Homecoming

Nimrod eagerly anticipated the reunion with Semiramis. He heard more rumors about her remarkable accomplishments as he neared Kish. He decided to visit his family and then travel to Uruk to spend the majority of his time with the Queen. Thereafter, he would oversee construction of Babel.

The population of Kish had grown tremendously since he had left. Laborers had converted more desert acreage beyond the city wall into usable farmland. Children tended sheep, goats, and cattle grazing the pastures. Farmers plowed fields with teams of oxen pulling bronze plows. Metal workers had forged bronze farm implements to replace the copper ones.

Nimrod noticed the conspicuous absence of priests laboring in the fields alongside their people. He heard they had acquired wealth and influence in Kish.

He entered an impressive gate, providing access to a main avenue leading to the city center. Six strong warriors guarded the gate and they recognized their leader immediately.

"I consider it a privilege to open this gate to the conqueror of the New World," the eldest warrior addressed Nimrod. "You will appreciate many new changes in this city since you left several years ago. The population has grown substantially, and our people have built magnificent structures."

"I have eagerly desired to return, and I appreciate the reception you have given me," Nimrod declared, as he passed through the huge gate. "I shall walk the city streets to interact with the people."

Young children played on the outskirts of Kish. Nimrod noticed several groups playing with wooden swords and spears. They had organized themselves into opposing troops and were playing military games. The children squealed in delight when they recognized Nimrod walking through the city. They ran to him, begging to hear stories of his campaign in the northern lands.

Nimrod looked down and smiled: "My battles are no more important than yours. Keep up the good work, young lads! I must depart to address the city leaders."

He continued walking toward the city center. The new temples of worship amazed him. Masons had embellished them with expensive stone and marble from the north. Artisans had adorned them with sculptures of Sumerian gods and murals extolling military conflicts in the heavens. Astrologers had designed each temple to align with the constellations. Prostitutes enticed worshippers ascending and descending steps to temple entrances. Nimrod heard noises of sacrificial cows and goats in the vicinity of each temple.

Merchants filled the city peddling their wares, and shops sold everything from food to farm implements. Most shops conducted a brisk business that day, and people of all ages leisurely strolled the city streets. They noticed the mighty warrior who walked in their midst. Many bowed before him, and others inquired about the welfare of their loved ones serving in northern lands.

"Fear not...your sons are healthy and have provided an

exceptional service to the Empire. When we have secured the northern lands they shall all return home," Nimrod promised.

Nimrod finally arrived at the government building in the city center. He hitched his mule to a nearby post then strode through the front entrance. He ascended two flights of stairs to the third floor meeting room. He found his father conferring with the council of elders, as usual. The council had grown significantly. Priests comprised four of the new positions. They wore black robes, contrasting the purple robes of other members. The elders immediately recognized Nimrod. The late afternoon sun entering western windows illuminated the fleece. He walked across the room and stood near the windows—his impressive silhouette superimposed on the silver Euphrates glistening in the afternoon sun.

A priest, presiding as leader, interrupted the agenda and addressed the council.

"I announce the arrival of Nimrod, son of Cush and hero of the Empire!"

All council members rose to extol their hero.

Nimrod bowed and briefly addressed them: "I appreciate the support this council has provided over the past several years. I have followed the gods to new territories in the north. The dark lord has directed me to develop five cities in that region. Residents of these cities are happy, secure, and devoted to the Empire. They embrace our gods and the Sumerian culture, as well. They have even sent revenue and workers to build the capital city. Our warriors have performed excellent work, consolidating the assistance of these people. Cities of the New World now stand united with one vision!"

The council rose once again to applaud Nimrod. The presiding elder then addressed him.

"We have eagerly awaited your homecoming, Nimrod. Construction of Babel has begun in earnest, but a fresh vision is needed to finish the work—a vision only you can provide. We need you to oversee the project and galvanize the people for this wondrous undertaking."

Nimrod, exhorted by the encouragement, replied: "The gods have ordained my return for this very purpose! I have delegated command of the military to responsible men. I have also appointed elders in each northern city and one man to supervise all of them. No major problems exist on the northern front at this time. I desire to join the gods and Sumerian people to create the 'Jewel of the Empire!'"

"What can we do to facilitate this work?" asked another elder.

"I must first meet with my father to plan the project, and then I will meet with the Queen. She will contribute substantially to the design and construction of Babel. Her architectural talents exceed most men of this city, and her workers obey without complaints. I desire to reestablish our eternal union. After all, I have not seen my wife for several years."

"Take time to restore your marriage. We have witnessed the gods' rich blessings on your excellent work. Continue to follow them as you plan this magnificent project. Call upon this council when you need help," encouraged the presiding elder.

"Thank you, my brothers," replied Nimrod. "I will cherish your support as we prepare for the culmination of our dreams."

Nimrod and his father left the meeting without delay and walked across the City Square to the King's palace. The palace now exceeded the size of the government building. However, the magnificent temple of An dwarfed both structures and all other buildings in the city.

"Your return brings me great pleasure, Nimrod." Cush affectionately embraced his son. "Your busy schedule permits little time for a proud father. Each member of our family dearly misses you. We must visit them immediately!"

"I fervently desire to see the family, Father."

"I have many sons and daughters, but you have surpassed all of them," boasted Cush. "You have a vision for the future and the power to execute it. The gods have blessed you, my son. You and the dark lord will soon overthrow Noah's God and achieve your destiny. Someday I shall die a satisfied old man with my greatest hopes fulfilled."

Nimrod felt proud, having finally won the favor of his father.

* * * * * * * * *

The majority of Nimrod's large family had already heard rumors of his arrival. They had homes in various parts of the city, but that afternoon most of them rushed to the King's palace for a grand reunion. Countless nieces and nephews mobbed him on the palace grounds. Other family members waited to welcome him in the first floor meeting room. All rejoiced to see Nimrod. Many nieces and nephews had grown to adulthood and had children of their own. Children were spellbound as Nimrod shared tales of military exploits in the northern lands. They all aspired to be mighty warriors. His grandmother, Marah, even gloated in pride. After many decades a huge smile appeared on her long face. The family had difficulty recognizing that unnatural expression.

"Happiness has finally replaced the bitterness of my early years! I have witnessed the fruit of my loins become ruler of a magnificent Empire. Only the gods know the extent of his overwhelming power!" Marah exclaimed.

Marah—mother of the Sumerian civilization—had lived nearly three hundred years in a world she hated. Dark wrinkled skin and a stooped posture gave her an ancient appearance. Nimrod had never seen her this happy, and nothing could have made his day any sweeter.

"I shall savor the honor of bringing such pleasure to you, Grandmother. Perhaps you will change your name when the Empire comes to maturity!"

Nimrod realized her behavior for 350 years had perfectly illustrated the meaning of the name, Marah—'bitterness.' She had repeatedly expressed a yearning for the Old World and resented Noah's God for destroying it. She harbored deep animosity towards Noah for 'evicting' her family from the northern lands.

"Noah's descendants in the north will never control our family again!" she boasted.

"My plans for the Empire will include my nieces and nephews. They will participate in building the capital city. The least of them will command legions of slaves!" Nimrod promised.

He smiled as the children and his grandmother shrieked in delight. Nimrod renewed many family relationships. Their fellowship continued over a delicious supper prepared by the King's servants.

Nimrod preferred to meet alone with Cush after supper. He always appreciated his father's wise counsel. They walked to the courtyard behind the house. A fading sunset provided adequate light for the conversation. They sat on a marble bench under a fruit tree.

"Do you still have the full backing of city leaders, Father?"

"These men honor me and generally do my bidding," Cush replied, "but the priests have become very influential in Kish. They wield a strong arm of power in the affairs of this city. You will even find them disagreeable at times. Several priests now sit on the council of elders. They have attained positions of authority because of their rising influence, wealth, and scribal skills."

"I know you scoff at the religious establishment, Father. I imagine you are bothered by the very notion superstition largely influences the advance of the Empire."

"You know me well, my son. Let me pick a fruit of wisdom for you." Cush reached to pick a fruit from the tree overhead. He handed it to Nimrod, who gladly ate it. "Would it not benefit these ignorant, superstitious people if famous men of the Empire were deified? At least our citizens would apprehend the tangible accomplishments of these great men as they bowed to worship them. Such a religion would make more sense than making gods of the sky, earth, and seas."

"You have made an excellent suggestion, Father. It merits consideration as we formulate the religion of the Empire. The priests will submit to my commands, I believe."

"We shall see, my son. I question the motives of these stubborn, power hungry priests."

Nimrod desired to discuss another issue.

"Father, have you heard any news from Uruk? Does the city run well under the present administration? And how does the Queen function in this new arrangement?"

"I sense your later question is more important than the former. You need not be diplomatic with your father." Cush smiled. "The population of Uruk swells by leaps and bounds, and its advances surpass those of our city. Agriculture has produced substantial revenue for Uruk. Artisans have created beautiful works using gold, silver, and gemstones acquired from the northern lands. Priests grow more influential there than in Kish."

Cush continued: "Perhaps the new temples in Uruk illustrate the most significant change that has occurred over the past three years. The number of temples has increased dramatically. People commemorate a new deity whose importance grows daily. She is Inanna—the goddess of love and procreation, who blesses citizens of Uruk with creativity, energy, and power. She reportedly brings order out of chaos.[24]

Nimrod was intrigued. He felt certain Semiramis had a motive in all this. His father continued the description.

"People adore Inanna, and her popularity exceeds all other gods. I suppose your Queen has a lot to do with that. Semiramis has promoted goddess worship above all other forms of religion. She has built a magnificent temple for Inanna. Furthermore, the Queen has commanded the schooling of children in the temples. Priests teach them the mystery religion of Babylon and demonstrate how to worship the gods. They groom the children to serve as temple priests and prostitutes. More children are schooled in the temple of Inanna than in all other temples combined."

"Does the Queen command the respect of her people?" Nimrod desired more information about his wife.

"I was getting to that before you interrupted, my son," teased Cush. "Semiramis is very popular among the citizens of Uruk. They practically worship her. Her appeal soars above the city elders. People consider her commands pleasures, which they jump to obey. It seems her beauty captivates them. I fear you cannot compete with Semiramis in Uruk. The Queen's popularity makes her a dangerous foe for anyone who tries to rule in that city. I hope you apprehend this as you rekindle your marriage. You have correctly assessed her architectural abilities. Laborers and brick masons love to work for the Queen. She has supervised many building projects over the past several years and some are truly spectacular!"

"Thank you for your insight, Father. Indeed, Semiramis is a worthy partner as Queen of the Empire. The gods have granted her remarkable abilities."

Nimrod did not know if he could share authority with his wife in the new Empire. He would permit her free reign in Uruk and support her projects there, as this was her home city. However, Nimrod doubted the dark lord would allow her substantial control over the capital.

"I believe Semiramis will insist on having authority over the construction of Babel," Cush declared, appearing to perceive the thoughts of Nimrod. "You will need to compromise with her on this project, or else the people we govern will witness the consequences of disunity. Do you understand, my son?"

Nimrod was amazed his father could read his mind.

"Uh... I ..will seriously consider your counsel, Father. I shall even present your concerns to the dark lord."

The courtyard darkened quickly as the night sky enveloped the city. They rejoined the family in the palace meeting room. An abundance of candles and several oil lamps illuminated it. The family interacted for several hours before sleep finally beckoned. Parents even allowed the children to alter usual sleep schedules to visit their famous uncle. He decided to depart for Uruk the next morning.

* * * * * * * * *

Nimrod anxiously anticipated the reunion with Semiramis, so he traveled night and day to reach her city. He entered Uruk through a massive wooden gate guarded by six warriors. They recognized Nimrod and hastily obeyed his command to open the gate. He was thoroughly impressed with the enormous wall that stretched higher and wider than the wall surrounding Kish. The guard towers were also larger and more numerous. Nimrod rode his mule over newly constructed roads, finally finding the tavern at the usual location. Afternoon customers busily shopped the fish market and other nearby businesses. He strode into the tavern just in time for supper. The cook was totally unprepared for him.

"We did not expect you today, my lord." The cook looked dismayed. "Why haven't you given us time to prepare a celebration for your homecoming?"

"Time is a precious commodity, my lady. The gods allow me little of it these days—not even enough to announce my visits. From one day to the next I do not know my itinerary. Where can I find the mistress of the tavern?"

"She has just returned to the tavern for the evening meal, my lord. I shall find her if you wish."

"I would like to witness her bewildered expression."

"I cannot possibly grant that request, my lord. She would never forgive me for surprising her."

"Then by all means, bring her to me before my patience wears thin."

The cook returned shortly with the Queen.

"My lady is here to greet you."

Semiramis stood behind the cook, smiling up at her husband.

"I have long awaited your arrival, Nimrod. Why have the gods brought you here on this day?"

He gathered her into his arms and kissed her affectionately.

"I preferred to return months ago, but a momentous work hindered me."

"What work could keep you from this place?" she teased.

Nimrod's memory of her remarkable beauty did not disappoint him.

"My lord has led me through the northern lands these past several years. He did not permit me an opportunity to return home."

"Speak more about your adventures in foreign lands."

Nimrod proudly recited his accomplishments: "The dark lord has given many people into my hands, enabling me to build large cities for them. He has made enemies bow before me. The very name, Nimrod, causes them to tremble!"

"My legs do not tremble at that name—nor do my knees bow," she declared defiantly, "but my heart has yearned for the presence of the man. I am happy to welcome you today. Let us eat the food my cook has prepared. We can share our adventures during the meal."

Nimrod knew this amazing woman would never cower to any man, and he admired that fearless spirit. They sat at a small table in the corner of the dining room, adjacent to a large window and watched boats docking on the banks of the Euphrates.

People occupied every table, and the noise of many conversations filled the room. Musicians played their instruments. The tenants recognized Nimrod but did not seem as fearful as they were several years earlier. His presence failed to dampen the vibrant atmosphere. Nimrod had missed the tavern as well as its owner. The aroma of fresh bread and fish filled the dining room. Servants promptly placed dishes of hot food before Nimrod and his wife. Nimrod was famished and did not wait to engulf the tasty food. A maid brought a large pitcher of beer and several glasses.

"Has the Queen's reputation grown in Uruk?" Nimrod asked between bites.

"The support of my people increases each year, and citizens enthusiastically obey my commands. They assist in all my projects and seem eager to please me. I have noticed no dissension."

"Describe these projects you have created for your people."

"We have completed the wall around Uruk, and it provides security for the residents. The workers have nearly finished the palace, where I now meet with my people. The gods have commanded us to build new temples. We have complied with these demands and added many new priests for service."

Nimrod thought each ambitious project was impressive, yet Semiramis had completed all of them in several short years.

She continued: "I consider the creation of a temple dedicated to the goddess, Inanna, my most important achievement. The dark lord has promised I will someday sit on the throne of this goddess. The new temple pleases him, and the citizens prefer worship here over all other temples in Uruk."

"Why is that, my lady?"

"Inanna is the goddess of creation. She has blessed us with the richness of this land and provides the fertility of our people, as well. Temple prostitutes regularly serve her with acts of creation, glorifying her attributes. The residents of Uruk do not feel compelled to worship Innana. They eagerly worship her and flock to the temple services. Innana's worshippers multiply weekly and revenues grow proportionately. Her devoted followers share their enthusiasm with others, and the new religion spreads like the wind."

This religion appealed to Nimrod. He would enjoy worshipping in the temple of Inanna.

Semiramis interrupted his thoughts: "I have ordered the formation of schools for the children and assigned priests to teach them the mystery religion. Children will someday graduate from the schools, becoming priests and temple prostitutes. The dark lord has repeatedly admonished, 'the future of the New World depends on the ideas we instill in the minds of our children.' He desires their allegiance."

"I believe our lord will use your creative talents to design the capital of the Empire. You will contribute substantially to this project."

Nimrod realized he just might have to share authority with his wife in the Empire.

"The dark lord will advise me in these matters," she replied. "I shall join you to create the capital city, and the gods will rule future generations of mankind from there. Our eternity will begin in Babel!"

Nimrod believed the dark lord possessed the very soul of Semiramis. He could see she yearned for enthronement as

Queen of heaven and earth.

"I marvel at your faith, my Queen! We shall enjoy the work of the Empire!"

Battle fatigue diminished rapidly. Harsh memories of war faded into the distant recesses of Nimrod's mind as he basked in the presence of his wife. They continued sharing their experiences.

"I shall tour the city with you tomorrow morning. I am anxious to worship in the Temple of Inanna," Nimrod declared.

Nimrod stayed with Semiramis in their usual third floor suite that night. He noticed idols of the goddess Inanna situated in various places of the room. The Queen's carpenter had anchored one of them to the headboard of the bed they shared. Excitement stole Nimrod's sleep. He pestered Semiramis with his plans for Babel, refusing to extinguish the oil lamp. Nimrod sensed her waning enthusiasm.

"I insist we cease this discussion at once, Nimrod. The events of tomorrow will demand your full attention. Adequate sleep will improve our temperament for the people."

"I have one further item to discuss. Please honor me with your attention for several more minutes," Nimrod pleaded.

"What else must you bother me with this time of night?"

He knew she needed sleep, and he couldn't expect her patience to last much longer.

"We have discussed our aspirations for the Empire and share excitement at the possibilities, but we have never talked about an heir for the throne, my dear."

"Do you desire a child at this time, Nimrod?"

"Of course, I desire a child, Semiramis. I long for an heir to the throne."

"Our lord has already answered your request," she stated coolly.

"Your words confuse me. Do you desire to conceive at this time?" Nimrod asked, hoping he correctly understood his wife.

"I have already conceived and expect to deliver a child in six months." She replied without emotion, hoping to calm a rapidly approaching storm.

Nimrod jumped from the bed, directly facing her. His temper rose to an immediate boiling point.

"How can this be? I have not seen you for more than two years. You could not conceive in my absence unless, of course, you have played the harlot. Now stand before me and speak the truth! You know I am a jealous man, and you have vowed your allegiance to me. I will not tolerate another man sharing the bed of my wife!"

Semiramis remained fearless. The Queen stood to face her husband.

"The child is not a gift from any man." She slowly groped for convincing words. "The dark lord conceived him in my womb. He has promised an eternal heir for our throne. A god-man will not face the reality of death. He will continue the dark lord's bidding long after we ascend to the eternal realm. Our lord has fathered this child, and I have obeyed as his lowly servant."

Nimrod could not apprehend this explanation, which flew in the face of reality. He vaguely remembered his grandfather's teaching about angelic visitations to women of the Old World. His grandfather said powerful men of renown had resulted from these unions, and they ruled the world. Noah's God had even sent the Great Flood to eliminate them from the earth. Could this be such a visitation? He was not convinced—the dark lord had never discussed this with him.

"Prove your claims! I will not tolerate the lies of a woman—especially my wife. My judgment will come swiftly if I find you are lying!"

Green fire seemed to radiate from those eyes.

"You have not communed with our lord lately, Nimrod.

You will find the answers you seek from him. I shall not defend myself further. I follow the dark lord, and you should do likewise. The door is behind you... I will finally have my rest."

"If my lord speaks to me tonight, I shall return after sunrise. Prepare yourself for my response, and pray you may escape my judgment if you are guilty!"

Nimrod pulled the fleece over his head and stormed from the room, slamming the door behind him. The tavern walls reverberated with the noise, and the clamor awakened several tenants. Nimrod quickly descended two flights of stairs and exited into the darkness. He would seek the dark lord that very hour for justification of his anger. He felt that throbbing headache returning and dizziness closely followed. He knew he could not walk for long. Fortunately, he did not have to pass anyone on the streets. He dodged stray cats and dogs hunting their late night meals. Finally, he made it to the wall surrounding Uruk. Nimrod pushed open the strong gate with such force the hinges suspending it bent irreparably. He stumbled out of the city, striving with all his strength to remain standing. He quickly found an isolated wheat field then collapsed on the ground, crying out to the dark lord.

* * * * * * * * *

Semiramis feared for her life. She extinguished the oil lamp, hoping those who awoke from the noise would not suspect it came from her room. She then reclined on the large bed contemplating her options. She had previously determined not to reveal her acquaintances to the King. He would surely execute them and then punish her with torture and even death. Semiramis had not intended to inform Nimrod about the pregnancy yet, but the door had opened and she had to walk through it. She had had multiple adulterous relationships over the previous years. The consequence of that behavior now reared its ugly head. Several weeks earlier she had made a pact with the dark lord, when she was certain of the pregnancy. She had agreed to rely on him when this inevitable moment arrived. He had comforted her, promising to rescue her from certain death when Nimrod became aware of the pregnancy. Of course, his assistance would cost her dearly. The dark lord demanded total allegiance. Obedience to him must take precedence over everything else. She knew this was his ultimate goal, and she had fallen headlong into the trap. He did promise huge rewards if she fulfilled his expectations. Should she trust him for deliverance or rely upon her own power to stand against Nimrod? If she chose the latter course, she would need to summon warriors that very night to assist her. Would they stand against Nimrod after observing his ruthlessness several years before? She would have to convince them he had threatened to end her life and harm the citizens of Uruk. Even then, a terrible war would certainly ensue and her days would be numbered. Yes... Semiramis decided her best option was to trust the dark lord. If he would not protect her, no man could. She determined to get some rest and appear confident before Nimrod the next morning. She would not alert the citizens to her imminent danger—at least not yet. She tossed and turned for several hours, finally drifting into a deep sleep nuzzled in soft animal-skins.

* * * * * * * * *

Nimrod could not believe the course of events that day. His emotions had literally dropped from the sky to the depths of despair within an hour. He had so loved this woman and trusted in her faithfulness. How dare she carry another man's child? Waves of nausea accompanied the dizziness and that terrible headache. Millions of stars illuminated the heavens, but Nimrod could not see any of them.

He dared not open his eyes for fear of worsening the misery.

He cried out in agony.

"Please lord, don't let me suffer this burden any longer. I cannot bear it!"

Silence greeted his pleas. He twisted on the ground, weeping and moaning. After some time had elapsed the gods began to ridicule him.

"N-i-m-r-o-d…(laughter)… did you presume you owned this woman?" (more laughter) "Will you share your glory with another man?" (yet more laughter)

Someday in eternity he would demonstrate superiority over these worthless gods. They did not care for him. Their laughter finally faded, and then silence returned once again until he could not endure it any longer. No cool evening breezes relieved the suffocating air.

"Lord…please answer me! I need you now!!!"

The dark lord finally responded after Nimrod lay on the hard ground for what seemed an eternity.

"Do you finally acknowledge your needs, my son? You are learning… I commend you. I have the key that unlocks your soul. Expose your heart so we can unite in purpose."

"Do you know the condition of my wife?"

"I know everything about her, for she is also my child."

"Semiramis claims she is pregnant. I cannot possibly be the father. She insists you have conceived the child. Is that true?"

The dark lord allowed him to burn with uncertainty for several minutes. Finally he answered.

"Semiramis has spoken the truth. She is pregnant with my child. The child is part god and part man. I will never leave my earthly throne vacant. Do not harm him. If you do, I will require your life in this world and your reward in eternity. I shall raise the child, and he will obey me. Do you understand, N-i-m-r-o-d?"

"I understand, my lord. I am honored you have chosen

my wife as the vessel to deliver your heavenly representative into this world. I shall care for the child as if he were mine."

"So you will, my son. Trust your wife—she also belongs to me. I will not tolerate any harm you might intend for her. Is that clear, or do you need further encouragement?"

The headache pounded mercilessly. Nimrod felt he could not survive it.

"I understand, my lord! I will not harm her or the child. You have my word!"

Silence returned once again, and Nimrod fell into a restless sleep for several hours. He awoke abruptly at sunrise with ants crawling all over his body, biting multiple locations. He forgot all other ailments at that instant.

"Ouwee... cursed ants! Surely they have better things to do than this! Perhaps those annoying gods have stirred them up to torture me."

He brushed off the ants and fiercely shook them from the fleece.

"I must make it to the tavern."

Fortunately, the headache and nausea had disappeared, so he slowly trudged through the massive gate and city streets. Though weak and wobbly, Nimrod finally managed to stagger to the inn. Fortunately, the citizens of Uruk did not see him in this compromised state because it was too early to begin city business.

The cook had already prepared breakfast. Semiramis sat quietly at the table, deep in meditation. She was dressed in a white silk robe, clinging loosely to her body.

"Her fair skin looks as soft as the robe she wears," Nimrod thought, observing her well-rested appearance.

He noticed several customers sitting at tables, waiting for breakfast.

"They gaze suspiciously at me. Perhaps I awakened them by the disturbance I caused," he reflected.

Nimrod sat beside the Queen and patiently waited until

she completed her meditation.

"My anger has subsided. Will you forgive me for that unreasonable outburst last night?"

"Have you communed with the dark lord? Has he vindicated me?" Semiramis inquired, looking directly into Nimrod's eyes without flinching.

"He has confirmed the truth of your statement, my dear. I shall raise the child as my own and continue as your devoted husband, provided you forgive me for doubting you."

Semiramis sat in silence for several minutes.

"I forgive you, my King. I do not blame you for doubting me. Indeed, it stretches my faith to believe the child in my womb is part god. Now let us eat breakfast so we can visit new projects in this city."

Chapter 12

The Jewel of the Empire

Construction of Babel had begun months before Nimrod and Semiramis arrived to inspect the work. They traveled to the capital with a contingent of warriors assigned to protect them at all times. Many servants also accompanied them with orders to satisfy the needs of the Monarchs. Nimrod permitted the Queen to have the majority of the slaves for her service, as she would likely need them during the remainder of the pregnancy.

They noticed the masons working at a feverish pace, having already constructed dwellings for priests, commanders, and common laborers. The masons had also built slave quarters, which were nearly filled to capacity. Worship centers and government offices were not yet visible in the city, but the slaves had prepared many wide roads. Nimrod intended Babel to house three-hundred-thousand people.

Fields of grain and vegetables were conspicuously absent from the area—laborers had not even prepared the earth. Wild grass and vegetation extended several hundred yards inland from the Euphrates River. However, the remaining landscape appeared dry, brown, and lifeless. Nevertheless, more than sixty thousand slaves and additional laborers from neighboring cities worked diligently to raise Babel from the desert sand.

"The pace of construction pleases me," said Nimrod, "but the work is just beginning. Other cities of the Empire provide the revenue to build the capital. Babel must some-day stand on its own."

"What needs to be accomplished before this city can function independently?" asked Semiramis.

"Carpenters must build boats to transport goods on the river, and farmers need to establish agriculture in the region. Irrigation canals require excavation to bring water to parched lands. The city must attract businessmen to support a thriving metropolis. Eventually masons must erect a wall around Babel for the security of its residents."

"Hopefully, the city planners have considered all these factors as they prepare designs for the capital," Semiramis commented.

Sounds of work filled the city—men hollering orders to subordinates, metal clashing with bricks, whips snapping on the backs of slaves, and even barking dogs. The slaves had caused no significant disturbances. They worked hard and obeyed the commanders. Even the Shemites submitted to the taskmasters, producing excellent work.

Nimrod sensed something amiss.

"This city is beginning to look like all cities of the Empire. It appears no different—except a bit larger. We had planned to make Babel the 'Jewel of the Empire,' but I can-not see one glistening gem here. Something novel in this city should cause it to stand apart from all other cities—something unique and impressive. After all, this is the capi-tal of the Empire. Babel should attract people from all over the world. Its uniqueness must entice people to build homes here. What is missing, my dear?"

"I worked hard to give Uruk a distinct appearance among cities of the Mesopotamian Valley. Babel must appear even more pleasing. I have pondered ideas for months. The dark lord directed us to build this city as 'the wonder of the Empire.' Babel is not only the capital of the Empire but also the city of the dark lord. His earthly throne will sit here. The name, Babel, means 'the gate of god.' People will come through the gate of this city to commune with their god. Did you and your father conceive the name, Babel?"

"Yes… we intended the throne of god to sit in this city so people can meet him here. The dark lord has proclaimed he will someday sit on the heavenly throne above the stars of God. The stars are angels, and our lord surpasses them all."

"Indeed, he prefers high places, where people can see him from afar," Semiramis added. "The largest building in each city is the temple dedicated to its god. The dark lord commands all the gods, so he must sit on a throne that towers above them."

"Our lord will greet the people in Babel, and they will worship at his feet," Nimrod thought aloud. "The gods will commune here to determine their purpose for the New World. Hopefully, they will shower blessings on citizens of the Empire. The most spectacular place on earth must impress the gods."

"And it must surpass all temples previously constructed," remarked Semiramis.

"Let's seize the vision!" exclaimed Nimrod. "The dark lord's temple will stretch far above all man-made structures of this world. The sky will barely contain this enormous tower as it pierces the clouds. People will see it for miles outside the city and praise its remarkable architecture. Citizens from every city of the Empire will create this wonder of the New World. The gods will yearn to dwell there. The concept of such an edifice has never touched the imagination of a man."

"Or a woman," Semiramis added.

Nimrod continued, oblivious to the comment: "This tower will appear imposing to the common man. Even a great flood from Noah's God will not submerge it!"

"Summon the priests, laborers, and slaves. Proclaim our remarkable vision, Nimrod! We must inspire the people— even possess them with this dream in order to achieve it."

"You speak the truth, my lady. We must assemble the people at once!"

Nimrod summoned the priests and warriors: "Gather all the people in the city center immediately. The Queen and I will share our vision for the Empire and its capital city."

It took several hours to convene the people. More than eighty-thousand were gathered in the city center. Carpenters hastily erected a platform where the King and Queen would address the people. Nimrod and Semiramis ascended it and sat on two large wooden chairs the high priest had provided—each carved with pictures of gods communing with serpents.

The City Square stretched several hundred yards from the platform. People assembled on three sides, while priests and astrologers stood on the fourth side—where the great Tower of Babel would one day sit. Warriors surrounded the platform to protect the Monarchs. Four-thousand soldiers guarded sixty-thousand slaves on the periphery of the crowd. Nimrod and Semiramis waited impatiently to present their wondrous vision.

Nimrod finally stood to address the crowd: "Citizens of this great city..." His deep booming voice projected easily across the City Square. "The Queen and I have come to inspect the capital of the Empire. We commend your excellent work, preparing the foundation of this magnificent city. You have already accomplished much, and we are pleased with the progress. The gods rejoice this very moment. We intend to dwell here and labor with you. Our Queen desires to share her thoughts."

Nimrod sat next to the Semiramis. She rose and stunned the crowd with her enchanting appearance. She wore a delicate purple robe, highlighting her fair complexion. Long brown hair flowed in ringlets over the robe. A gold turreted crown adorned her head, symbolizing the wall that would one-day surround the city. Nimrod knew the crowd's full attention was focused on the Queen.

People applauded wildly, waving in the air. Semiramis turned to face spectators on all sides of the platform, giving everyone a full view of her beautiful body.

"We have planned this remarkable city as the centerpiece of the Empire. A rock cannot compare with a diamond. Likewise, no city in this world will compare with Babel. It will feature remarkable accomplishments of men and women. Babel will demonstrate how rapidly human civilization has progressed and prove people can join together to achieve a standard of living only the gods know. We shall become like gods when our achievements advance sufficiently in this world!"

Applause and shouts of exultation filled the air, temporarily interrupting her address.

"Babel will attract the gods who have given us life, and they will dwell here in all their glory!"

She sat next to her husband as the crowd chanted— "More! More! More!" and "We love our Queen!"

Nimrod stood to address the crowd once again.

"The Queen and I desire to share our vision for this unique city. The gods have instructed us Babel must stand apart from all cities of the Empire. It will attract people from everywhere in the New World because we shall rule the world from here!"

The crowd cheered the King. He wore the mysterious fleece, which reflected golden light from the afternoon sun. A crown of bullhorns sat upon his head.

Nimrod paused, allowing the emotion of the moment to capture the crowd.

"Babel must demonstrate its superiority over all cities. People will imagine walking on streets of gold instead of dusty roads when they visit here. This city will feature achievements worthy of the capital of a great Empire. We have selected the name, Babel, because it means 'the gate of god.' The gods will come here to commune with us, and people of the New World will pass through the gates of Babel to worship their gods. We will welcome all people and gods to this magnificent city. Babel will feature the newest forms of worship. The finest priests will dwell here, and they will assist the people to commune with gods."

Nimrod paused to gather his thoughts.

"The Queen and I have authorized construction of a magnificent tower of worship in the center of this impressive city. It will sit directly behind this platform, where you presently observe the priests and astrologers. The tallest of us will stand in front of the edifice and appear as ants before an enormous tree. It will soar into the clouds where the gods dwell. Its appearance will differ from all other temples. Citizens of the Empire will see it for miles beyond the city limits. People will recognize this Tower of Babel as the wonder of the New World. Gods will have thrones in the awesome tower. An observatory will sit in its pinnacle, where people can peer into the heavens. Astrologers will map the constellations and decipher messages from the gods. The most capable workers in the world live here. I suspend all construction in this city until the Tower of Babel is completed. This new project will begin tomorrow morning."

Nimrod delivered the climax of his message:

Come now, let us make bricks and bake them thoroughly. We will use tar for mortar. Let us build ourselves a city, with a tower that reaches to the heavens, so that we may make a name for ourselves and not be scattered over the face of the whole earth.[25]

The people stood and screamed their approval of the wondrous vision.

* * * * * * * * *

Initially, excitement for building the Tower of Babel consumed the people, but the staggering requirement for clay and bricks quickly dampened their enthusiasm. Nimrod's commanders drove the slaves at a feverish pace. Workers began the laborious process of making bricks from clay. Commanders assigned slave women and children to gather the clay. They had difficulty maintaining the pace of this backbreaking work. Nimrod kept his promises to nieces and nephews by giving them command over women and children slaves.

Building the immense structure required millions of bricks, so the Sumerians fashioned huge ovens to bake them.

Taskmasters worked the slaves for hours without rest, permitting them minimal food and water. Illness or injury did not excuse the slaves from work. Commanders punished those who fainted and forced pregnant women to toil with the workers. These unfortunate women carried clay and bricks even while laboring to deliver their babies. Weary, malnourished mothers simply could not care for the infants and often died from exhaustion. The newborns usually perished shortly after birth. Building the Tower of Babel was more important than human life—especially the lives of slaves.

* * * * * * * * *

Nimrod and Semiramis lived in Babel during construction of the tower. They met daily with architects and astrologers in a brick building which housed them. A third floor meeting room contained windows on several walls facing the city center. The city planners enjoyed a comprehensive view of the immense project. Architects and astrologers sat at tables, busily designing models of the tower. Each morning Nimrod prodded the process forward.

"This planning takes an inordinate amount of time," he announced one morning. "I shall hold you accountable to complete these designs by the end of the month."

"But we must work together to align the tower with important constellations and propose a structure acceptable to the gods," one astrologer implored.

"The dark lord will not accept it unless you speed up the process. Do you understand?"

The architects and astrologers nodded their acknowledgment. They finished the design on the last day of the month and presented the plan to the Monarchs.

"The tower will appear like a huge pyramid with seven mammoth layers—the largest on the bottom and smallest on top," the chief architect explained. "Each layer will slope slightly inward, enhancing the pyramidal shape and enabling rainwater to drain from the structure. The receding tiers will progressively diminish in height and total base area. Dimensions of the first step will extend three hundred by three hundred feet in length and width. Its height will soar one hundred and ten feet. Adding the remaining steps will stretch the height of the tower to three hundred feet."

The Monarchs watched quietly as the architect pointed out the highlights on a large clay model they had created.

"The entire structure will rest on an eight-foot foundation of sun-baked bricks," he continued. "A triple staircase will ascend the huge tower. The main stairway will span thirty feet in width and perpendicularly intersect the front face of the tower."

"That should allow plenty of room for worshippers to access the tower," the chief astrologer interrupted.

The architect continued: "The staircase will ascend from the ground to the base of the seventh and highest level. Two other stairways will perpendicularly intersect the main stairway at the second level." [26]

"What are those openings at the base of the clay model?" asked Nimrod.

"They represent large storerooms in the first tier of the tower which will contain tons of grain obtained from temple farmlands. The tower will function both as a temple of worship and an economic distribution center for the Empire. Priests and their servants will live in dwellings surrounding the tower."

The chief astrologer continued the presentation.

"The gods will dwell in specially designed rooms in upper sections of the tower. Each god will have a throne, but the important gods will occupy the top rooms. The highest throne will belong to the dark lord—King of the gods."

"Where will the priests conduct worship services?" asked Semiramis.

"They will conduct services in large rooms in the second and third tiers. However the most important worship will occur in the pinnacle of the tower. We do not intend the common people to observe these services. Only those closest to the gods can practice the secret rituals. Priests, astrologers, diviners, and the Monarchs all number in that chosen group."

"Where will the astrologers do their work?" the chief priest asked.

"We will have a commanding view of the heavens from atop the huge tower. We will track movements of the gods from that vantage point and identify new constellations portraying the mystery religion of Babylon."

The astrologer sat down and the chief architect continued.

"Bitumen will cover the first two layers of the tower, coloring them black. Plaster will cover the third, fourth, and fifth layers—each painted a different color. Pictures of bulls and lions will also decorate these layers. The priests have instructed the top two layers be left mud brown, as this is the most sacred color for Sumerians. It symbolizes the gods' greatest gift to mankind—the earth itself. Mud is the purest of substances."

"How will you design the tower so that it doesn't deteriorate over time?" Nimrod asked.

"We will use fire-baked bricks on the exterior of the tower because they will resist the erosive effects of weather. The outer façade of plaster will further protect it. A sloping pavement covered with bitumen resin will surround the base of the tower on all four sides, protecting the foundation from rain damage."

"Can you guarantee the tower won't fall to the ground from the sheer weight of the structure?" inquired Nimrod.

"We believe that sun-baked bricks and massive cedar trunks from the northern mountains will support the tower from within, rendering it indestructible."

Nimrod was satisfied with the design and eager to press on with the construction.

The Monarchs assigned the best artisans of Mesopotamia to decorate the interior walls of tower rooms. They instructed artists to paint murals of Sumerian gods, illustrating legends of the mystery religion. Semiramis and Nimrod selected much of the artwork. One morning they met with artisans, priests, and astrologers. Semiramis addressed them first.

"The dark lord has informed me he desires the premiere Sumerian artists to illustrate his achievements. He requires a mural in the pinnacle of the tower depicting a colorful serpent communing with the first woman of this world, directing her to administer the affairs of men. Portray this woman with my face, wearing a gold turreted crown. The crown will symbolize the wall and guard towers that will someday surround this great city."

"The dark lord has also approached me regarding artistry in the highest rooms of the tower," volunteered Nimrod. "He requests portraits of the King in several murals. One must reveal him bowing to a great dragon.

Another will depict him as 'MARDUK—god of war and fortresses.'[27] Inscribe that name beneath these images, and illustrate citizens of the Empire bowing at my feet."

Semiramis gave additional instructions, not showing much interest in her husband's ideas.

"Illustrate the Queen holding her infant son in several murals. Suspend golden halos above their heads to symbolize their god-like qualities. Images of this male child will represent the precious gift the dark lord has bestowed upon me. The infant will have both human and godly characteristics, for the dark lord has conceived him without the assistance of a man."

Priests, astrologers, and architects looked at one another in disbelief.

"Portray this infant to reveal the face of my child. I am expecting in five months. Artists may come afterwards to sketch his likeness."

Chapter 13

Building the Great Tower of Babel

A rchitects completed the final model of the tower then began to plan the city. They determined the Tower of Babel, the palace, and the immense wall surrounding the city were the three most important projects. Laborers must first complete the tower—the paramount project of all.

Babel was designed as a large rectangular city. All main avenues would converge on the City Square, where the Tower of Babel would loom over the city. The palace would also sit in the city center, directly opposite the tower. Nimrod and Semiramis spent months designing their palace. They planned a magnificent structure, fit for Monarchs of the Empire.

"Embellish many rooms with paintings of the terrifying animals I have slain. Mount the heads of fearsome beasts on the walls of large rooms," Nimrod instructed the artisans. "Paint a mural of my courageous leopard. She accomplished a great service for the Empire but died years ago in an unfortunate accident—crushed under the feet of a huge dragon. Portray my military conquests also."

"Illustrate people bowing before the Queen and her son in several paintings. Exhibit idols of the goddess Inanna in various rooms, revealing different legends attributed to her. Emphasize her fertility powers most of all," Semiramis directed.

"Use bricks, huge stones, and marble to construct the palace. Make bricks from the clay of this region, but transport the stones from northern territories and slabs of marble from foreign lands. Cover interior floors with marble," Nimrod ordered. "Remember, our palace must not detract from the Tower of Babel."

Masons planned to construct the huge wall surrounding the city after completing the tower and elegant palace. Eight chariots would easily ride alongside one another atop the massive wall.

* * * * * * * * *

Sixty-thousand slaves and thousands of laborers toiled feverishly to accomplish the visions of the designers. The majority worked to construct the Tower of Babel.

"The Tower of Babel will attract thousands from all over the world, so complete it first," Nimrod commanded. "This will accelerate growth of the city."

Slaves made bricks and gathered clay near the river. They labored endlessly, often acquiring illnesses from swampy, mosquito infested lands. Mules pulled carts loaded with bricks to the base of the tower, where slaves carried them to masons constructing the edifice. Taskmasters punished those who dropped bricks, but when slaves fell from the lofty heights of the tower their bodies were removed with little remorse. Many slaves died constructing the enormous tower.

Priests, diviners, and astrologers performed their unique services during construction of the great tower. Diviners conjured the gods' artistic preferences for the throne rooms.

Astrologers aligned the tower, its rooms, and ascending stairways according to signs of the zodiac. They worked in harmony with the architects. Astrologers designed the throne rooms to reflect legends illustrated by the constellations.

Priests ordained construction of the tower as a religious act. They taught each job was an act of worship. They sacrificed goats, rams, and cows continuously during the project. Priests even performed human sacrifices after completing each layer of the tower. Masons erected a huge altar at the base of the tower for that purpose. Priests communed with the gods in secret rituals, restricted from public participation. These services became standard practice in the mystery religion of Babylon. Priests commanded the people to habitually worship idols of the gods.

Temple prostitutes busily celebrated the fertility of gods with priests and influential leaders of the city.

* * * * * * * * *

No one could predict the King's behavior during his dark moods. The dark lord often visited late at night, expressing displeasure at the slow pace of construction.

Temporary living quarters of the Monarchs sat next to the city planners' residence. Neither Nimrod nor his wife enjoyed the modest quarters, but they made the sacrifice for the sake of the Empire. The two-story brick home had only ten rooms, and the servants of Semiramis occupied half of them. Nimrod's second floor room was the largest in the house. It had brick walls with windows on two sides of the room. Windows on the western wall allowed a view of the Euphrates River. Nimrod viewed the growing tower from windows on the southern wall.

Sticky, suffocating heat bothered Nimrod one summer night. He extinguished the candles and oil lamps but could not relax. The Euphrates River produced no breezes to cool the midnight oven. Plans for the Empire swirled in Nimrod's mind as he lay perspiring on the bed. He could find no comfortable position for his large aching frame.

"Wretched heat and pricks in my mind linger endlessly," he muttered. "Semiramis refuses to console me and the hours drag into forever!"

The gods taunted him.

"The mighty warrior cannot conquer his thoughts!" (laughter)

"Nimrod—the King without a throne!" (hissing and more laughter)

"The powerful Emperor—impotent to father a child." (still more jeers and laughter)

The annoyance provoked Nimrod's fury.

"I cannot wait to sit on my throne in your midst. As Marduk, the god of war, I will make my greatest conquests in the heavens!"[28]

The laughter increased following that admonition. Chattering voices and ceaseless racket continued unabated then stopped suddenly, giving way to a long period of silence. Nimrod thought the sweltering heat and eerie silence was even more intolerable.

"Please spare me this endless torment, my lord! What message do you bring on this night of madness?"

Silence prevailed for additional minutes, and then the dark lord's raspy voice rumbled forth—even more oppressive than the heat of the night.

"Why are you irritable, Nimrod? I do not enjoy communing with you in this condition."

"I apologize, my lord. I have experienced more sleep deprivation in Babel than during all the military exploits of previous years. Harassing thoughts are my only excuse."

"I am unhappy with the construction of my home. The capital of the Empire grows at a turtle's pace!"

"I can not find a way to drive the workers any faster, but

I am willing to consider your suggestions."

"Slaves from Shem's family do not suffer enough for their procrastination. Persecute them for lack of enthusiasm, and hold their commanders accountable. The Tower of Babel must soon stand as the symbol of my dominion over this world! Do you understand the importance of this project, Nimrod?"

Nimrod perceived the question more as a threat.

"I appreciate the importance of completing the tower in a timely fashion. I shall impose greater suffering on the slaves if they do not speed up the construction."

"No less a commitment will satisfy me!"

The stifling heat continued through the night, but sleep eluded Nimrod.

* * * * * * * * *

Workers operated under significant stress because of burdensome demands from their superiors. Irritability and fatigue hounded them continuously. The early morning sun burned their weary backs. Nimrod stood at the base of the tower, surrounded by twenty warriors. He observed men toiling diligently on the heights of the uncompleted tower.

"The gods are not pleased with the slow pace of constructing their home!" His booming voice carried to all the workers. "The dark lord will punish the people of this Empire should work not proceed more quickly. He will not tolerate laziness or disobedience! Throw the slaves presently delivering bricks on the tower to the ground below! Priests will burn their bodies as a sacrifice on the altar. Hopefully, this will appease the gods for delay of this project."

Commanders reluctantly obeyed because their leader closely watched them. Nimrod ordered the murder of a dozen slaves that day. Taskmasters instructed the slaves to lay their bricks down, and then four workers pushed each struggling slave off the backside of the tower. Screams of terror and agony filled the air as each slave was consecutively shoved to his death from the heights of the tower. Several fell without a sound. Horrified onlookers witnessed the sight. Friends and relatives of the executed slaves mourned them dearly.

Chapter 14

The Escape

Nimrod assigned command of women and children slaves to his nephews. Slaves occasionally escaped these immature taskmasters. Daring escapes usually occurred in broad daylight, when Nimrod's young relatives were occupied in distracting activities. One such escape took place several months after construction commenced on the Tower of Babel.

Many Shemitic slaves worked in Babel. Among them were the two sons and widow of the young Shemite from Akkad, who had volunteered his life to save his brethren. They were assigned to gather clay in the swampy marshes. Slaves were forced to dig trenches angled obtusely to the Euphrates River. These would eventually become irrigation canals for the farmlands. Slaves harvested clay from the ditches, which extended fifteen feet deep and twelve feet wide approaching the Euphrates. Children commanding slaves avoided the thick tenacious mud. Priests taught them gods had planted diseases there, and they only permitted slaves in the ditches. Milcah, the Shemite widow, worked daily in a trench with her sons, Jared and Seth. They talked quietly in the deep ditch as they gathered clay. High banks shielded their conversation from Nimrod's commanders.

"Mother," whispered the older son, Seth, "our commanders do not watch us closely. They prefer to laugh at the misery of our brethren."

Milcah was thankful for her muscular sons. Despite meager food provisions, they had somehow managed to grow to adult size. Her sixteen-year-old son, Seth, had red hair and a fair complexion, which always burned in the hot desert sun. She was thankful he usually worked in the shade of the ditch. Her fourteen-year-old son was somewhat smaller, with curly black hair and tanned skin.

"We must carefully look for an opportunity to flee," Milcah replied. "Nimrod will surely execute anyone caught trying to escape. He regularly makes examples of disobedient slaves. The Lord has blessed us by not allowing the division of our family. We have strength in our unity with God, Who binds us together."

"Jared and I will plan an escape, Mother. We have toiled in these muddy ditches for two months, and I worry about your health. You grow weaker by the day. Please pray God will grant us wisdom," Seth requested.

Milcah had witnessed her once shapely figure dwindle to a shadow of its former beauty. Bones of her face and trunk had become increasingly prominent with each passing day. Sad brown eyes remained the only attractive feature of her gaunt face.

"I shall petition God for wisdom," Milcah whispered. "Now go with your brother and seek the Lord's guidance."

Milcah filled large shallow pottery vessels with the sticky clay. Sumerians had provided her an ample supply of those vessels. She could not lift the clay-filled containers. She knew the muscles in her lean arms would not endure the difficult work much longer. Taskmasters had provided a bronze spade and other digging implements, but Milcah found the soft mud was simpler to remove by hand. Sweat and smudges of dark brown clay covered her face. Her sons and several other slaves alternated retrieving the containers she had filled. They transported the clay-filled pots approximately one hundred yards along the bottom of the trench until they reached crude steps ascending to normal ground. At that point they transferred their loads to fellow slaves, who carried the containers atop their heads one-quarter mile east of the Euphrates River. Designated slaves squeezed the clay into rectangular forms there. Nearby ovens baked the clay into bricks, while other slaves gather wood to stoke the hot ovens. Laboring near the ovens on summer days was nearly unbearable. Slaves tending the ovens routinely passed out from the heat. Milcah recalled relatives she and her friends could not revive after they had succumbed to heat exhaustion.

* * * * * * * * *

Seth and Jared had labored two months in the trenches and sported strong muscles from the work. Though poorly fed, they were among the healthiest Shemitic slaves. Seth preferred labor in the cooler trenches despite the filthy work and abundant mosquitoes. He believed the work was more pleasant than jobs given to other slaves.

The boys had worked the same trench with their mother for several weeks. Each day they exchanged ideas for a possible escape. One morning Jared initiated a quiet discussion with his brother while transporting clay from the ditch.

"I think the Lord has given me a plan," Jared whispered.

"I hope it is a good one, Jared," Seth returned. "Mother cannot tolerate this work much longer."

"Have you noticed the reeds of bamboo in swampy areas near the river?" Jared asked.

"I have noticed them. Now divulge your plan before our conversation is discovered."

Seth tried to act busy.

"We must cut a sturdy large bore reed for each of us. A short reed will do for mother," stated Jared.

"How will these assist our escape?" asked Seth, fearful of being overheard.

"Mother will need to excavate a hole along the side wall of this trench—large enough to fully contain her. We must conceal it from the commanders. At the appropriate time she will crawl into the hole and we will cover her with clay. Our commanders must not see any suspicious alterations, which might suggest the burial chamber. Mother will poke her reed through the wall of the enclosure and draw air for as long as necessary to avoid detection. She might need to stay in the chamber for a long time."

"That sounds interesting, but what is our role in this daring escape?"

"We will have a more dangerous assignment, Seth. Do you remember the swimming lessons Father gave us years ago and the games we played in the water? We competed, holding our breath and swimming long distances underwater."

"Yes, I remember." Seth perceived where his brother was leading the discussion. "I also recall times we dove into the Euphrates River and swam nearly to the middle. We let the currents bring us slowly back to shore, far down-stream from the original point of entry. Father taught us these skills in happier times. I am thankful we had those opportunities with him."

"God used those experiences to prepare us for this present time of danger. I believe we may soon entertain Nimrod and his commanders with a similar swim."

"Are you saying we will swim for these people?" asked Seth incredulously.

"Well, yes … sort of. We must make a spectacle of the escape for the commanders. They will witness us stroking to the middle of this huge river but will not see us swim to our potential. They will perceive us as novice swimmers. Then the currents of the mighty Euphrates will simply take us under—forever. Hopefully, they will reach that conclusion, but we will have our reeds. We will drift underwater with the current until they think we have drowned. We can then discreetly swim to shore and hide in the swampy marshes until nightfall."

Seth could not compare this daring escape to games of their childhood. He knew winners on this occasion would live but losers would surely die.

Jared continued: "After nightfall we will cautiously steal into the city to this very ditch, where mother will be concealed. We will silently remove her from the chamber and hopefully find her alive. If we survive the ordeal our family will leave Babel under the cover of darkness."

"How can we be sure the commanders won't find her in the ditch?"

"We must take that chance, Seth. Perhaps, if we stagger the escape we will give the impression she dove into the river ahead of us. When they see us, I hope they will reach that conclusion."

"That would mean I will be the last to leave this city, with enemies in hot pursuit," Seth muttered quietly.

"You are the strongest swimmer and fastest runner. Age brings a distinct advantage, my brother. Don't you agree?"

Jared grinned.

"I suppose so, Jared. But later, I will collect your debt— after this game of swimming in the river!" Seth returned the smile, trying to suppress the anxiety in his soul.

"We will need to watch the river for several weeks to determine the pattern of boat traffic. We must avoid boats during the escape," declared Jared, carrying a large clay-filled bowl.

Seth carried a larger load of clay on his head but only noticed the crushing burden of fear in his mind.

"We must observe the habits of the commanders. Mother will need ample time to prepare her chamber," Seth whispered as they ascended the steps of the ditch.

Two weeks passed slowly. The boys discreetly gathered reeds from the swampy marshes and tested them underwater when they were permitted time to bathe in the river.

"I feel confident we can draw air from these reeds," Seth declared after an evening bath in the Euphrates several days later.

"We must allow them to dry for a week, and then store them in the ditch," remarked Jared. "My excitement grows daily as I anticipate the escape."

"I wish I could share your enthusiasm," grumbled Seth. "Dread more accurately describes my feelings."

They closely monitored boat traffic on the river, determining it was lightest just before sunset.

"Nimrod's warriors will have to peer west into the setting sun to locate us swimming in this wide river," Seth commented one afternoon. "They will find it difficult to track our position at that time."

"Commanders yearn to return home to their families at the end of these long days," added Jared. "Furthermore, Nimrod's nephews lose interest in the slaves by early afternoon and often play games thereafter."

"The time prior to sunset will provide the best opportunity to escape this wicked city," Seth concluded. "Hopefully, mother will only spend several hours underground if the plan succeeds. She will have a better chance to survive if that time is abbreviated."

* * * * * * * * *

Milcah needed the two weeks to prepare her chamber. She worked in different locations of the trench to avoid giving clues she was excavating it. She figured the clay she retrieved from the hole would make many bricks for the Tower of Babel. She would perform her duty to the very end. With bare hands she scooped the thick, tenacious clay from one side of the ditch, carefully shelling out a small chamber, just large enough to fit a slender woman. She would have no room to wiggle about. The sides of the hole would likely collapse when she crawled into it. She believed the commanders would fail to notice the defect from the top of the ditch—especially late in the afternoon, when the ditch was shrouded in dark shadows. Milcah agreed a late afternoon escape had the greatest likelihood of success.

Nimrod demanded hard labor until sunset each day. Slaves wore scant clothing because of the filthy working conditions. Men and boys wore a leather girdle supporting garments covering their genitals, and women dressed in light robes. Commanders permitted the women to wash their robes in the river at the completion of each workday.

* * * * * * * * *

The fateful day finally arrived. Slaves had completed a long day's work, and women began to emerge from the trenches. They desired to clean their garments and filthy bodies in the river. The late afternoon sun shone brightly, making it difficult to look across the Euphrates River. Milcah did not emerge from the ditch that afternoon. She quietly crawled into the small cave. Seth closed the entrance with a generous portion of thick clay. Dark shadows disguised all defects in the side of the trench. His mother poked a large bore reed through the wall of clay, and Seth quickly removed it to blow out the mud. He then replaced the reed in the original hole and concealed it from above.

"I love you, Mother. We shall return in the middle of the night. The Lord will guide us."

Seth worried about his mother who was beginning this

ordeal in a considerably weak condition. He silently prayed God would bless the foolish escape.

"I shall seek God for your safety, my son."

Seth could barely hear his mother's muffled voice.

The boys had instructed their mother to exit the chamber if they did not return within several hours after nightfall. Hopefully, she would detect the fading daylight through the end of the reed. They instructed her to flee the city before sunrise.

"The Lord will have the victory. You will see. Goodbye Mother..." Seth spoke softly at the end of the reed.

The time to escape was now or never. Seth knew he and Jared must move quickly. The sun had neared its most brilliant point on the western horizon. Seth's heart pounded wildly as he moved to the steps exiting the trench. He felt droplets of perspiration dribbling down his forehead into his eyes. Seth signaled Jared to get to the river as quickly as possible. Jared had transferred his reed to a swampy area close to the river. He swiftly moved there without being detected. He found the reed and tied it firmly to the girdle around his waist.

The women washed their robes in the river. Their commanders were fully occupied with lustful thoughts and failed to notice Jared slipping quietly to an area far downstream. He silently slid into the water then began swimming underwater towards the middle of the river. He periodically surfaced for air but remained unnoticed.

Seth allowed Jared enough time to make it out of arrow range then quickly grabbed his reed, hidden in a swampy area close to the ditch. He secured it tightly in front of his girdle, where the commanders would not see it. He would not face them directly. Taskmasters prodded the slaves together, preparing to herd them into the evening residence. They were eager to get home. Suddenly they realized several slaves were missing. One of the commanders looked back and saw Seth standing a distance behind them.

"You have not finished your work today. I do not intend to join you. You may pursue me if you wish!" Seth taunted from the top of the ditch, approximately a hundred feet away.

"I order you to come at once! We have no time for games! Your companions are hot and weary," shouted the nearest commander.

"I regret making your work more difficult."

Seth lunged forward, running full speed toward the river.

Surprised commanders blew their horns and several rushed after him in hot pursuit. However, they could not keep pace with this speedy young lad. Seth quickly doubled the distance between himself and the commanders. In an instant he was beyond range of their spears. Archers were several minutes behind the commanders. By the time Seth reached the river he was nearly a quarter mile in front of the commanders and much further ahead of the archers. He dove headfirst into the wide Euphrates. Commanders guarding the women noticed the commotion, but they were a quarter mile upstream. Seth quickly stroked toward the middle of the giant river. His brother swam several hundred yards ahead of him. Arrows began to enter the water behind Seth.

"Mother, swim across the river to safety!" Seth shouted for the benefit of Nimrod's men.

The commanders had difficulty seeing through the blinding sunset. Jared was now past the middle of the river—well beyond arrow range.

"Keep stroking Jared! You still have a long way to go!" Seth shouted loudly.

Once again, Nimrod's men clearly heard Seth. Jared's hands began flailing above his head, which bobbed up and down in the water. He appeared to be tiring rapidly.

Seth screamed one more time, "Jared, don't give up! Swim to the other side!"

Then Jared's head disappeared below the surface and did not appear again.

Seth knew the archers would now focus totally on him. He also realized those swimming behind him would be intent on his capture. He stroked hard, but was still several hundred feet short of the middle of the river. As he neared the middle several arrows came dangerously close. He screamed loudly after an arrow struck within inches of his face. He started flailing arms and bobbing below the surface. Archers assumed one of the arrows had made a direct hit. Then Seth disappeared underwater for good. He had not planned to dodge arrows as he swam, but it did provide a convenient excuse to dip below the surface. He swam downstream underwater for several hundred feet then carefully pulled the reed from his girdle and pushed it gently above the surface. He exhaled to force water from the reed and then inhaled the precious air. It was wonderful! He could breathe underwater! No part of his body broke the surface.

Currents of the great River Euphrates carried Seth swiftly downstream, while commanders peered frantically into the sunset. They looked for the boys and their mother but could see no signs of human life in the river. They gave up the search after the sun sank below the horizon, convinced the boys and their mother had perished. Women slaves viewed the events from the river as they finished the evening bath. They talked quietly and lifted many prayers for the family. When the sky darkened the commanders summoned the women and herded them into a dwelling for the night.

* * * * * * * * *

Nimrod received the news about the escape and was happy the family had met their death in the river.

"Enki, the god of the waters, will give these souls to the

goddess of the underworld,"[29] he commented.

However, he was furious the commanders had allowed the family to escape. He was especially displeased with his nephews who had guarded that particular family. He punished them by removing their authority over the slaves and sent them home to Kish. He then instructed the commanders.

"Separate the children from their parents when working them each day. Use whatever means necessary to control these slaves, preventing future escapes. Do you understand?"

The commanders nodded affirmatively.

However, slaves continued to escape. Some heroic slaves evaded capture, but the commanders caught many others. They tortured and executed them as examples for their brethren.

* * * * * * * * *

Meanwhile, the boys drifted several miles downstream until far south of the city and then swam underwater to the eastern shore. They had planned to swim ashore after the sun had dipped below the horizon, hoping to make it before the sky was totally dark. They would then silently locate one another. Seth first identified his brother as they neared the shore. He quickly reached Jared, overjoyed to see him without injury. Excitement of the escape was fresh in their thoughts.

"I was nearly on the wrong end of an arrow!" exclaimed Seth. "But the miss permitted me safe passage underwater. God's angels surely protected us. I hope they still protect Mother."

"We shall soon find out. Let us move inland to find the road to Babel. The moon is absent from this dark sky. We must travel by starlight and may find it difficult to see our path," Jared cautioned.

No other humans braved the dark night. Seth and Jared

saw no living creatures, but the ever-present cries of wild animals frightened them. Seth trusted God to prepare the way.

"Surely, God will guide us to the city," Seth remarked.

They prayed for safety and sought Divine protection for their mother.

"God has provided thick calluses to replace the sandals we should be wearing," declared Jared, as they began the return journey. "Hopefully stones and briars will not bother us this dark night."

Their eyes grew accustomed to the darkness, and they made rapid progress back to the city. They entered Babel about two hours before midnight, carefully avoiding the slave quarters where attentive warriors stood guard throughout the night. They moved stealthily to the swampy marshes and finally found the ditch where they labored each day. They climbed into the trench and located Milcah's burial chamber, silently praying they would find her alive. Seth began removing the clay from the entrance of the hole.

"Mother, we are here! Please come out of the cave," Seth softly encouraged.

They heard no response. Panic immediately consumed them, as they feared the worst. The boys frantically tore clay from the front wall of the chamber, throwing it in all directions.

"Seth, I feel her arm, but it's very cold," Jared whispered ominously.

"We must pull her from this hole at once," Seth instructed.

The boys quickly found Milcah's other arm. Together they extracted her—each boy pulling an arm. They shook her and briskly rubbed her limbs. The stiff body did not respond.

"Please, dear Lord, save our mother. We need her!" Seth pleaded with tears pouring over flushed cheeks.

Seth felt guilty for not fully considering the danger to his critically weakened mother. He brushed the hair from her face while Jared continued to massage cold limbs. Seth noticed the twitch of a lip. He blew a deep breath into her mouth and watched closely.

"Jared, I saw her lip move! We must try to warm her!"

Tender love and nervous energy helped a bit, but it was God's response to heartfelt prayers that brought warmth to a lifeless body. Finally, Seth noticed his mother taking slow shallow breaths. Lips quivered, but her eyes remained closed.

A soft but audible voice came from stone-cold lips: "Lord, take me home. I am ready to meet you and see my husband once again. Please protect the boys."

"Mother, do not leave us!" Seth vigorously shook her shoulders. "We are here, Mother! We must leave this city together or not leave at all. Wake up and speak to us!"

Milcah began moving her arms and eventually caught hold of the boys. Eyes opened slowly, and blue lips parted.

"Seth...Jared?"

A single tear coursed slowly around the angles of her gaunt face.

"I prayed so long for you. I lost all hope you would return, and I was so cold. I thought the Lord had come to take me home."

She reached to embrace her sons and then all wept tears of joy.

Jared spoke first: "Mother, do you feel warm yet? We must not delay fleeing this wicked city."

"I feel warmer and my strength is slowly returning, but I have been lying in this mud for hours. I worked in the mud for a long day before I made it my bed. I must wash and clean this robe before we can leave. Perhaps a dip in the river will strengthen my arms and legs."

"Very well, Mother," Seth responded, "but we must distance ourselves from Babel by daylight or risk being caught by Nimrod's men."

The boys assisted their mother to the river. Milcah

preferred to bathe in the area designated for women slaves. Several large boulders sat on the riverbank. The boys sat beside one of them, and she draped her robe on another while bathing. Milcah promptly bathed and washed the robe. While she dressed, the boys heard a rustling commotion.

"Mother, be still!" Seth whispered. "I hear someone or something approaching from behind us."

They crouched behind the largest boulder and peered into the darkness. Sure enough, a man approached from the direction of the city. He muttered words that were not quite audible. Milcah and the boys suddenly recognized this large dark man. He was Nimrod! Terror filled their souls. They refused to move or make a sound, but Nimrod continued walking toward them as if he knew their hiding place. He had no companions and did not appear armed. Seth tensed his muscles, preparing to pay the ultimate price if Nimrod should discover them, but he did not seem to be searching for anyone in particular. Nimrod walked to another large boulder, not more than twenty-five feet from Milcah and the boys. He climbed the boulder and sat in silence.

* * * * * * * * *

Nimrod began speaking in a monotone voice: "Lord, I beseech you in the darkness. I seek your guidance in building the Tower of Babel—your new home. Do you approve of the progress we have made since our last meeting?"

Silence followed the question. Nimrod waited patiently then spoke again several minutes later.

"My priests teach the people you have supreme authority over all gods. Citizens of the Empire submit to your will, bowing before you and the gods. The memory of Noah's God fades rapidly from their minds. The faith of the slaves weakens daily. Shem's teaching is losing its power on his family. I am breaking their will and soon I will own their souls. Then we will lead them like sheep. What more can I do, my lord?"

Nimrod sat silently, waiting for a reply but none seemed forthcoming. Suddenly, he noticed that familiar headache returning. Despite the blackness of the sky, he began to see sparkling lights. He peered toward the river but could not focus his vision on anything. Dizziness recurred with a vengeance.

"Oh.... that wretched dizziness..."

Nimrod felt nauseated as trees and boulders swirled in a myriad of lights. He shifted his position, attempting to identify landmarks along the riverbank. Suddenly he tumbled off the boulder, unable to maintain balance. He turned, directly facing Milcah and the boys. They desperately tried to conceal themselves behind the boulder.

"He is looking right at us, Mother!" Jared whispered. "Surely he has discovered us."

They were terrified.

"Do not speak or move," Milcah whispered. "The Lord will go before us."

Nimrod peered through the darkness toward the family. He thought he detected movement—but everything was swirling about. Suddenly, brilliant flashes of light blurred all in his field of vision. He dropped to his knees and vomited repeatedly.

"Oooooh... why does this keep happening to me?" he muttered between bouts of retching.

"Because you have chosen to follow God's enemy. You have persecuted His children, and you will answer to the One True God!" Seth answered, stepping forward and gathering courage.

Milcah held her breath and tried to restrain Seth.

"Who speaks to the mighty Nimrod!" he demanded, trying to look toward the sound.

However, Nimrod only saw dazzling streaks of light coming from every direction. Lights twisted and turned, worsening the dizziness.

"I know you taunt me and you will pay with your life!" Nimrod threatened.

"You will pay with your soul for eternity, Nimrod!" Seth boldly proclaimed. "God does not trifle with such arrogance!"

Nimrod struggled unsuccessfully to identify his accuser. He crawled to his feet and stumbled up the path toward the city, vomiting repeatedly along the way. He held to any support he could find to prevent falling. The pounding headache and vertigo were nearly unbearable, but the brilliant lights disappeared, leaving only blackness and pain.

* * * * * * * * *

Milcah and the boys hurriedly escaped the city. Only four hours remained before dawn. They determined to head north to Akkad, traveling under the cover of darkness. Seth felt vulnerable after their experience.

"We risk discovery if we travel along the river," he remarked. "I think we should trek east of the Euphrates and off the main road."

"You are right, my son. We shall walk until sunrise then find a place to rest and gather strength."

Seth remembered his mother was once a strong woman, but the previous night's adventure had nearly sapped any strength remaining in her frail body. She could not keep pace with the boys, despite their assistance. They even carried her short distances—her arms draped around their muscular shoulders. They traveled ten miles north of Babel before the eastern sky began to lighten.

"Please find a resting place," Milcah pleaded. "When we settle, you can search for food and water."

They looked everywhere for a suitable hiding place but

could only see dry arid land. They finally found several large boulders. The boys scouted the site and determined they could rest in the shade of these boulders. Seth thought humans would not likely travel in that area. He knew his mother was exhausted. Sleep overcame her in several minutes.

Seth and Jared left to find sustenance for the day. They traveled two miles west to locate the first farmable land. They found a large field of grain and several small vegetable plots. Irrigation ditches coursed nearly a mile from the Euphrates River to water them. Seth noticed pottery vessels lying behind a brick storage building. They used two pots to gather water for the day and gleaned ripe vegetables from the gardens—carrying all this to their concealment. Morning sun fully illuminated the sky by the time they returned. People began traveling the roads and working lands adjacent to the river, but no one approached the hiding place. Milcah and the boys rested safely until mid-afternoon then awoke to consume the meal.

"Let us give thanks to the Lord, our Provider. Indeed, He was a cover of protection for us last night. God richly supplies our needs," Milcah declared.

They bowed to praise the Lord and seek His guidance. They waited patiently, enjoying each other's company. Seth did not mind the hot summer day as long as they were together. At sunset they departed, traveling north. Only the cries of nocturnal animals accompanied them, but the sounds did not frighten the boys that night. Stars illuminated the way once again. They moved quickly, covering approximately twenty miles.

"My sons, we rarely take time to appreciate the stars our Lord has created for us. He gave them as signs to reveal deep truths."[30]

"What do you mean, Mother?" Seth asked, puzzled by the comment. "How can stars reveal truth?"

"God created the stars to testify of His work in this

world. That is their primary purpose. God arranged them in groupings called constellations. He designed each constellation to illustrate a story, and He revealed these stories to our godly forefathers. Our patriarch, Shem, understands God's testimony in the constellations. He instructed me about the heavenly signs when I was a young girl. I still recall some of these truths."

"Will you please share the secret truths of the stars, Mother?" Seth asked.

"Seth, these truths are not secret or mysterious as the wicked astrologers from Babel teach," Milcah insisted. "Nimrod and his astrologers have corrupted the messages God revealed by the stars. They have distorted the signs of the constellations to justify their wicked religion. Their zodiac credits God's wicked enemy for creating the universe. The mystery religion of Babylon teaches Satan will someday assume control of the world and ultimately displace God from His heavenly throne. Astrologers claim this foolishness is illustrated by the constellations, and it is widely accepted by the people of Mesopotamia."

"What are the truths God reveals in the constellations, Mother?" Seth asked once again, somewhat frustrated his original question was not satisfactorily answered.

"Constellations reveal the unfortunate story of man's fall. It occurred many generations ago when Adam and Eve ate forbidden fruit in the Garden of Eden. Satan authored that wicked deception. God has portrayed this story in heavenly pictures, my son. Furthermore, constellations bear testimony God will provide a solution for the fall of man. They reveal He will send a Redeemer to free the creation from the curse of sin and sting of death.[31] His Redeemer—the promised Seed—will defeat Satan. Although the Redeemer will suffer injury, the outcome is certain. He will crush the head of the evil serpent.[32] God has destined us for eternal life with Him. That was His plan from the beginning, and He has revealed it for our benefit in the constellations. They portray this extraordinary conflict, which has been fought since the beginning of time. These heavenly signs bear witness that God will ultimately have the victory in this battle of the ages. No one will ever displace God from His throne. His celestial signs assure us His dominion will continue for eternity. Do you comprehend this?"

"I understand, Mother," Seth replied, "but I would like you to demonstrate how stars create these pictures."

"I cannot fully answer that question. Your great, great grandfather, Shem, can illustrate these pictures for your inquisitive mind. Someday I shall introduce this wonderful man to you. Your father could identify these heavenly pictures. He would often show them to me on clear nights. He told me God named every star,"[33] Milcah remarked, as several large tears coursed down her bony cheeks.

Milcah regained her composure and continued: "I remember there are twelve signs of the zodiac. Each corresponds to a month of the year, and it is only visible during that particular month. They all correlate with the movement of the sun through the heavens. I remember the first and last of these signs. The first is Virgo, 'the virgin woman.' The last sign is Leo, 'the Lion.' The constellation, Virgo, reveals God's promised Seed will come from a virgin woman. That child is the hope of mankind. Virgo contains three constellations. Each describes God's Seed, who will someday rule the world. The last sign of the year, Leo, portrays God's Seed as the Lion who will destroy Satan in His terrible wrath. Pictured within the constellation of Leo are three other constellations. The first is Hydra, the old serpent, who the Lion will conquer. The second is Crater, Cup of the Lion's wrath, which He will pour out upon Satan. The third constellation is Corvus, The Raven—bird of prey who will devour the evil one."

"Each sign of the zodiac contains three additional constellations, making a total of forty-eight. They tell the amazing story of Satan's rebellion, man's fall, man's redemption, and finally Satan's destruction. Our great father, Shem, will someday teach you the significance of each constellation."

"We are presently in the sign of Cancer, which means 'The Redeemer is safe, and His possessions are secure.' Look for a crab in a grouping of stars. I can see it in that region of the sky!" Milcah exclaimed, tracing the outline with her finger. "The crab is our God, holding tightly His Seed and offspring. They are secure in His care. Three other constellations appear in the sign of Cancer. One is Ursa Minor, 'the little bear or sheepfold.' The second is Ursa Major, 'the great Bear.' These describe the sheepfold and flock as God's permanent property. The third, Argo—the Ship, reveals 'the pilgrims have arrived home safely.' I can show you Argo as we look towards that portion of the sky. Can you see the outline of a huge ship made by the stars? We ride in the security of that ship. God is the ship, and He protects us against dangerous floodwaters of wickedness that envelop this world."[34]

Seth was mesmerized by these marvelous truths. He pondered them while gazing at the stars.

They stopped just prior to sunrise. Once again, the boys gleaned vegetables from the fields and collected water from irrigation ditches. They found a suitable hiding place for the day. After traveling for several nights they neared the city of Kish. Seth knew this was the hometown of Nimrod and his father. He had heard armed warriors guarded the city, so they would prudently avoid detection. After obtaining their daily nourishment, they found a suitable hiding place six miles east of the city—well inland of the Euphrates. Once again, they rested between several large boulders, standing alone in a dry arid plain. Seth noticed no humans traveling in the area. They did not leave their concealment until dusk.

Seth observed more rocks and trees as they traveled further north. The boys easily found hiding places. Seth eagerly anticipated their homecoming, and he discussed it with Jared every day of the trip. The journey to Akkad took a week, traveling in this fashion. A crescent moon sufficiently illuminated the city for a night tour.

"Akkad has changed dramatically since our forced departure several years ago," Seth commented. "Masons have constructed new buildings, and workers have built additional roads."

"An immense wall surrounds Akkad—just like other Sumerian cities. Have you noticed the new temples for false gods, Mother?" asked Jared.

"Yes, my son, and I also perceive more people have moved here. Perhaps they were coerced to move. The military presence discourages me, and I do not feel safe. Shemites who follow the Lord are not welcome in Akkad."

"We shall glean from the fields as usual and then find refuge outside the city for the daylight hours. It does appear too dangerous to stay," Seth agreed.

"I remember an isolated grove of trees north of the city. Perhaps we can relax there," Jared volunteered.

They welcomed the shade of those large trees and obtained a restful sleep.

Jared spoke first after they awakened: "Where will we go now, Mother? Must we travel endlessly? Will we ever find a home?"

Seth saw his mother teetering on a cliff of hopelessness. She quickly composed herself, attempting to conceal the fear. Seth admired her courage. He knew there were no good answers to Jared's questions.

"I feel the Lord's prompting to continue northward. We will follow the Tigris River, which originates near the home of our forefathers. Shem and Noah will advise us. God will give them wisdom for our predicament, my son."

"Perhaps we should tell them about the horrible conditions in Mesopotamia," offered Jared. "Shem will grieve when he hears Nimrod has killed father."

"Shem is a godly man, Jared. The Lord may have already informed him about the rebellion of this wicked enemy," Milcah replied.

When the sky darkened, they left their concealment and traveled several miles east to the Tigris River, then followed it northward.

"This land requires more work to cultivate than farmland along the Euphrates," Seth remarked, pointing to huge rocks sitting in plowed fields.

Milcah nodded in agreement.

After traveling for a week they arrived at the outskirts of a small city named Asshur. They quietly toured the new city at night.

"Asshur is designed like cities along the Euphrates River—complete with a defensive wall that nearly surrounds it," Seth commented. "It even has temples to worship heathen gods!"

The boys gleaned vegetables from gardens and moved several miles north of the city to find a resting place.

"Is this city named after our great Uncle Asshur, Mother?" Jared asked.

"I feel certain it was named after him. I wish it were not so."

"Did he refuse to heed his father's instructions?" asked Jared.

"Shem instructed all his children of God's intentions— that we spread over the earth and not congregate in cities," Milcah replied.

"Did we err by living in Akkad?" Seth asked, feeling confused.

"Your father and I traveled with several Shemitic families to the region of Akkad. We decided to make our home in this beautiful land. We did not intend for that small settlement to grow into a large city, but many people followed us because of the proximity to both the Tigris and Euphrates Rivers. We did not organize Akkad into a city like those in the Mesopotamian Valley. Descendants of Shem, Ham, and Japheth settled this region, but Nimrod's warriors forcibly moved them into the city under a central ruling authority."

Seth pondered the explanation, and then asked: "Why is it wrong to gather people into a city under the rule of men? People seem more productive when they work together. City walls appear to offer protection from animals and wicked men."

"Our minds do not reason like God," Milcah answered. "Evil, rebellious men initially built cities in the Old World. They did not rely upon God for provision but satisfied their needs apart from Him. Cities enabled them to achieve independence. Pride consumed them, and their visions became idols. Memories of a personal God quickly faded. Therefore, God destroyed the Old World as you have been taught."

Seth listened intently, and then asked another question: "Mother, do we sin by living in a city?"

"No, my son... living in the city is not a sin. We sin by depending on it to provide our needs and desires, especially when that dependence pushes God from our lives. Satan uses cities to destroy the personal relationship God has with His children. This close relationship protects us. Sin grows to evil proportions when that relationship is compromised. Nimrod followed that path and closed the door of his heart to God. He pursued worldly success by arrogance and domination. His father and grandfather contributed to that deception. Cush named him 'to rebel,' and Nimrod fulfilled his father's expectations by rejecting a relationship with God. You must teach your children to seek God for their needs, or they will build their lives on shifting sand—like Nimrod."

Seth remembered his father's similar counsel—years before.

Milcah continued: "Someday many cities will exist in

the New World—provided God does not destroy it, as He
did the Old World. Cities will arise as the world's population
increases, but evil will also multiply. God embraces only
One City—the City of Righteousness, also known as the
City of Peace. It does not need walls to defend its people
from animals and human invaders, and warfare does not
exist there. The hands of men did not make one brick for
God's Holy City. God created the City of Righteousness,
where people dwell in Peace. God's Holiness demands the
righteousness of His people there. Its inhabitants exalt
God—not their creations. They walk with God like Adam
did before his original sin."

Milcah paused momentarily, and then continued: "Do
you realize we have walked in that City for several weeks?
We have not depended on cities of men to provide our needs
in this wilderness but have totally relied upon God. We walk
in His City though we cannot see it. Someday people will
see God's City of Righteousness with their eyes."

Seth was fascinated as he contemplated God's Holy
City.

"I believe it is easier to enter God's City when we are
insecure in the cities of men. Life is comfortable in man-
made cities, but danger causes us to walk in God's City and
rely on Him. Is this how God desires us to live, Mother?"

"Yes, my son. Whether we live in a city or in the wilderness, God desires us to depend on Him. He has not promised
security from the evil of this world. He has only promised to
provide our needs and walk daily with us. God has said:

I will never leave you, nor forsake you.

So we can say with confidence, 'The Lord is my helper;
I will not be afraid. What can man do to me?'[35]

When God removes Satan from this world we will enter the
City of God, as He has planned from the beginning of time.
We will dwell safely within the eternal boundaries He has
established, and we will apprehend His awesome City in its

totality. Wild animals and vicious men will not hunt us there. God's presence will provide security to men. These times are different because our eyes cannot see God's City. Nevertheless, we dwell there by faith."

"Mother, I long to walk in God's city," Seth declared, hoping to share these truths with others in the New World.

They slept soundly that day and awoke mid-afternoon to eat a meal, and then they continued to journey northward. They traveled along the Tigris River for several more nights before reaching the city of Nimrod. It was smaller than the previous cities but built in similar fashion. They rested outside Nimrod during the day then continued the trek by night, traveling rapidly on a good road that paralleled the Tigris. They passed through Resen and Rehoboth Ir, continuing north. Finally, they arrived at the outskirts of Nineveh. Seth was amazed at the arrogance of a man who would name cities after himself.

"Does this man assume he owns the people in these cities?" Seth inquired.

"I won't pass judgment on Nimrod's motives, but God knows his heart. Our Holy God will someday expose these motives before all created beings and then toss 'the rebel' into the eternal fire of His wrath," replied Milcah.

They stayed concealed outside Nineveh during the day. Hills and trees covered the landscape, providing excellent hiding places. They rested on a hill under the shade of several trees.

After awakening, Seth and his family sat in silence, enjoying the sights. They watched farmers carrying produce on mule-drawn carts. They observed warriors entering and leaving Nineveh. Children played delightful games on the city streets. Finally, at sunset they resumed the journey.

* * * * * * * * *

Many years had passed since Milcah had left the northern lands, and she cherished memories from that time. She was impressed with the growing population along the Tigris River. Most of these people now lived in cities. When Milcah and the boys finally passed through the last of them, the population thinned out considerably. Small settlements of extended families dotted the countryside. Many in these settlements believed in Noah's God, and Milcah was related to most of them.

"We can now travel by day, as the danger of capture is considerably less," Milcah declared one morning. "You have never experienced the majestic mountains, my sons. Observe the trees covering mountainsides and large boulders peppering the terrain. Creeks weave through valleys and wild animals run freely. Colorful birds own the skies. We shall enjoy the wonderful creations of our Lord today!"

"For once, I will see scenery beyond my feet!" Jared joked.

"Nights are much cooler in these lands. We shall travel to the home of my cousin, Eber. Perhaps he will invite us to stay with him. We can trust this man of God," Milcah assured.

Time whizzed by as they soaked up sights and sounds of the mountainous lands. Milcah picked up the pace as she approached a small group of homes at sunset.

"My cousin lives in that small house—the one built with stones," Milcah gestured. "Houses are routinely built from stones in this area. We shall stop here to rest, if the Lord permits. Hopefully my cousin will welcome us."

"Is anyone home?" Milcah called at the entrance.

Momentarily, a tall handsome man of thirty-four years came to the door. His sandy hair and tanned skin were exactly like Milcah remembered.

"Milcah!" Eber exclaimed, embracing his long lost sister in faith. "We have worried about you and your family. No one has informed us of your whereabouts for several years."

Tears flowed freely, reflecting a joyous reunion in dangerous times.

"You have lost so much weight. Your once shapely figure is now replaced by a skeleton wrapped in bruised skin, and your countenance suggests years of hard burdens," empathized Eber.

"Indeed, I have borne my share of tribulation, Eber," she replied, "but the Lord has provided during these trials. He always stands by my side."

Her chest heaved and she sobbed uncontrollably.

"Please come into the house," Eber encouraged. "My wife, Leah, has cooked a generous meal this evening."

Leah stepped from the shadows and warmly embraced Milcah and the boys. They walked to the dining room and reclined at a small table. Leah served food and then sat to join the company.

"Your sons have nearly grown into men, Milcah. They are tall and handsome, favoring their father in so many ways. Where is your husband? Does he not travel with you?" Eber inquired.

Milcah wept once again. She appreciated her cousin, but these memories were terribly painful to dredge from a wounded heart.

"Nimrod executed him before us. My mind relives that terrible scene many times each day. My only solace is that he willingly gave his life for our family and the brethren in Akkad. That sacrifice enabled us to return home. I have joy, knowing he is in God's hands. However, sorrow and suffering have walked in my footsteps ever since that time. I yearn to join my husband and the Lord, but I have endured to preserve my godly testimony and minister to these boys. Instead, they have comforted me."

"Share your sufferings with us so we can pray for you," requested Eber.

Milcah remembered Eber's compassion and dedication to serve the brethren. God would use Eber and Leah to tend their emotional wounds.

"Nimrod enslaved us immediately after murdering my husband. He ordered his men to march us through the desert of Mesopotamia to the new city of Babel, where they placed us in forced labor. He subsequently sent many of the brethren to join us, and we have all worked as his slaves. Nimrod is erecting an enormous tower to God's diabolical enemy. Slaves are working this very moment, making bricks and transporting them to masons constructing the tower. Nimrod has abused and executed many of the brethren. Our people are weak and their number diminishes daily, but their faith in God grows in the midst of great suffering."

"That is tragic news. This world is rapidly becoming like the Old World. Hearts of men are evil, and wickedness has no boundaries. How did you escape and return home?"

"The Lord has been good to us, Eber. God gave Jared a plan after many months working as Nimrod's slaves. God's angels helped us escape, and His grace brought us home."

Milcah described the harrowing escape and their travels through new cities of the Empire. She shared about the living conditions of slaves and the suffering they had endured. Eber and Leah listened patiently as Milcah recounted these things, interrupted only by her tears.

"I have finally returned to find a home among my people—God's children."

"The population of the world grows rapidly, but the number of God's people declines even faster," Eber lamented. "People who yearn for security flock to the cities, and those fearing persecution from Nimrod's warriors settle there also. They refuse to seek God in these dangerous times and are losing their spiritual vision. People would rather trust in what they see, than in God who brought them into this world. My dear sister... you and the boys have suffered terrible trials, yet you have kept the faith. God will reward that faithfulness, but now your blessing is in drawing close to Him. Eat your fill and get some rest. We shall continue this discussion in the morning."

Milcah did not realize how exhausted she was. She and the boys immediately fell into a deep slumber. They slept till late the next morning then awoke to the sounds and aromas of a busy kitchen. Eber and his wife had prepared a large breakfast.

Eber greeted them with a smile. " 'This is the day the Lord has made. Let us rejoice and be glad in it.'[36] Leah has prepared a wonderful meal of eggs, meat, and bread. She even picked fresh grapes from the vineyard. We must eat and strengthen our bond of friendship."

"Two cooked meals in a row is more than my mind can fathom, Eber," Milcah declared. "More than two years have passed since we have enjoyed such luxuries."

Milcah felt rested and refreshed. She drew strength from Eber and his wife. Morning sunlight streamed through the windows and added to the warmth of their fellowship.

"My wife is pregnant with two children!" Eber proclaimed, gesturing toward Leah's burgeoning midline. "We hope to celebrate the birth of these infants in six months. We have waited many years for a child, but God desired to keep Leah lean with an empty womb. Now He has blessed her with two children!"

Eber and Leah beamed in delight.

He continued: "An angel informed me God will bring a prophetic message to the world at the birth of these sons. Will you join us to celebrate this coming event as we partake of the meal?"

"We are pleased to join you and very hungry besides. I hope you are practicing to feed two hungry boys! Has the Lord provided names for these young lads?" Milcah asked.

"He has named one of them. 'The child will be called

Peleg, for in his days, the earth will be divided.'[37] An angel of God spoke those words. I suppose God has given us liberty to name the other son."

"I wonder how God intends to divide the earth," mused Milcah. "I am thankful He will intervene once again in the affairs of men. Events occurring in this New World have surely enraged Him. I desire Him to intercede this very moment!"

"God will intervene according to His timetable. His timing is always perfect. Unfortunately, we do not often wait for Him," Eber responded. "When we finish this meal I shall take you to our great grandfather, Shem, and his father, Noah. You have not seen them for years, and your sons have never met them. What a blessing they have missed! A wonderful surprise awaits these young lads!"

"I eagerly desire to meet the man who fathered all the people of this New World!" exclaimed Jared.

They quickly finished breakfast and prepared to leave.

"Shem and Noah have mined extraordinary treasures of God. I shall never approach their godliness," Eber remarked, "but I hunger for the wisdom that fulfills the soul! I often sit at their feet as they teach believers, and occasionally I stay for days at a time. However, Leah cannot travel safely, and she needs me until the children are born. Therefore, I will not linger at the home of our great grandfather."

Leah remained at home while Milcah, Eber, and the boys journeyed further north. They traveled on Eber's mules, covering many more miles than Milcah and the boys had trekked in a night of walking.

"Your endurance amazes me, Milcah," remarked Eber.

"My physical condition is strong enough to walk these mountains, Eber," she retorted playfully. "God has not blessed me with an opportunity to ride mules for several years!"

They passed many settlements of Shemites but did not stop until they reached Shem's home late that afternoon.

Eber announced their arrival at the entrance, and an elderly man soon greeted them at the door.

"I have expected you Eber! The Lord informed me you would bring guests," Shem declared, as he turned to examine Milcah and the boys—his moist eyes glistening with happiness. "I am honored with the blessing of more godly children, Milcah! I know you and your husband have reared these boys in the wisdom of our Lord, and I rejoice. Come and join the fellowship. Father and I have dearly missed you. Each new child brings rich blessings to our souls, but every lost child causes us intense anguish. I understand you have suffered for Him, and I am eager to hear your testimony."

Milcah remembered Shem's large house. She had even visited Noah's apartment years before but had never met his wife. God had taken her to His eternal City decades prior to Milcah's birth. Milcah had played childhood games in Arphaxad's apartment on numerous occasions.

Shem led them to the meeting room where Milcah once sat at the feet of the patriarchs to hear God's wisdom. She still remembered many of those teachings. Milcah recalled comparing God's great truths to the immense stones in the walls. Sunlight illuminating the room always reminded her of God's purifying light.

The believers in Shem's large family sat quietly, anticipating something special. They anxiously awaited the guests of honor. Several hand-carved chairs sat on opposite sides of the room. One was reserved for Noah and the other belonged to Shem. The patriarchs taught from these chairs without growing weary.

Noah sat in his chair, looking more frail than Milcah had ever recalled. His wrinkled skin was weathered from years of harsh conditions in the world. A bent back and twisted joints made it impossible for him to sit upright. He squinted at the guests entering the room, and a gentle smile of recognition appeared. Tears of joy still flowed from those ancient eyes.

"My children, your arrival warms this old heart of mine. Our Lord has blessed you to suffer for Him. That is a great honor! You have dwelled in God's City, and I know He has personally walked with you. I hope all of us will someday have that privilege," Noah declared.

Milcah totally lost her composure. She ran to embrace Noah then bowed before him and wept freely. Her sons stood silently, marveling at the sight.

Noah bent down to caress his great, great, great granddaughter.

"Please, my daughter, do not bow before this old man. I am just wrinkled flesh and crooked bones. As the years have aged my body, sin has also stained my soul. I am no different than you. We must bow only before God! Now rise to stand here beside me."

Milcah rose slowly and gazed into that loving old face. Earlier memories of this godly man flooded through her mind in an instant.

Noah continued: "You are broken, my daughter. The Lord has touched you—cherish the moment. God reaches into the depths of a broken heart. We experience His tender love through suffering. Only then does He mold our character to glorify His name."

The family was amazed at the scene. No one had heard Noah speak this way for decades. Years of suffering and despair had shaped the temperament of this godly man.

Milcah looked around the room for the first time. At least fifty members from Shem's family were gathered, but to Milcah the room seemed filled with thousands of God's chosen. She recognized everyone but the young children.

All the believers gazed warmly at Milcah, and many rose to embrace her. She and the boys sat with the family at Shem's feet after the greetings. Their ears were open and their minds thirsty for God's Word.

Shem rose from the chair and sought the Lord's guidance

for the family. When he concluded the prayer, he slowly folded his crooked legs beneath him and sat on the floor—a difficult feat for a 350 year old man.

Shem gestured toward the empty chair and spoke to Milcah: "My daughter, we have reserved this chair for you today. We desire to hear your testimony of God's work."

Milcah looked around the room, fearful to sit in that large chair.

"I am not worthy to address this group of godly brothers and sisters." A blush of embarrassment lit her face.

"Our worthiness is in the Lord, my dear," Noah chided gently.

Milcah reluctantly rose from her position on the floor and sat in the comfortable chair, gathering her composure. She prayed the Lord would use her to exhort the brethren.

"Brothers and sisters… I am not here to teach God's wisdom. My sons and I only desire the fellowship of this family. We come, having lost our home, our possessions, and even my dear husband and father of these boys. We have realized our needs are not met by cities or the creations of men. We abide in God—our home is in Him. We have journeyed here to join the few believers left in this troubled world. He has prepared us to face a difficult future in a dangerous time."

Milcah paused to wipe a river of sorrow from her cheek.

"Nimrod has forcibly moved many of our brethren to Mesopotamia and made slaves of them—men, women, and children. He has violated their dignity and mocked their faith. His commanders drive them mercilessly to build the vast city of Babel. They work from sunrise to sunset gathering clay and making bricks for his huge tower. Nimrod has even ordered our brethren thrown from the heights of this enormous edifice when their work fails to please him. He has not yet stolen their Hope, and they still refuse to bow before him."

The family praised God, but all were saddened, hearing

of the terrible persecution of their relatives.

Milcah continued: "Nimrod's commanders monitor the activities of all slaves. His men guard them day and night. Our brothers and sisters are herded like cattle into multiple one-story brick buildings after every long work day. Often, more than fifty slaves occupy each windowless building, which would normally house a family of eight. Only one latrine is available, and its odor drifts through the entire house. Rows of slaves sleep on animal skins laid on the floor of each room. They are given inadequate nourishment and rest then pressed into labor at the break of dawn. Pregnant mothers are forced to work through the delivery of their infants. The sick are driven without mercy, and many fall from sheer exhaustion."

"How do they maintain the faith, Milcah?" Eber asked.

"The slaves pray and worship for several hours every night, developing strong spiritual bonds with God and each other. In these brief times of fellowship—in deplorable conditions, our Lord nourishes their spirit and strengthens their faith. Yes... a faithful remnant from our family is alive in the darkest place of this New World. They remember God saved only eight of their ancestors from among millions of wicked people in the Old World. They have determined to number among the blessed few if He chooses to save a handful of righteous ones from this present world. Many perish from illness, starvation, or execution, but their faith continues to grow. They know if wicked men kill them, God will spare their souls."

"How do people escape this evil man and his commanders?" asked Shelah.

"Some have escaped but more have died trying. Several armed men guard the only entrance to each dwelling. They catch most slaves attempting nighttime escapes and execute them before the brethren. This instills fear in those remaining. Nimrod and his commanders torture the slaves, attempting to extract information regarding the whereabouts of escapees. Slaves intending to escape usually do not share their plans with the brethren, to avoid endangering more lives. They hope Nimrod's men will grow weary of this useless torture."

"How did you and the boys flee this horrible place?" asked Arphaxad.

"The Lord gave Jared a plan. We prepared for several weeks, knowing the escape would be dangerous, but God strengthened our faith. His angels delivered us at a time of great peril. I must admit we feared for our lives."

Milcah described the harrowing escape and concluded with this testimony: "When we were preparing to leave the city that night, we found one more terrifying obstacle to our departure. Nimrod inadvertently walked within twenty-five feet of our location at the edge of the river. He did not see us, though we were certainly not hidden from his view. He came to converse with Satan, the great enemy of our Lord. Nimrod speaks with Satan as we commune with God. The Lord struck him with a terrible malady. I do not know what it was, but Nimrod fell to the ground. Seth stepped forward to convict him with God's Word. I feared Nimrod might capture us that very moment, but God kept him on the ground like a harmless beetle. God's angels blinded him, but the Lord did not stop his ears. I am certain Nimrod heard God's Word. He crawled up the path and stumbled into the wicked city. Thereafter, we fled from Babel and have traveled northward by night ever since. The Lord protected us and gave my sons the strength and character of godly men. We give Him the glory!"

Many were concerned about their loved ones, whom Nimrod had taken into slavery. Milcah answered their questions truthfully. Her answers evoked many tears but also increased their faith and brought glory to God.

Finally, Shem stood to address the family.

"My children... this world is very young. In fact, it is less than the age of a healthy old man. In this brief time God's enemy has spread evil deception to the minds of all who populate the earth. Unfortunately, we live in a very dark hour in the history of mankind. Few faithful followers of God remain. These perilous times are like the last years of the Old World. The wicked serpent has pressed his advantage mightily upon men and women of this age, and he has usurped the rule of this world from our Lord. Satan has granted Nimrod remarkable strength and authority, and Nimrod uses it without mercy, according to the ways of his dark lord. God has informed us the world is under a curse. Satan operates freely in this cursed world, and he will do so until God sends His Seed to redeem the creation. God's Redeemer will eliminate evil from the world, and He will remove the sting of death from the enemy. Someday God will deliver the mortal blow to Satan and abolish the curse from His creation. These promises are written in the Holy Scriptures, passed down from our forefathers. Adam recorded God's promise,[38] but we do not know when He will accomplish it. God desires our faithfulness. He has granted us a sure hope—an anchor for our souls during this precarious time."[39]

Shelah interrupted: "Grandfather, the number of believers in the New World is rapidly declining. Most of the world's population is gathered into cities. Impenetrable walls surround them, and the citizens feel secure and fulfilled. Warriors protect the cities and they mock our faith even as Nimrod does. Soon they will move to exterminate the remaining believers in this world. Is this not Satan's real agenda? What is God's plan for us? How can we resist this bloodthirsty evil looming on the horizon?"

Shem paused to seek wisdom from the Lord before responding to this thoughtful question.

"God has not given us answers for these difficult questions, but He always keeps a remnant of believers in the world. Such is the case even now. God has promised to provide for the faithful, and He fulfills His promises. We do not know His plan at this dark hour, but He often protects us in our ignorance from fears that would certainly overwhelm us. Nevertheless, the Lord will fight this battle, and He will redeem His creation. God only asks us to faithfully endure with Him until He is ready to intervene."[40]

"Do we just sit and wait as the believing remnant shrinks?" Eber asked.

"No, my son, we do not just sit, but we must wait upon the Lord. He is pleased when we do so. For now it is our privilege to pray and seek wisdom until the dark clouds lift from the path before us."

This was a difficult teaching to grasp—even for Milcah. Most of the believers were ready to take up arms and fight for God if Shem had encouraged them to do so.

Shem hesitated briefly, and then continued: "I have prayed and fasted for God's wisdom. Once again, I sense God is about to intervene in the affairs of men. I have some evidence to support this prediction, and now I will share it with you. First of all, God has opened the womb of Eber's wife after years of infertility. Recently an angel visited Eber in a dream and told him Leah carries two children in her womb. The angel instructed Eber to name one of these children, Peleg. God attaches great significance to names because they often portray His intentions. This may provide some insight about His plan. The name, Peleg, means 'to divide the world.' I have no additional information, but I can only assume God is poised, once again, to change the course of history."

"Secondly, an angel of God also appeared to me during an evening prayer. The angel instructed me to proclaim God's Word to Nimrod. I do not know what that Word is, but God has summoned me a second time to confront this evil man. I shall leave in the morning with two witnesses. God will use these men to minister to me. I cannot guarantee our safety, but I know God will go with us. I will take Shelah and Seth, the son of Milcah. Together we shall travel to the wicked city of Babel. Arphaxad will mentor you in my absence. We will need your constant prayers for courage to be God's ambassadors in this evil world. Together we shall petition the Lord for faith to face the unknown."

The women and children wept, and fear overwhelmed the entire family. Several men pleaded to go in Shem's place, claiming their loss would be less traumatic for the believing remnant.

Shem flatly refused these requests.

"The Lord has spoken to me about this matter. I shall follow God, and He will empower me to accomplish His command. We shall depart at sunrise. Arphaxad and Eber will prepare for the journey."

Shem hugged Milcah who quietly wept with her head bowed.

"Welcome home, my daughter. Do not be anxious. Your son will be in the best of hands. The Lord Himself will accompany us."

"I cannot bear the loss of a son and great grandfather to this wicked man."

"Do not carry this burden, Milcah. God knows what He is doing. He will provide for us and supply your needs also. Rest with the family and allow them to minister to your soul."

Shem hugged her one last time then left to spend several hours communing with God.

Milcah met with her sons to pray with them.

"I am proud of you for seeking God during the terrible events of the past several years. My heart is not prepared to turn you loose, but this is precisely what God requires. I shall pray for you, Seth. God will richly bless you. You have the best spiritual mentor in this world. Heed his wise counsel, and pray for your mother in the days ahead. The Lord still has much work to perform in me, my son."

"I shall pray often for you, Mother. I am certain God will keep me in the center of His Will. Pray I might minister to Father Shem. He will need strength. This long journey would challenge the endurance of a young man. Do not worry if we are delayed. We shall return according to God's timetable."

Seth kissed and hugged his mother. The day's activities had exhausted them, and the boys quickly fell asleep. But Milcah lay awake, pondering the events of that day. She felt an assurance that Shem and Seth were in God's hands, yet sleep did not come easy for her that night.

Chapter 15

The Journey to Mesopotamia

S hem, Shelah, and Seth were ready to depart after eating a large breakfast. Arphaxad and Eber had prepared five mules for the journey. They had loaded food, tents, and other supplies upon the two extra mules. After hugs and many prayers they departed for the southern lands. Seth would guide the party, as he was more familiar with the territory through which they would travel.

Seth noticed they covered many more miles each day on mules than they previously could on foot. They traveled by day and rested each night in tents hand-crafted by Shem's family.

Shem informed his companions: "We need not fear traveling in daylight. God does not miss His appointments. He has ordained a meeting with Nimrod, and He will accomplish it. He would not have his children journey in fear of the unknown."

Traveling through the cities did not bother Shem, but he avoided them at night.

"The Lord has commanded us to spread over the earth. If we conduct business in these cities, temptation to settle there might afflict our soul. We must avoid such temptation.

Only a tiny portion of the world is settled at this time. I will not change my habits until the Lord instructs me otherwise," Shem insisted.

They spent substantial time in the cities, however. Shem often stopped to greet the people. Everywhere people knew him, and all respected this faithful man. Armed warriors guarded each city, and they knew a godly man moved in their midst. Yet, no one challenged him. Warriors either feared Shem or did not consider him a threat. Seth saw Shem encourage many to turn from their false deities to faith in the true God. Several acknowledged their spiritual needs, but very few pursued a relationship with God. Children eagerly desired to seek the Lord, however. In city after city they hungered for spiritual Truth. Their parents had never taught them about God. Seth thought this a sad commentary on the condition of the New World. It only took six generations for Satan to suppress God's Truth. What would happen if no one shared this good news? He shuddered while contemplating the thought. Seth knew this was the intent of God's foremost enemy.

Children followed Shem, and he instructed them about God. Many requested to join him.

He always replied, "Remain with your family until you reach the appropriate age to leave. Perhaps God will use you to win your parents to His Truth! I shall return if God permits and answer the questions you might have."

* * * * * * * * *

They journeyed through Nineveh, Resen, and Nimrod. They reached Asshur after five days of travel. Shem was particularly interested in this city because it was named after his son. He anxiously desired to find his son and restore their ailing relationship. Many Shemites populated Asshur. Shem recognized grandchildren and great grandchildren.

Guilt from their rebellion caused many to avoid him, but the youth swarmed after Shem, begging to hear about God.

Shem observed a malnourished boy searching for food scraps in garbage littering the streets.

"Where can I find Asshur, young lad?" Shem asked.

"Asshur is a powerful man, and he has no time for children. He works in a big building in the city center," the boy volunteered. "It sits next to the temple. I hope he will have time for an old man like you!"

"Thank you, son. I am concerned he may not find time for an old man if he cannot spend time with children, but the God of creation can change a man's heart. Don't you agree? Let us pray for this important man."

The three companions dismounted and gathered in a small circle, holding the young boy's hands. They prayed for Asshur and the boy—that their hearts would soften to accept God's Truth. The Lord answered the prayer before they left that spot.

"Do you realize that abundant food exists beyond the walls of Asshur?" Shem asked. "You must hunt and plant vegetables, but God provides a much bigger harvest than garbage in city streets."

"My parents forbid us to leave the city," the boy replied.

"Perhaps your family will hear about a loving God who supplies the needs of His children. Share God's Truth with them. Your faithful testimony will honor Him, my son," Shem encouraged.

"I will tell them about God, but they usually ignore me."

"You will bless God with your faithfulness, nonetheless. Perhaps your parents will permit us an evening at your home someday. Then we will share God's Truth with them. Inform them Shem and his sons request an opportunity to spend time with the family when we return."

"Will you really stay with our poor family, Mr. Shem?"

"I would consider it a privilege and honor, my son."

"When will you return, Mr. Shem?"

"I shall come when God permits. We have an important assignment in the city of Babel, and it may take several months before the work is finished. We shall return thereafter—as God leads."

The answer appeared to satisfy the boy. He ran to relay the good news to his family.

The three companions walked to the city center and identified a large three-story stone building, which sat beside a larger temple dedicated to false gods. Shem was dismayed his son lived in the heart of enemy territory. They tied the mules in front of the building and walked through the main entrance, finding a worker on the first floor. Shem spoke first.

"Can you take us to Asshur? We desire to meet with him."

"His schedule is filled with appointments this morning," the man replied.

"God has ordained my appointment. We will see Asshur at once," declared Shem, not deterred by the man's delaying tactics.

"Yes sir!" The worker looked puzzled but did not argue with this old man who commanded such authority. "Follow me to his office."

They ascended stairs to the second floor and walked past the entrances of many rooms opening onto a long hallway. Their escort finally stopped at the end of the hall and knocked on a thick wooden door. Shem allowed several seconds to pass then opened the door himself and entered the room. He found Asshur sitting alone at a large wooden desk, occupied with records of city transactions baked on clay tablets. Asshur looked up to identify the intruder. Shem noticed thinning patches of gray in Asshur's once curly black hair.

"My long lost son! Do you have several minutes in your

busy schedule to meet with an old man?" Shem spoke before Asshur could address him.

Asshur smiled and gestured his father and the others to enter the room. "I recognize my nephew, Shelah, but I do not know this other young man accompanying you. I have not had the pleasure to meet him."

"This is Seth, the son of Milcah. He was once a slave and now he is still a slave, but he has a different Master. He currently answers to God! His previous master forcibly enslaved him, but God broke the bonds of that master. Seth willingly submits to his present Master. He accompanies me on this journey. In fact, he is our guide and my great grandson!"

"I am pleased to meet another member of our distinguished family," Asshur addressed Seth, extending his hands to embrace the young man.

Asshur also embraced his father and nephew before they sat.

"And where does this journey lead you?" Asshur asked.

"Hopefully it will lead me to the key that unlocks your heart, my son."

Shem detected Asshur's discomfort after sensing the real purpose of the visit. Asshur began drumming his fingers nervously on the desk.

"I am not prepared to listen to religious foolishness, Father. I will enjoy hearing news about our family, however."

"I shall reveal this news—at your request. Nimrod and his warriors have killed many of our family. Your relatives have left this world for a higher calling. Nimrod has enslaved countless others. His warriors have abused and persecuted them, depriving them of dignity. The world is not worthy of them either."

Asshur looked at the ground, fidgeting under the uncomfortable pressure.

"I am sorry, Father. I grieve for them and their families."

"That is a lie! You fear for your flesh! You do not care

about our family or the people of this world! You should at least worry about the condition of your soul!"

"My family should strive to accomplish their potential. This is only possible in cities, where people combine skill and intellect to achieve marvelous works!" responded Asshur.

"That opinion is a deception from God's foremost enemy. You rationalize your desires to make them appear as truth. God gives absolute Truth. You have run from God your entire life. Your rationalizations have caused harm and death to thousands of people. God calls you to change your ways and let Him command your life."

"Years ago I grew weary of these erroneous fables. Even the superstitious people in this city worship gods. There is no difference—it is all nonsense! We create our world, Father," Asshur insisted, picking the lint off his robe to avoid an emotional connection with his father.

"The world you create is the world of God's enemy! Sin in your heart pushes you rapidly down the mountain in his direction. You are totally deceived! You have awesome responsibility and authority in this world. The fate of many people hangs in the balance, to be determined by a word from your mouth. Therefore, you will drink the full cup of God's judgment. God has granted you authority over men. Nimrod did not give it to you. Someday you will stand before God and answer for what you have done with the people under your command. Remember that, my son. God has numbered your days in this world. Soon He will call you before His throne!"

Shem noticed Asshur looked pale and avoided eye contact. He began wringing cold clammy hands.

"I have chosen my destiny, Father, and I am content with that decision."

Shem delayed a response, allowing those words to convict Asshur's heart. Shem's stern countenance broke as tears filled the ancient crevices in his cheeks. He understood the eternal consequence of Asshur's decision.

"Indeed, you have chosen your path. God grants you that privilege. Your path leads to eternal torment—not happiness. Your vision is nothing more than a mirage in the desert. I have spoken from my heart. Now I shall leave you to deal with this truth. You will remember these words when you stand before the God of creation—when He, alone, will determine your destiny."

Shelah and Seth hugged their uncle—tears also misting their eyes. Shem embraced his son with a heavy heart.

"I shall continue to pray for your soul, my son," Shem stated, finally establishing eye contact with Asshur for the last time.

Shem turned and exited the room with Shelah and Seth close behind. They left Asshur alone with his thoughts. He took no further appointments that day.

* * * * * * * * *

Shem refused to speak for a long period. Seth knew he was praying and grieving over the fate of his son. Seth would not interrupt the meditation of this godly man. The three walked their mules beyond the city limits then paused to pray for the souls in Asshur.

"We must proceed to Akkad, my sons," Shem instructed.

Shem now traveled in unfamiliar territory. Seth guided the group from that point, preparing them for the desert and merciless sun of Mesopotamia—'the land between the rivers.'

"I am not fond of this region," Shelah remarked. "The land is too flat, and the weather is oppressively hot. I prefer the mountains because they remind me of God's majesty."

"I agree, Shelah," Shem declared. "This sun is hard on an old man, but I am fascinated by the variation in God's creation. I am curious to see the rest of the New World.

Perhaps God will grant us an opportunity to visit more of it someday."

Seth remained silent, but hungrily consumed every word of his mentor. Maybe God would lead him to these new lands. They traveled quickly, covering twenty-five miles each day and sleeping the nights in the wilderness. They stopped to greet people along the Tigris River. Shem shared God's Truth with each of them. They were friendly but rarely requested to know God. His Light did not pierce their dark souls, because they refused to open the sin-stained door of their heart. Once again, spiritual ignorance among people of the New World saddened Seth.

"My father repeatedly proclaimed God's truth to thousands during the last century of the Old World. Day after day and year after year Noah faithfully preached God's message. Not one person who heard him accepted the Truth. They continuously joked about Noah. Members of our own family openly mocked him," Shem explained, after sharing God's Truth to a farmer.

"Why did Noah endure this humiliation for one hundred years?" Shelah asked.

"Because God asked him to proclaim His Word. Noah simply obeyed God. Obedience has no time limits, my son. Noah loved those people despite their hurtful behavior. He knew God's judgment would one-day come, and he hoped to take many on the ark."

"Why did they reject Noah's invitation?" Seth asked.

"The evil one deceived them, and each person deliberately chose to reject the protection of God's ark. People are no different today and their deception is no less. Most will choose to believe Satan's lies and enter God's judgment for eternity. They will refuse to enter the covering our Lord provides for every human soul.

"God permits each individual to choose a path," Shem declared. "Two pathways lead to eternity, and the correct path is not the most attractive. Only the crooked, narrow path leads to glorious riches in eternity with our Lord."[41]

"I am grateful we walk that narrow path," asserted Shelah. "I do not intend to deviate from it."

"You choose well, my son. Remember... God calls us to obedience as He did Noah. He commands us to share His Truth. We must not strive for praise from men who falsely credit us for enlightening others. Joy comes from obedience to God's commands. This is the faith that pleases Him."

Shem's godly wisdom amazed them, but his living witness impressed Seth most of all. Shem lived in the center of the Truth he shared, and his life reflected that godly wisdom. He was like an old tree whose deep roots drank from God's life-giving Truth. Seth imagined his own life like that, with branches bearing fruit for others.

* * * * * * * * *

They traveled five days before reaching the outskirts of Akkad. Shem knew many people, although he had never traveled in this area. He greeted grandchildren, nieces, and nephews, proclaiming God's Truth to all. As always, children seemed more interested in him.

Seth guided them through the city of Akkad. He showed them his previous home—a humble appearing stone building on the outskirts of the city. Several of Nimrod's warriors occupied the house, and garbage from their careless neglect littered the front yard. A once productive garden behind the house now grew weeds and briars. Seth's heart ached as he viewed the small home through misty eyes. He then led them to the city center, where his father had given the ultimate sacrifice for his family and the brethren.

"I miss my father," remarked Seth after describing the horrible events of that fateful day.

Seth found it difficult to dredge up those memories

without feeling intense hatred towards Nimrod.

"You have witnessed the greatest gift a man can leave his family," declared Shem. "Your father lived his faith fully, serving God to the very end. But he accomplished more in one fateful moment than he did in his entire lifetime. Living for the Lord is a very challenging task, my son. However, laying down one's life for others is far more difficult.[42] Your father achieved both these goals. God has given him a crown of glory and will someday avenge his blood. Now you must forgive the man who slayed him."

"I can never do that!" Seth countered defiantly.

"You will find strength in doing so, Seth. A man cannot grow in godliness with hatred in his heart. However, if he releases that bitterness to the Lord, he will have a powerful testimony in this world. God loves you Seth—even more than your father did. He will take this burden from your heart. Give Him an opportunity," Shem gently coaxed.

Seth felt pain and hatred well up from the depths of his soul. He turned toward Shem, yearning for guidance but struggling with conflicting emotions.

"You are right. I shall seek the Lord as you have recommended. Perhaps He will free me from this bondage and return my joy. The burden grows heavier each day, and it consumes my thoughts for long periods. I came so close to executing this murderer when he crawled on the ground like a wounded viper! I confess I do not want to relinquish these bitter thoughts. Many fingers in my mind grasp the desire for vengeance. Please pray this tightly closed fist will open to release its burden and embrace God's grace."

"That is not good enough, Seth. Wishful thinking can never remove this deep infection. Its removal requires the sharp blade of God's pure Light. Man's sinful heart prefers to feed on resentment for an entire lifetime. This burden produces greater suffering than death at the hands of an executioner. You must choose to relinquish this yoke like you chose to accept God's Truth. The choice is not easy. God's enemy will strive with all his power to convince you happiness will come only through retribution, but vengeance can never produce happiness. You will experience the joy of the Lord only when you release that yoke and let God avenge the innocent."

Seth dropped to his knees at the precise spot of his father's execution.

"Please pray for me now! I hunger for God and yearn for His deliverance!" Seth cried in anguish. "God, take this resentment from my soul!"

"Father in Heaven, forgive this young man for the bitterness in his heart. Remove this heavy burden. Give him the joy of drawing near to You—joy which comes through obedience to Your will. Grant him wisdom to accept that vengeance belongs only in Your hands."

"Thank you Lord." Seth lifted his hands to the God of creation.

Seth immediately felt a heavy load lift from his heart. He experienced a freedom and joy he had never known. Seth brushed the tears from his eyes, and the first image he beheld was a purple wildflower growing at the site of the execution.

"The Lord answered my prayer! Your counsel was true!"

Seth picked the delicate flower as a fleeting but tangible sign of God's work in his heart.

"God's counsel is always true. Remember this as you walk that narrow path." Shem smiled as he assisted Seth from his knees.

Suddenly Shem began laughing—a laughter emanating from the joy in his soul. Seth saw nothing humorous about the situation.

"Didn't you know that flower was there all the time?" Shem asked. "God had already accomplished His work. Only your eyes were blinded to it as you held so tightly to that burden. The same holds true for all of us at crucial times of life. Man's wicked mind chooses blindness over God's glory. Darkness seems more comfortable in the immediacy of life, but God's glorious light exposes the rottenness smothering the soul and replaces it with eternal joy."

"I am grateful for your receptive heart, my son. Your desire for obedience brings joy to my soul. Never allow your passion for God to fade," Shem exhorted.

Seth completed the guided tour of Akkad. He then led Shelah and Shem to the outskirts of the city—beyond the wall. Several families of believers lived there and had successfully evaded detection from Nimrod's men. They lived in four small brick homes standing in a wooded area. The houses were not in the usual path of travelers entering and leaving the city. Seth knew the families and felt they needed encouragement from their patriarch. Years had passed since Shem and Shelah had seen them, and the reunion brought joy to all. Seth imagined the trials these families had endured, but God had faithfully provided.

"How has God directed your lives in this wicked place, my brothers?" Shelah inquired, as they communed around the dinner table in the largest home.

The wives had prepared a meal of vegetables, fish, and hot baked bread. The aroma of fresh bread aroused Seth's hunger.

The spiritual leader of the families responded: "We continually seek God's Will. He has not instructed us to move, though we would prefer to do so. We have seen many brethren killed or enslaved, and we hope to avoid this fate for our families."

"Hasn't the Lord protected you?" Shem asked

"God has cared for us, but we live a fearful existence," he complained.

"The Lord often leaves a remnant of believers in the center of enemy territory. He will continue to provide for you,"

Shem encouraged. "Don't let fear persuade you to move. God will prompt you to leave if that is His desire. He will turn your fear into faith, my children."

"That is easy for you to say," replied another young man. "I intend no disrespect, but the northern lands are much safer."

"The Lord has instructed our grandfather to go to the most dangerous place in the New World," Shelah responded, giving Shem an opportunity to eat. "We are traveling to Babel to meet with Nimrod!"

"You have reason to tremble!" exclaimed the father of the third family. "This man has the heart of Satan!"

"God is greater than the ruler of this world!" Shem declared. "Wicked leaders will come and go in the history of mankind, but God will surpass all of them. Our Lord has established the birth and the precise time of death for each of these rulers. He will limit their authority when He chooses. We must not allow emotions to push us toward decisions that lessen the impact of our godly testimony. We walk by faith—not by fear. I do not advocate taking unnecessary risks, but we must remember God uses us to speak to those who do not know Him. If we hide from the world's dangers, God will raise the stones to proclaim His message. Personally, I would rather be His mouthpiece to these lost children."

"Amen, amen!" All agreed heartily.

The fellowship of these believers continued for several days. Shem encouraged them with wisdom and faith. He received needed rest and nourishment in return.

"I do not know when or if I shall return from Babel. Please pray God will use us to accomplish His work there. Petition the Lord to give us opportunities to encourage our brethren in their horrible circumstances."

The believers held hands and bowed on their knees before the Lord of creation. They lifted heartfelt petitions, and their prayers ascended to God's throne as sweet incense before Him.

"The sacrifice of our prayers pleases God more than animal sacrifices, my children," Shem remarked, as they prepared to depart.

They saddled mules and packed provisions. The hot sun rose quickly that morning as they resumed the journey into Mesopotamia. After leaving Akkad they traveled along the less turbulent Euphrates River.

"Have you noticed the scarceness of stones in this Valley, Grandfather?" Shelah asked. "I presume God won't raise stones from this area to proclaim His message!"

"You are right, my son," laughed Shem. "Nevertheless, we shall proclaim His Truth!"

"I believe He can make bricks cry out to glorify Him!" declared Seth.

"He can indeed," chuckled Shem.

* * * * * * * * * *

Their journey to Kish required two days. Shem knew this city was named after his nephew, Cush, and it was also the birthplace of Nimrod. Perhaps Shem could find his brother and visit his family. He trusted God to supply the message of Truth he would share.

Shem noticed mule-drawn carts filled with grain traveling toward the city. On the outskirts of Kish he observed archers, warriors, and chariots in military training. Boats of various sizes rode the currents of the mighty Euphrates. The massive wall and guard towers surrounding Kish dismayed Shem.

"Works of men appear impressive, but they are foolishness compared with the least accomplishments of our Creator," Shem remarked.

Warriors stationed at the gate barred their entrance to the city.

"What business do you have in our distinguished city?" demanded a guard.

"I am the uncle of your King and the brother of his father, Ham. I have come to visit them," Shem stated.

The soldiers looked puzzled.

"I did not know the King had an uncle. I will permit your passage, but if you stir up trouble, justice will come swiftly," a second guard threatened.

Shem chose not to respond to the arrogant sentry. A response might evoke calamity, and he intended to visit his family.

They passed through the gate into the impressive city. They did not notice any Shemites walking the streets of Kish. All the people in this city descended from Ham. Most had darker complexions than the Shemites. Descendants of Cush had the darkest skin of all.

Shelah hailed a tall, dark man crossing the street: "Excuse me, sir. We are seeking the house of the King. Can you assist us?"

"You desire to meet with King Bel? He does not see commoners without a thorough screening by his sentries and a prearranged appointment," the man responded, eyeing the strangers suspiciously.

"We have an appointment, sir. God, Himself has established it," Shelah stated.

The man looked confused and skeptical.

"His home sits in the city center, over there," he gestured. "The King dwells in one of the largest buildings in Kish. Only the temple of An exceeds its size. Warriors guard the entrance to his palace. You will need a good reason to meet with the King."

"Thank you, sir, and may God bless you," Shelah stated, bowing his head slightly.

The young man stared at them, more bewildered than ever.

They walked the mules to the city center and identified a large structure, dwarfed only by a nearby temple to a false deity. Shem felt disgusted as he stared at the ornate temple.

"This temple stands as an abomination to God, my sons. It portrays the foolishness of men," Shem asserted.

They tied the mules to hitching posts and walked a short distance to the entrance of the King's home. Shem considered the palace an arrogant extravagance in a city filled with needy people, but he did not voice that concern. Four muscular warriors guarding the entrance quickly diverted his attention. They were armed with spears and daggers.

The largest, most intimidating guard hailed them: "What business do you have with King Bel?"

"I am the King's uncle and these are his cousins. We have come to visit him," replied Shem.

"The King has not warned us of your arrival," the guard declared.

"We journey from a land far north of this city and were unable to send word of our visit. Nevertheless, he will welcome us," Shem insisted.

"Excuse me," said the guard. "I must confirm your visit with the King before you can enter. He just returned from a long meeting with the city leaders. I know he is weary."

The sentry left them waiting for several minutes but subsequently returned with the King.

Cush peered through the doorway cautiously... curiously.

"Uncle Shem? Is that you, or do my eyes deceive me?"

Shem smiled broadly, extending his arms to embrace his nephew.

"My... you have aged since I last saw you. May the Lord bless you and your family!"

"Your body cannot disguise the ravages of time either." Cush laughed. "Who are these young men accompanying you?"

"These are also your relatives from my family," Shem answered, as they stepped into the foyer. "The older is Shelah. He is my grandson—the son of Arphaxad, whom you might remember."

"I do remember my cousin, Arphaxad, and his brother, Asshur. Do they still live in the northern mountains?"

"Arphaxad lives in the mountains of your childhood, but Asshur has moved several hundred miles south, into a large city named after him."

"Umm... that is interesting. Who is this younger lad accompanying you?"

"This is Seth, and he is my descendant of the fifth generation. He has escorted this old man on a very long journey from the north."

"I am pleased to meet the children of my honorable uncle," declared Cush. "Please let me introduce my children, grandchildren, and several additional generations of descendants. My wife is also here, of course."

Cush introduced his family, who happened to be dining with the King that evening. Shem was impressed with their size and dark complexions. They politely extended greetings but appeared rather aloof. Shem wondered if Cush had previously biased them against followers of God.

"My servants have prepared a large meal. Join us to partake of this excellent food, Uncle Shem," Cush offered, leading the way to the dining area.

Shem and his companions gladly accepted. Shem wondered what it was like to eat in the house of a King. He was grateful the King's slaves were not his descendants.

"What brings you this long distance from the northern mountains?" Cush asked, as they sat at a table filled with an abundance of strange delights.

"May I bless your family and the food before I answer that question?" Shem asked.

Cush hesitated then replied reluctantly: "Certainly you

may ask a blessing—but to which god will you make this request?"

"To the One and only God, of course. There is no other. Surely, you know that."

"Very well... you may proceed," Cush sighed.

Shem sensed his nephew's concern but he petitioned the Lord's blessings, nevertheless. He ate several bites, figuring he might have to talk awhile. He finally responded to Cush's earlier question.

"An angel brought me a message from God. He instructed me to make this long journey to Mesopotamia. Specifically, He directed me to meet with your oldest son, Nimrod, in the new city of Babel. I have eagerly anticipated this visit with you and my brother's family."

Shem perceived Cush did not accept this explanation.

"Uncle Shem, all these years have not changed you one bit. You speak of God and His angels as if you know them personally. How can a loving God speak to you and ignore the rest of us in this world? I doubt the authenticity of these angelic visitations, and I am skeptical your friendly God even exists!"

Shem was hungry. He decided to eat more delicious food before responding. He had never seen such extraordinary delicacies. Rare tasty vegetables, fresh baked bread laced with cinnamon, and exotic fruits filled the table, in addition to the usual fish and vegetables from the area.

"I commend your servants for preparing this wonderful meal. I have never tasted such treats in all my years!" Shem exclaimed.

"That is because you have chosen to live in ignorance your entire life! I taste only bitter memories from years long past."

"I am surprised you do not enjoy this delicious food."

"Answer my question! Prove your God is superior to the Sumerian gods," Cush challenged. "I think it is all rubbish."

"Cush, I have not come this far to strive with you. Nor have I come to prove the existence of God. His destruction of the Old World and creation of the New World confirm His existence. Your father and I were eyewitnesses to those remarkable deeds. Indeed, God revealed His unfathomable love to our family in the Old World. He instructed Noah to build the ark, which provided our safe passage into this world. Does that not validate His existence? Surely your father, Ham, has informed you of these miraculous events. God has blessed you with wealth, a wonderful family, and authority in this world. This bears testimony of His love for you," Shem declared, then paused to fill his mouth with more tasty delicacies.

"The abilities of my children account for their impressive accomplishments. I have earned riches and command authority over my people by intelligence and hard work! God did not grant these to me!"

"You are terribly wrong. Pride deceives your brilliant mind. Give God a chance for your family's sake, at least," pleaded Shelah.

"I have directed my questions to your grandfather! I have not asked your opinions!" Cush reprimanded.

Shem had eaten his fill, and he felt the Lord prompting him.

"God has reached out to you, Cush, yet you harden your heart. He desires to speak with you, but you stop your ears. He stands before you in all His glory, yet you close your eyes! Eternity stares you squarely in the face. Please... soften your heart and make a home for God—for the sake of these children. You cannot know joy from these riches around you. They merely bring temporary pleasure. Only God can provide eternal joy. He has created you with a void in your heart that only He can fill. Open your ears to hear His soft but audible voice. God beckons you—enter His rest."

All present at the table noticed the beads of perspiration

appearing on Cush's forehead. Everyone knew he was angry, but he had no intelligent response. His children wondered why their father did not silence the old man. Cush had easily refuted their spiritual concerns in times past.

Cush spit the food out of his mouth.

"This is nonsense! We waste precious time speaking of intangible things. I am convinced we create our world, and I don't need superstition or silly fables to complicate my life. I am content and have no desire to change."

Shem perceived pride had totally blinded Cush to the Truth. Shem knew the futility of pressing the issue any further but felt the Lord encouraging him to establish a spiritual bond with his nephew.

"God's love is unquenchable. I have come to extend His love to you and your family. We have missed you since you departed from the northern lands many years ago. My father grieves at your absence."

"Let Noah grieve! I will rejoice if despair kills the old man. I hope never to see him again!"

Now Shem understood Cush's spiritual problem. Bitterness had consumed his soul. He hoped Seth discerned this.

"Noah has no animosity toward you. He never meant to harm any in your family. He loves you and prays daily for your success in this world."

"That is a lie! A man who prides himself in proclaiming truth now speaks with a forked tongue! Noah always preferred you and Japheth to my father. He treated our family as vermin. Noah evicted us from our homeland, invoking God's curses—but we have disproved them! We are not your slaves. In fact, our family enslaves many of your descendants! It appears these curses were false prophecies. If God exists, would He not authenticate His Word?"

Cush appeared pleased with this argument.

"I apologize, Cush." Shem knew he would not persuade

him by debate. "I never intended to harm you or your family. A loving God never commands us to enslave others."

"Then why did God make Noah prophesy our family would become your slaves?"

Shem perceived Cush had not apprehended the true meaning of the curse. Hopefully, his explanation would clarify the confusion.

"First of all, the curse did not involve the entire family of Ham. It only involved Canaan and his descendants. The curse stated Canaan's own brothers would enslave him, and it also specified his enslavement to Japheth and me.[43] Slavery does not apply to the rest of your family in the context of God's Word. Furthermore, the curse actually foretells events in the distant future. As you know, neither you nor our families enslave Canaan. This will take place beyond our lifetime. I do not know how the prophecy will be fulfilled. Nor do I know how many generations will pass before it occurs, but I am certain God's Word is true. Someday descendants of Canaan will fulfill this prophecy. God has predestined it and we cannot alter His Word. Nevertheless, God does not desire slavery for people. His righteous character cannot permit even the thought of such wickedness. These things will occur because evil dwells in the hearts of men. Slavery presently occurs for the same reason—not because God desires it. I intend to speak with Canaan about this. Japheth and I yearn for his friendship."

"I must consider this further, Uncle Shem. I admit, I did not view past events in the way you have described," Cush remarked, appearing confused.

"You were a young man at the time. Emotions influenced your interpretation of those events. God desires us to have His mind as we try to comprehend His Word."

Cush rose from his chair.

"I acknowledge this discussion has diminished my bitterness somewhat. Hopefully, we will discuss these issues further as opportunities arise. I will provide directions to the house of my brother, Canaan. He lives in Kish and my parents also reside there. I hope you can encourage them, but I cannot guarantee that result. My weary mind spins with thoughts generated by this discussion. I shall retire to my room. You are all welcome to stay here tonight. We have many rooms in this large home. You may roam the city and renew old relationships in the morning. Good night."

Shem embraced his nephew. The Lord had made some progress softening this hard heart, but complete excision of the bitter root was still necessary. Shem knew spiritual healing was only possible in a heart given completely to the Lord. The three companions prayed for Cush and his family.

Shem felt refreshed the next morning after sleeping in the house of a King. The servants had prepared breakfast, but Cush was not present to enjoy it. He had departed to meet with the city elders. Many of Cush's grandchildren, descending to the fourth and fifth generation, shared breakfast with Shem and his grandsons. They ate in the large dining room.

Shelah had enticed the children's attention with stories about the northern mountains.

Seth then spoke: "Did you know God shares the wonders of His creation with children of this world?"

They shook their heads in disbelief.

One of the children spoke timidly: "Our parents have taught that danger lurks beyond this city. Our fathers built the city to protect us from it."

"Magnificent sights lie beyond the wall surrounding this city!" Seth's eyes sparkled. "Buildings and walls do not compare with the wonders God has fashioned for us. God desires us to leave the city and enjoy His creation. He loves each of us and His protection surpasses the great wall of Kish!"

Shem noted the children sitting quietly, enthralled with

the teaching.

Seth continued: "Someday you will have an opportunity to see these wonders. When you do, remember the One and only God has created them for you!"

The children nodded their heads.

Shem and his companions finished breakfast and bade farewell to the remaining family members. Shelah invoked God's blessings upon the family, and then they departed to find the house of Canaan.

They followed Cush's directions, and late that morning they arrived at Canaan's home in a wealthy section of Kish. Shem marveled at the large sprawling house. It consisted of six apartments surrounding a central courtyard. Apparently many people lived there, yet the King's palace dwarfed its size. Shem called at the entrance.

An older woman greeted them: "Good day, my lord. Whom do you seek?"

"I seek my brother, Ham, and his son, Canaan. If you lead us to them, I will be grateful."

Shem thought the woman appeared anxious.

"I...I did not prepare to entertain the brother of Ham," she replied, looking nervously about. "I am Canaan's wife, and we have many children—as you will see. Ham and his wife, Marah, live in an apartment adjoining the house. I am certain they will warmly receive you. Canaan is meeting with the elders of Kish in the city center. He will come later for the evening meal. Please, let us share our home with you today."

She escorted them to the main apartment, overflowing with children of all ages.

"Our children are grown, with children and grandchildren of their own. The men of this house work in the city or surrounding farmlands. Their wives and I tend these children you see."

"I believe your work is harder than your husbands',"

Shem responded, while embracing several children.

"Canaan and I have eleven sons and many daughters. Our daughters have married and live elsewhere. Six of our sons live here with their families."

"I hardly know where to start with all these children."

Canaan's wife pondered Shem's statement then replied: "Perhaps you should first visit your brother and his wife. I shall accompany you to their residence."

"I appreciate your desire to serve us," declared Shem gratefully. "I am eager to reestablish a relationship with my brother and his wife, but later I intend to spend time with these wonderful children!"

Giggles and peals of laughter came from several young girls. She led them to the entrance of Ham's apartment and called for her father-in-law. Ham appeared at the doorway after a short delay. He squinted at the visitors, and then his jaw dropped.

"I have waited many years to embrace my youngest brother," Shem announced. "God has richly blessed me to see you and all these children. Can you still count them?"

"That is a difficult task, Shem," Ham chuckled. "We have much to share. Please come into my humble dwelling."

They entered a modest living room, illuminated by sunlight from windows viewing the courtyard. Ham gestured toward several wooden chairs partially covered with thick, soft animal skins. They sat, facing one another across a small wooden table. A small bedroom adjoined the room.

"I intend to record the names of your descendants during my visit," Shem stated. "Will you assist me with this daunting task? I plan to chronicle the genealogy of our family to benefit those who follow in the New World.[44] Much work remains in this project."

"I shall assist you," Ham volunteered, as he gestured his wife to bring refreshments for the guests.

Marah provided drinks and then sat with the men.

Memories of events generations before had molded the personality of this woman. Resentment had deep roots in her soul. She refused to greet these guests with open arms, and Shem felt the bitterness. He had hoped one-day to see Marah rise up and refute the name her parents had given her. He was amazed a simple name could define an entire life. Shem delayed addressing the problem, wisely deciding to redeem the time with his brother.

"I am truly grateful to see my youngest brother once again. How is your life in this hot valley?"

Ham smiled warmly then answered: "My old body has decayed over the years, like a boulder worn to sand by the mighty Euphrates. Mortality is an ever present thought—more so than in my younger years. I truly apprehend the curse of death."

"Do your fear death, my brother?" asked Shem

"In some respects I do, but in other ways I acknowledge God has granted me a rich life with the blessings of many children. I do not deserve what I have received."

"Would you alter anything from your past, given that opportunity?"

"Unfortunately, I would change many things. I deeply regret not teaching my children the ways of God. If I could alter just one thing, I would change that."

"Why is that, my brother?"

Shem wasted no time piercing to the heart of this important issue.

Ham pondered the question, taking a long drink from the cup of water Marah had provided.

"I suppose my desire to know God was not a priority in earlier years. I witnessed His remarkable works and never doubted His existence. I believed God had a plan for this New World, but I would not embrace His plan for my life. I did not believe God cared for me. In recent years I realized I had not shown interest in Him. Decades ago I envied you,

Shem. I craved the attention Father gave you and coveted God's blessings in your life. I did not consider you surpassed all of us, striving for God's attention. Now I understand your desire to seek God enabled Him to intimately commune with you. I selfishly expected fruit without watering the tree that bears it. Do you apprehend this?"

"I understand, my brother. Please continue. Your words minister to my soul."

"Because of pride and selfishness, I did not cultivate a relationship with God. Therefore, the tree bore no spiritual fruit in my life." Ham looked at the ground as he spoke. "There was no relationship to pass to my children. None of them know God, Shem."

Ham's chest heaved and tears flowed before he could continue.

"I have lost the opportunity. They have all aligned with Satan and refute God's existence."

"You are not responsible for this, my dear," Marah reassured Ham. "Your father caused it to happen. Do not carry this burden on your shoulders."

"No, Marah... I must accept responsibility. I have reaped the consequences of my behavior," Ham lamented.

"All these children continue to dwell here. Your heart is ripe to cultivate a personal relationship with God, and He will supply fruit to pass to these children. Even your older children will benefit," Shem encouraged. "Do you doubt God's ability after witnessing His works many years ago?"

"I do not doubt God's ability. He could easily accomplish that. I suppose I feel sorry for myself. My knees buckle under the heavy burden of guilt that I carry."

Shem considered the long journey to Mesopotamia was worth this one conversation with his youngest brother.

"Ham, you are presently cultivating that relationship with God. You have accomplished much by admitting the wickedness in your heart. God now has an opportunity to fertilize the tree He planted. The relationship you desired was diminished only by your refusal to acknowledge your sin. Confession is God's path to the heart of every man. I must still admit my wickedness for God to show me the way out of it. I shall make many confessions before God delivers me from this body of flesh."

Shem knew Ham's tender heart was ripe for God's loving touch.

"I have missed you, my brother," acknowledged Ham, "and I have missed the family. I yearn for God most of all. Please pray God will restore these relationships."

"He already has restored these relationships at your request, but I shall pray for you. I will also pray for your godly influence in the lives of these wonderful children."

Marah sat quietly, but Shem knew vengeful thoughts stirred her bitter mind. God's time to expose that spirit had not yet come. Shem waited patiently for His leading.

"I have not introduced these young men who accompany me. The older is Shelah, and He is my grandson. The younger is Seth who numbers among my descendants of the fifth generation. I am blessed they came from my loins. They have richly ministered to me during this long journey. Now your numerous grandchildren will minister to my spirit. I must learn their names before Canaan returns. We have much work to accomplish."

Ham and Canaan's wife introduced the children. They not only provided names and identified parents, but also explained unique characteristics about each child. It took several hours to meet all the children of Canaan's household. Shem determined to know them individually, and recorded every name for future generations. Marah sat in the background, refusing to volunteer any information. She appeared very unhappy with this unwelcome intrusion. Afterwards Shem turned to his brother.

"Tell me about your sons, and describe their relationship

to God."

"Cush is my oldest son. You have already met him and know his heart. Canaan is my youngest and favorite child. Unfortunately, he does not know God. He worships the Sumerian gods. Mizraim and Put are my middle sons, and they also seek the gods of Nimrod. All my children worship regularly in the temples of Kish. Each has many children and grandchildren. In fact, six generations of my descendants are present in this city alone! You have met very few of them during your time here."

Canaan's wife and several young women had prepared a large supper for the family and guests. Canaan arrived after a long day's work as the women served plates of delicious food to each person. Shem noticed Canaan had a medium build with straight black hair and beard. His fair skin contrasted the dark complexion of Cush, and sad brown eyes mirrored the condition of his heart. Canaan did not appear excited to see Shem. Nevertheless, he politely extended the customary greetings. Shem discerned Canaan's temperament was strikingly similar to his mother's—a smile rarely appeared on their faces.

The entire family gathered in a huge dining room and sat at a long wooden table. Children occupied the majority of seats. More than one hundred surrounded the table. Canaan stood to address the family.

"I last saw Uncle Shem when I was a child. Years have passed so quickly since that time. I am not fond of those memories. Perhaps, after many decades we shall restore our broken relationship. Let us eat this meal the women have prepared."

Shem turned towards his nephew and spoke: "Your older brother, Cush, entertained us with a lavish meal—similar to this one. He gave me an opportunity to invoke God's blessings upon his household. May I have the same privilege to bless your family?"

Canaan looked down, purposely avoiding Shem's eyes. He did not respond quickly enough for his father, who sat across the table.

"Yes, my brother, please ask the Lord's blessings for us," Ham requested.

Canaan's scornful glare towards his father did not evade Shem's observant gaze.

"Thank you, Ham. Let us bow our heads to the God of all creation." Shem bowed and sought the Lord with a pure heart. "Father in heaven, I am deeply grateful You have given me the opportunity to renew relationships with this wonderful family in my later years of life. Indeed, these children are a blessing from Your hand. I am thankful You have provided for this large family in a remarkable way. I praise You for this, and I pray the reality of Your Presence will blossom in the heart of each one here. Please bless this food you have provided... Amen."

Canaan wasted no time dealing with the spiritual threat.

"This food is not from your God, Uncle Shem. We obtained it from fields belonging to Sumerian gods. Our gods have bestowed these provisions, producing such a bounty the priests had no room for it in the storehouses!"

Marah gave Canaan a nod of encouragement.

"We have no difficulty eating the wonderful food you have prepared. We may differ in our understanding of who provided it, but it is a delicious meal nonetheless. I commend your wife and daughters for preparing it," Shem replied, wisely avoiding unnecessary conflicts.

Shem preferred to avoid issues skirting the core problem in Canaan's heart. Furthermore, he desired to minister to the children. They needed his attention during this hour. He was concerned the Lord would not grant additional time with these vulnerable souls. Shem sensed Canaan was preparing to ignite the fuel for another argument, so he preempted the attempt.

"Children, let me tell you about the vast mountains of the north. My grandsons will also share this exciting story." Shem quickly commanded the children's attention. "My home sits in the midst of high mountains. Your great, great grandfather, Ham, also lived there many years ago. The jagged mountaintops are covered with God's storehouses of snow. The snow is whiter than a cloud, and God gives it to illustrate His purity. It reflects the sun's bright light with such intensity that one's skin burns red on the coldest days. The snow is a delight to the little ones! Bundled in warm clothes and sitting on smooth boards, they fly down mountains of snow faster than your father can ride his mule!"

The children giggled at the thought, and then Shem resumed the story.

"Waters near the peaks of these high mountains are frozen harder than bricks in the wall surrounding Kish! Children walk on the frozen waters. The Tigris and Euphrates begin their long journey from these snow-covered mountains and frozen waters. Droplets of water melting from God's cold treasures grow to mighty rivers in this Valley. These great rivers are born near the spot where God landed the ark that carried our family into this New World. The huge ark was created from trees of the Old World, and it was many times larger than any boat presently navigating the Euphrates. Noah and his three sons labored to construct God's ark for one hundred years—much longer than it took to build Kish and its encompassing wall. Your great great grandfather, Ham, and I were two of Noah's children. We enjoyed building the ark because we were obedient to God's command."

Shelah continued without interruption, allowing his grandfather time to eat.

"Trees standing at the base of the mountains are taller than any building in the cities of men. Our children climb them to find a view of the world that only birds enjoy.

Children build tree houses and play in them for hours at a time. They watch frolicking animals, created by the hand of God. Small furry creatures chase one another across the branches. God has painted colorful birds that peck out musical rhythms on tree trunks. He gives them food at the bottom of holes they bore. God provides trees to build houses for many families. Carpenters use them to construct boats that traverse the mighty rivers. We bring God's treasures of gold, copper, and silver in these boats."

Seth continued the adventure story.

"Children delight watching animals on the mountains. God created them for our enjoyment. Mountain goats balance themselves on the smallest rocks over the highest cliffs. They lead their kids to safety on these frightening heights. Deer run swiftly, bounding over rough mountain terrain. The doe gives birth in a secret place, but as soon as her spotted fawns can stand on spindly legs she brings them to show our children. Even the fastest children cannot keep pace with them. Wild donkeys and horses dwell at the base of the mountains, and they are not tied with the ropes of men. God has given them hills for their pastures. They laugh at the commotion of the cities.[45] Proud eagles soar to the heights of the clouds at God's command. Rocky cliffs are their strongholds. They raise their young there and teach them to fly.[46] From atop a mountain an eagle can spot a snake in the valley and have it for a meal faster than you can swallow a bite of this delicious food."

The children were absolutely enthralled as they listened to these stories. Most could not even finish the meal. However, Shem had finished his and was ready to complete the message.

"God loves you even more than the amazing animals He has created. He desires you to explore His creation and enjoy its wonders. Did you know cities prevent us from appreciating God's creation? Has anyone ever told you the huge wall surrounding Kish separates God's children from the treasures He has reserved for them? God formed our eyes and ears to experience these pleasures. He bestows gifts freely to His children so His joy can reside in their hearts. God has granted us dominion over animals of the New World. We must follow Him to unexplored lands to exercise that dominion. God's children cannot explore His creation if a wall blocks their path! I invite you to visit me in the mountains of the northern lands! I will show you God's hidden secrets, which are superior to the inventions of men."

"Can we...can we visit Uncle Shem, Father?" asked several children. "We desire to see these treasures."

"Your uncle speaks nonsense," declared Canaan. "His imagination runs faster than currents of the Tigris River. Creations of men are far more useful than these animals he describes. The weakest Sumerian gods are mightier than the God of Shem. Now go and play in another room. We have subjects to discuss that don't pertain to children of this family."

The women hurried the children into another room. Some of the curious ones sat close enough to eavesdrop on the conversation but far enough to avoid detection.

Several minutes after dismissing the children Canaan aired his feelings.

"I do not appreciate your unwelcome influence on my children, Uncle Shem. Our philosophy of life does not agree with yours."

"I am sorry to hear that, Canaan. God did not intend for us to disagree on such basic issues. These are not just opinions we have discussed. His Word is absolute Truth, and He does not compromise with philosophies of men."

"Don't preach to me! I do not need your impotent God!" Canaan scoffed. "Sumerian gods have served me well all these years. I have not asked you to bring this foolishness back into my life."

"Surely your father has not reared you to believe these absurdities," Shem remarked, as Ham hung his head in despair.

"Father does not influence my thoughts. I know what is right, and I determine my own destiny. I am a grown man with authority over many, in addition to my family."

"Perhaps you should consider the honor of being a humble host to your uncle and his family, my son," Ham encouraged.

"I command authority in this house, Father, and I will decide how to interact with the guests."

Ham hung his head lower than before and did not speak again. Shem could not fathom Canaan's disrespect.

"I have not traveled hundreds of miles to cause divisions in this family. I came to renew our friendship and bring the love of God."

"Your God does not know love. He only knows curses and judgment. This family will have none of it!" Canaan vowed.

"Shem, your family and God have caused considerable hardship for us. We lived a humiliating existence for years because your family rejected us. Your God has never given us anything. If He exists at all, He has only created trouble. Please leave Him out of our lives. Our relationship will improve if you do," Marah interjected.

"Mother is correct, Uncle Shem," confirmed Canaan. "We have done well in this New World without your God. He only hinders our advances by the teaching of fanatics like you. Our people have created wonders in these magnificent cities in spite of your God. All you can boast about is birds and squirrels!"

"I grieve to see bitterness rooted so deeply in your heart. I cannot say a word to dislodge it but I would if it were possible. Only you can speak that word, Canaan. God will heal your heart if you sincerely ask Him. He permits you that choice. Like all humans, He designed you with the freedom to choose your fate, though He desires your commitment. If you choose to build on a foundation of bitterness, He will honor that choice. Beware... if you choose to walk that lonely path you will never know love and true joy will flee your grasp. The seed of bitterness you sow will blossom for your children in future generations. Your path will lead directly into the arms of God's foremost enemy. Eternal damnation awaits you. Choose your destiny."

"I made my choice many years ago, and your frail words will not alter it. I have set my course to steer far from the God of Noah. If that means I must align with the enemy of God, so be it! I have long considered myself God's enemy. I shall persecute those whose minds are feeble enough to follow Him. I regret if your family numbers in that category, Uncle Shem."

Marah nodded her agreement.

"Canaan, I have no desire to enslave you or any man. God's righteousness does not permit slavery," Shem stated, hoping to allay Canaan's resentment.

Canaan spit on the floor.

"You mention this because you fear the power of Nimrod and my family. Your words will never influence my thoughts or behavior!"

"I do not fear men who can only destroy my body. I fear God who can destroy both my body and soul. I shall align with Him until my path ends in this life."

"Then we have no basis for a relationship. I will not allow you to expose my family to further teaching about your God. You must leave my home in the morning."

Shem wished it could be different.

"I shall honor your request... May I commune with my brother for the remainder of this night?"

"What is that to me? Do as you wish," replied Canaan, as he hastily exited the room.

Shem knew he would never see his nephew again. He grieved at his inability to penetrate the thorny shell encasing Canaan's soul. However, he had faithfully borne witness of God's Truth and he could do no more. Canaan must decide to embrace God or face His wrath. Shem determined to address his brother's spiritual need. The women hurried the children to bed. Only Ham, Marah, Shem, Shelah and Seth remained at the table.

"Can we move to your private quarters?" asked Shem. "I would like to converse before retiring. I am anxious for my grandsons to spend time with their long lost Uncle Ham."

Shem realized Ham was not in a mood for conversation. In fact, he appeared quite depressed, but this would likely be their last time together.

"I apologize for my son's disrespect. I had hoped the reunion of our family would produce happy memories." Ham hesitated an instant. "Please accompany me to our apartment. We will talk further there."

Ham led the way with Marah, Shem and his grandsons following close behind. They sat in the front room after Ham lit several oil lamps.

Shem began: "Please do not mourn over the previous discussion, Ham. We could talk about superficial matters but it would merely produce a superficial happiness. God desires us to forge spiritual bonds, which produce true joy and friendship. The risk of achieving this is substantial, as you have seen. When God becomes the topic of sincere dialogue His enemies readily identify themselves. If they choose to embrace God, fellowship between believers is fulfilling. However, an attitude of rebellion destroys any possibility of establishing a spiritual bond with God's followers. Enmity with God produces hatred of God's children. We have witnessed this tonight. You could not have altered the outcome even though you fathered this household."

"I struggle with such guilt over the spiritual condition of

my family," Ham lamented. "I wish my children would welcome God in their hearts. I feel responsible for the condition of their souls."

"You must leave them to God. The prayers of a faithful man can accomplish much,[47] and the life of a godly grandfather can significantly impact future generations."

"Shem, why have you traveled so far to visit us? Tell me your real purpose here."

"I yearn to follow God each day of my life. I have not journeyed here because of idleness in my home country. I am not touring strange lands in my old age. The Lord has directed me here in this troubled time."

"Please elaborate for your ignorant brother," Ham requested.

"An angel of God appeared to me one night. He directed me to travel to the city of Babel and meet with Nimrod. I do not know what I shall say, but God will supply His words."

Ham contemplated this momentarily and then asked: "Do you anticipate a difficult meeting with Nimrod?"

"God has prepared me for the worst. Nimrod has openly declared war on God and His followers. Nimrod's hostility towards God is no secret."

"Describe your assessment of this New World," Ham requested.

Shem felt certain Ham knew that answer.

"This world has quickly deteriorated to the level of wickedness present in the Old World. Men's hearts are continually evil in God's eyes. Most people have chosen to trust in the wisdom of men, which is foolishness to God. They have proclaimed Nimrod as their leader, and he has assumed the authority of God in their lives. Nimrod has killed or enslaved those refusing to bow before him. His wife has commanded priests of Satan to deify her. False priests lead people to worship idols of false gods in false temples. Priests and leaders of the Empire practice divination, astrology, magic, prostitution, slavery, and murder. God holds Satan accountable for this abomination. Nimrod will stand before God as the one who led the people of this world to submit to Satan's rebellion. God will severely judge this man in proportion to the many souls he has delivered into Satan's hands. God is poised, once again, to intervene in the affairs of men. When He intervened in the Old World the result was catastrophic, as you remember."

"But God promised He would never flood the world again! His bow in the sky is a sign of the covenant He made with us!"

"You are correct, Ham, but this covenant does not tie God's hands. He can intervene in other ways. The wickedness of mankind has kindled His anger. Our Holy God will not stand for this enormous rebellion in His creation. God determined His plan for this world before He created time, and He will accomplish it!"

"What can I do to help, Shem? Do you have wise counsel for your brother in this precarious time?"

"There is nothing you can do to make my meeting with Nimrod any easier. Only God has that power. I cannot dilute God's message to him." Shem responded to Ham's second question: "I advise you to obey God and pray frequently for Nimrod and your family. We must redeem the little time we have in this world. Time is more precious than gold. An investment of faithfulness in God over time will reap a bountiful treasure in eternity."

Shem perceived the tentacles of bitterness were loosening from Ham's soul.

"Shem, my love for you is greater than a brother's love. It transcends fulfillment of my desires. I have never known such love, but you have loved me for years without desiring personal gain. On the contrary, I have returned your love with insolence and persecution."

"God has richly rewarded my small efforts to extend His

love to others. Indeed, I consider the love of my brother a priceless reward!"

Shem and Ham embraced one another as spiritual brothers. Shelah and Seth also rose to join them, but Marah refused to stand. Shem perceived her jealousy and resentment.

"Marah, I love you. You are more than a sister because our loving God has uniquely created you," Shem appealed.

Marah rebuffed him.

"I have grown tired and bored with this conversation. My bedtime has passed and I require sleep," she replied, then quickly exited the room.

Shem, Ham, and the boys continued sharing their experiences. Friendship and love increased as the hours passed. Finally, Shem gathered them together to bow before God. They held hands and prayed in unity for Ham's wife and family. They prayed for Canaan, Cush, and Nimrod. They interceded for Shem's upcoming encounter with Nimrod. God heard each of these petitions and considered them a worthy sacrifice before His throne.

* * * * * * * * *

Marah also heard the prayers, for sleep fled from her weary eyes. The prayers fueled her bitterness as she tossed and turned. She used those long hours to concoct a plan, which would bring her revenge to fruition.

* * * * * * * * *

Shem and his companions awoke mid-morning refreshed. They felt ready to depart from Kish. Ham had already awakened and was preparing breakfast. Many children were stirring in the house. Shem noted Seth and Shelah had engaged them in conversation.

"Where is Marah?" Shem asked.

"I do not know. She was gone when I awoke. Perhaps she went to the market," Ham responded.

Shem avoided further discussion of the matter. He would enjoy the remaining time with his brother. They sat at the large table in the dining room to enjoy breakfast together. Seth and Shelah taught the children about God using examples in God's animal creation.

Shem hoped this interaction would stir Ham to engage these children in discussions about God.

After the children's attention waned, Ham encouraged them to play in the courtyard. Ham, Shem, Shelah, and Seth spent their final hour making lasting memories.

Finally, the time for their departure came. They included the children in one last prayer. Shem and his grandsons had made a favorable impression. Shem hoped Ham would now mentor them to follow God. Shem and his companions left the city hours before Marah and Canaan returned.

Chapter 16

The Sabotage

Marah was determined to find Canaan that morning. She knew he would be working in the largest temple of Kish. After all, he was administrator over temple affairs. He managed the grain fields and appropriated revenue for city use and temple functions. Marah had encouraged him to skim profits for himself, reasoning their large family deserved generous support. Canaan was also the liaison between priests and city elders. He marketed the Sumerian gods and hired artisans to create idols for worship. He worked closely with priests, developing forms of worship that appealed to the common people. Marah had encouraged her son to learn from the Queen's success—that prostitution in temple worship attracted multitudes. She did not even consider the fact it sanctioned immoral behavior, and that small problem never seemed to trouble Canaan. Marah had commended Canaan for shrewdly using astrology to appeal to people's intellectual curiosity and divination to appease their superstitions. She often boasted Canaan was the first to recognize the value of these elements in popularizing the religion. He enticed thousands of worshippers and then indoctrinated them with the mystery religion.

Marah found Canaan in the temple of An—just where she had suspected. Canaan was meeting with the priests in a room next to the sanctuary. Natural light was never permitted in the temple. Oil lamps and candles illuminated the rooms. That day several oil lamps and a large candle lit the room from positions on the wooden table. Canaan and the priests sat around the table. The priests wore long black robes with small animal bones dangling from their necks. Flickering lights hit the priests, casting eerie shadows that danced across the walls.

Marah strode into the room as if invited to attend the meeting. She did not stop to announce her arrival. The priests paused the discussion to allow Marah to address her son.

"May I request an audience with you, Canaan? I have a very important issue to discuss."

She knew Canaan was not pleased with the interruption, but he excused himself and directed her to a smaller room.

"Mother, why have you disrupted this meeting?" Canaan demanded.

"I must speak with you about our guests. I was lying in bed last night, listening to your father speak for hours with Shem. Sleep escaped me due to their troubling conversation."

"Why do you bother me with this? Can't you see I am a busy man?"

"I apologize for interrupting the meeting, but the discussion I overheard revealed enlightening information—vital to our cause. You will only have a narrow window of opportunity if you choose to act."

"Don't keep me guessing, Mother. Tell me about the conversation...quickly!"

"Shem revealed his God summoned him to Babel to meet with Nimrod. He intends to leave Kish this morning to travel to the capital. Since you shortened his visit, he believes he is supposed to proceed without delay. Shem is not sure what he will say but he is certain his God will relay an important message. In fact, Shem declared his God is on the verge of destroying everything our family has worked for in this New World."

"What do you expect me to do?"

"I spent the night contemplating that question, my son. If it seems reasonable, I think you should promptly send messengers to Babel, notifying Nimrod of Shem's pending arrival. Warn him about Shem's intentions. Nimrod is a smart man, and he will prepare appropriately for the meeting. The gods will give him a plan to deal with this intruder."

Marah was proud of the plan she had concocted.

"I will heed this counsel, Mother. Nimrod would appreciate more warning than we had before Shem showed up on our doorstep. The dark lord will advise him how to handle the problem. Perhaps Nimrod will eliminate Shem from our world, once and for all. What a pity that would be. I would welcome the praises of men and rewards from the gods. Shem's execution would devastate the worshippers of his God. His following would surely crumble."

"The family of Ham would dominate the world forever!" Marah exclaimed.

She kissed her son then left him alone with his thoughts.

* * * * * * * * *

Canaan promptly decided the next course of action. He summoned messengers from the city. The priests' slaves quickly brought them to the temple to meet Canaan.

"I command you to leave at once with this message for Nimrod—King of the Empire," instructed Canaan. "Tell him Shem currently journeys with several companions to Babel. He plans to relay a message from his God. Shem intends to harm the King, so travel as quickly as your mules will ride. Request an audience with Nimrod immediately, regardless of your arrival time in Babel. If his guards postpone the meeting, explain this message from his Uncle Canaan is vitally important."

The messengers saddled mules and left the city without delay. Canaan hoped Nimrod would receive the message with ample time to plan the elimination of this menace.

"Revenge on Shem and his God will satisfy my soul," muttered Canaan.

* * * * * * * * *

Meanwhile, Shem and his grandsons slowly traveled south with their five mules. They did not hurry to the wicked city of Babel. Each day Shem instructed Shelah and Seth from his treasures of godly wisdom.

Shem had enjoyed the fellowship of his grandsons during the long trip. They had ministered to him and spiritual bonds had strengthened. He knew the journey was rapidly approaching an end. He really didn't mind the sweltering heat and desert terrain, realizing it was only a minute particle of sand in the scope of eternity. Shem intended to make good use of the remaining time.

"We have learned a lot about God and His creation, my sons. Please share what you have discovered during our time together."

The request was difficult to answer for both Seth and Shelah. They had received many nuggets of wisdom from their patriarch. Which of these were gems of eternal value? They traveled for several minutes before Shelah responded.

"God has spoken to my heart countless times. Perhaps the most valuable lesson I have learned is that a man can significantly impact humanity during his short lifespan. He may touch people for God, leading them towards eternal glory, or he may push them towards God's enemy for eternal judgment. I hope to influence people to draw near to God."

"Your revelation deeply touches me, Shelah," Shem remarked, then turned to Seth. "I yearn to discover what God has revealed to you. Please share it with me."

Seth looked at the ancient mentor then glanced at his mule before speaking.

"Grandfather, I have learned I behave like this stubborn mule. My wicked heart holds tightly to sin. My soul dwells in sin's darkness much of the time. Without even realizing my condition, a vengeful heart consumed my soul. I have seen that same sin devour the lives of Cush, Canaan, Marah, and even Ham. I would never have identified their problem had I not relinquished my sin to God."

Shem lifted his hands toward heaven and praised God.

"Thank you, Father, for revealing these precious stones of wisdom."

"Only God could have revealed this to you, my sons. Let me share an event that occurred many generations ago, which will highlight the wisdom God has revealed. It ultimately determined the destiny of the Old World. Several thousand years ago the mother of mankind gave birth to her first son, Cain. God soon blessed her with a second son, Abel, who desired to seek the Lord with a sincere heart. Cain's jealousy burned towards his younger brother, and one day Cain slew him. God judged that wicked act of murder by banishing Cain from the family's presence to wander the wilderness of the Old World. Cain could hardly bear the punishment. His bitter mind nursed vengeful thoughts for an entire lifetime. Satan sowed seeds of rebellion into that fertile soil."

Seth interrupted, "Cush and Canaan also considered themselves banished from their homeland and wandered the deserts of Mesopotamia, harboring feelings of bitterness until now."

"The similarity is obvious, my son. The root of bitterness in Cain's heart blossomed to fill the Old World with an abundance of wicked fruit. He spent his life rebelling against God and imparted that vengeful spirit to his children. The life of this one man influenced the destiny of the Old World. The achievements of his descendants brought the praises of mankind. They invented music, agriculture, and metallurgy, but they also developed cities where evil deeds flourished. Polygamy, prostitution, murder, and idol worship filled the Old World. The rebellion of Cain's descendants kindled God's anger and eventually provoked His judgment—the worldwide flood. Satan uses bitterness to accomplish his purpose, but God uses repentance and holiness to achieve a work of eternal merit. You have witnessed both during our journey."

They traveled south through the hot desert towards Babel. The Euphrates River flanked them on the west. Shem noticed considerable boat traffic. He enjoyed traveling in lush green lands near the river. He marveled at the amount of acreage converted to productive farmlands. Sumerians had constructed many irrigation canals to feed the parched land.

It took three days to travel to the outskirts of Babel. Several miles outside the city they identified the Tower of Babel, even though it was only partially constructed. Shem thought the tower looked as evil as Seth had earlier described it.

Shortly thereafter, Shem noticed a large company of soldiers approaching them from the direction of Babel. The troops marched with purpose. As Shem and his companions neared the city they noticed the warriors divide into three equal parts. One part detoured left and another deviated right. The third group approached them directly from the front. Shem surmised the troops likely had hostile intent.

"Have you noticed the troop movements, Grandfather?" Seth asked. "I believe they have discovered us. They are not on a mission of peace. I have previously observed soldiers as they prepare for battle. I feel certain they have targeted us!"

"Our God has many more warriors, Seth. His angels will

protect us. I have an appointment to keep, and God also intends to appear. A handful of Nimrod's men will not thwart God's plan!"

It did not take long for the troops to complete the operation. They completely surrounded their prey within five minutes. Shem identified Nimrod leading the procession on a large black mule. He was fully armed with a spear, sword, and several sharp daggers. He wore the divinely fashioned garment under his armor. Nimrod stopped several feet in front of Shem and ordered the troops to halt.

* * * * * * * * *

Shem initiated the conversation: "Does it take an army of warriors to capture three defenseless men and their mules?"

Nimrod scowled at Shem and his companions. He thought he recognized the youngest of these men but could not recall where he had seen him.

"You have arrived at Babel—capital of the Empire that extends to the perimeter of the New World. I am the King and ultimate authority in this Empire. You have come without requesting my permission," Nimrod accused.

"I did not realize your permission is necessary to travel in this world. God previously commanded us to roam freely without restrictions and have dominion over the New World."

"I have dominion over the Empire and control those who come and go from this city. Neither you nor your God have any authority in this Empire. I do not welcome enemies in the capital city!"

"I have not come to fight, Nimrod, nor have I traveled this far to argue these preposterous accusations! God has directed me here to give you His prophetic word. I have journeyed to Babel solely for that reason."

"I will hear this message from your worthless God.

Now speak...before I render you and your companions speechless!"

"Nimrod, your thoughts and actions are hostile to God, your Creator!"

Nimrod interrupted at will: "You have spoken the truth, Shem. I have never considered your God a friend!"

Shem opened his mouth and God spoke:

> 'Come now, let us reason together,' says the Lord. 'Though your sins are like scarlet, they can be white as snow; though they are red as crimson, they can be like wool. If you are willing and obedient, you will eat the best from the land; but if you resist and rebel, you will be devoured by the sword.'[48]

Nimrod spat on the ground.

"I have not sinned as you say. The dark lord has honored my works as obedience, and he has already given me the best of the land!"

God continued, using Shem to deliver His message:

> I am the Lord; that is My Name! I will not give My glory to another or My praise to idols. See, the former things have taken place, and new things I declare; before they spring into being I announce them to you![49]

Nimrod rudely interrupted once again: "I share my glory with the dark lord! Our idols proclaim his authority. Lesser gods are also powerful. The least we can do is make idols of them. When we worship idols, we worship our gods!"

Shem's tongue continued to proclaim God's Word:

> Before Me no god was formed, nor will there be

one after Me. I, even I, am the Lord, and apart from me there is no savior. I have revealed and saved and proclaimed—I, and not some foreign god among you. You are My witnesses,' declares the Lord, 'that I am God. Yes, and from ancient days I am He. No one can deliver out of My hand. When I act, who can reverse it?[50]

Nimrod's men stood in awe of this old man who would dare challenge the authority of their leader.

God was not finished.

In the pride of your heart you say, 'I am a god; I sit on the throne of a god in the heart of the seas.' But you are a man and not a god, though you think you are as wise as a god.[51]

Nimrod clutched his head between his hands as Shem persisted:

All men are like grass, and all their glory is like the flowers of the field. The grass withers and the flowers fall, because the breath of the Lord blows on them. Surely the people are grass. The grass withers and the flowers fall, but the Word of our God stands forever.[52]

"Enough of this nonsense!" Nimrod shouted. "My head pounds with each foolish word."

He had come prepared to slay this man as an example for the entire world, but he had not anticipated this recurring headache. Furthermore, dizziness overwhelmed him, and he did not wish to appear foolish before the warriors.

"Apprehend this man who sows rebellion in my Empire! Let Shem and his lackeys labor with their brethren, making bricks for the great Tower. We shall see if this old man can endure the demands of hard work. Those who resist me will build the tower to my god! Now take him away! I will hear no more of his endless prattle!"

Nimrod's warriors bound the hands of Shelah to the neck of Shem. They bound Seth behind Shelah in similar fashion. Nimrod confiscated their mules and belongings.

"Make them walk before me into the city! Citizens of Babel will see who controls this Empire, and they will apprehend whose god rules the world!"

The troops goaded Shem, Shelah and Seth forward.

"Bring five strong warriors to walk on either side of me as we proceed into the city," Nimrod ordered, fearing his dizziness might cause him to topple from the mule.

The warriors prodded Shem and his companions for several miles through city streets, displaying them before the residents of Babel. Warriors mocked Shem and shouted insults against his God. The parade finally ended at the unfinished tower. Nimrod intended to make Shem bow before the Tower of Babel—the symbol of his dark lord. However, he felt miserable. Despite riding the mule, he was in much worse condition than Shem. Nimrod could not even focus on the huge tower as everything spun wildly before him. The "mighty hunter" fell from the mule while his men watched helplessly. Nimrod lay prostrate in the dirt before the Tower of Babel. His stomach expelled its contents in paroxysms of retching.

"Take these fools to the slave quarters! Their presence brings this sickness upon me. Have the commanders prepare them for hard labor!" Nimrod instructed between waves of nausea.

Six of Nimrod's strongest men lifted him from the ground and carried him to his residence, where he remained desperately sick until nightfall.

* * * * * * * * *

Warriors took Shem and his grandsons to the slave quarters but did not permit them to enter the building. They ordered them to stand in the sweltering heat for the remainder of the afternoon—tightly bound to one another. Seth was concerned Shem's frail body would buckle under the searing heat, but God's strength was sufficient to see him through the ordeal. Commanders finally removed their bonds after sunset, when the slaves were gathered from assigned work locations. Soldiers threw Shem and his partners through the entrance of a large building, where several hundred slaves were housed. Shem was exhausted and dehydrated, but still alive.

"Our father has endured a fiery ordeal today, and he will need water and some nourishment to survive," Shelah addressed the slaves.

"Please, do not allow him to succumb to the wicked plans of God's enemy," pleaded Seth.

Many slaves sacrificed their allotment of water that night to save the life of their patriarch.

Thousands of slaves were forced to construct Babel at the expense of their health and dignity. They had grown accustomed to daily arrivals of men, women, and children, who were added to the swelling population. However, this eventful day changed their lives forever. Most had heard of Shem, and many had known him personally. At least half the slaves had descended from him. Shem was the patriarch of a very large family. Many Shemitic parents had told their children stories about the faithful exploits of this courageous man. Only several individuals living in the New World had floated upon God's floodwaters of judgment generations before. Shem was one of those distinguished few, and he was also considered a godly man of faith—second only to Noah. That evening, many of the slaves found themselves living with this famous man of God.

Chapter 17

Slavery for the Patriarch

Word spread quickly that Nimrod had captured and enslaved Shem. Conflicting feelings of joy and fear tore at the slaves. They rejoiced because this prominent man of faith dwelled with them and encouraged them to face trials and persecution. Yet the slaves feared Nimrod more than ever. They realized Shem might die in slavery or be executed by Nimrod, and this would surely deliver a mortal blow to the dwindling population of believers in the New World.

Shem, Shelah, and Seth labored daily with the slaves. Nimrod's commanders did not treat them any different. They were given small food rations and assigned strenuous work. Seth was reassigned the job of transporting clay from ditches. His previous commander recognized him as the boy who escaped by swimming the Euphrates River. The commander did not even inquire about his mother and brother. He probably assumed they perished trying to escape, Seth thought. The taskmaster punished Seth by doubling his workload, and he watched him more closely than before to prevent another escape. Seth knew Nimrod would require the commander's life if he allowed another mishap, but Seth was not interested in escaping. He was totally consumed with keeping Shem alive. Seth believed God had assigned him to protect the patriarch. He felt he had disappointed God by not considering the risk of capture before they approached the city. Nimrod had easily apprehended Shem without even a complaint from Seth. Now, Seth's overwhelming passion was to care for Shem and make sure he was not harmed.

* * * * * * * * *

Taskmasters ordered Shem and Shelah to carry bricks to masons erecting the Tower of Babel. Their job was difficult and dangerous. The tower now reached a height of over two hundred feet. Climbing the high tower was difficult for a man Shem's age. There were days when slaves were pushed from the tower for not working as fast as their commanders desired. Shelah labored continuously at his grandfather's side, assisting him whenever possible. Commanders and warriors enjoyed seeing Shem toil with the other slaves. They felt this was another sign their mighty hero was consolidating control over people of the New World. They boasted about the powerful King who had humbled the famous Shem. This surely proved their gods were more powerful than Shem's God.

However, taskmasters found it difficult to mistreat Shem. This old man never complained of his workload, even though he could not labor at the pace of younger men.

Shem used every opportunity to encourage his brethren.

"You do not have to believe in Sumerian gods to perform an honorable day's work," he often exhorted.

Shem fearlessly proclaimed God's Truth. In fact, his living testimony exposed many of Nimrod's warriors to God. Shem impressed them because he wore humility as a badge of honor. Nimrod could not break his spirit or cause him to despair. Indeed, it amazed the Sumerians this frail old man commanded greater respect than the powerful Nimrod. Slaves and Sumerians alike were mysteriously drawn to this godly old man. Shem realized the mantle of leadership came by serving others.

＊ ＊ ＊ ＊ ＊ ＊ ＊ ＊ ＊

The horrors of slavery exacted a heavy toll from the Shemites. Families were torn apart as children witnessed the torture and execution of their parents, and parents lost their children from disease and starvation. Some Shemites had endured several years of slavery in Babel. Unending misery and persecution drove many to despair. Initially their faith was strong but hopelessness ultimately prevailed. God brought Shem and his companions to Babel at the opportune time.

Night after night they met with the slaves, encouraging them and ministering to their souls. The believers' faith increased even as their numbers declined.

One night Shem encouraged those faltering in the faith. He was acutely aware of the hopelessness overwhelming many slaves. Shem had shared in their tribulation and felt compassion for them.

"Wicked men can persecute us even as they mock our faith. They can kill our bodies and take our loved ones, but no man—not even Satan—can steal our Hope. Our blessed Hope is certain because God has promised it. A godly man once said, 'Our faith rests on the Hope of eternal life, which God, who does not lie, promised before the beginning of time.'[53] Our father, Noah, was given the Hope of God's promise. He labored for one hundred years building an ark during an age when rain did not exist on the earth—the Old World's inhabitants had never even imagined such a thing! During those long years people repeatedly mocked him. He shared God's Truth with thousands, but no one received it. Nevertheless, Noah's faith was anchored in the Hope of God's promise. That promise was sure because God's Word is always true.

For one-hundred grueling years Noah remained faithful even though he could not grasp the promise."

"At least we have the support of many more believers," one man remarked, "and we have only worked for a few years in these wretched conditions."

"That is correct. Noah's enduring faith finally apprehended the Hope of God's promise. We live today as a result of this man's faith. Unfortunately, some will die before their Hope is attained, but Hope is no less real. Nothing can cancel it—not even death. Those who die will acquire their promise in eternity. We will all realize the Hope of eternal life with our Lord. Erase all doubt from your minds. God's promise is an anchor of certainty in this present time of tribulation. Our Hope is secure and no one can ever steal it from us."[54]

"How long must we endure these deplorable conditions?" one woman asked. "Our children have lost their childhood."

Shem believed God would soon intervene, but the timing and nature of His intervention was still unclear. Shem did not feel led to share this with the brethren.

"I am certain God will take care of us. We may miss the benefits of a peaceful life in this world, but the blessings of living by faith in God far surpass any worldly benefits. Take comfort in this truth."

Chapter 18

A Child is Born

Semiramis met repeatedly with the priests to plan attractive worship services for the masses. She influenced the artisans as they created sculpture and artwork for the Tower of Babel. She delighted in the progress she had made. Priests and artisans desired to please her. She felt her most important achievement was an agreement with the priests to incorporate mother/son adulation in the worship services. Semiramis, first and foremost, desired commemoration by future generations of mankind. The birth of her child was imminent and she eagerly awaited it.

Late one-night labor pains suddenly seized the Queen in the midst of a restless sleep. She awakened everyone in the house by her shrill cries. Servants and midwives rushed to assist her. Nimrod remained in the house through the labor but did not hamper the work of the midwives. He stayed in his room, praying for assistance from the dark lord. He remembered the story of his mother's death, and he feared for his wife.

This was the Queen's first pregnancy, and she had not anticipated the severe pain generated by each contraction. Several midwives attended her throughout the labor.

"Let us give the Queen beer to lessen her pain," one mid-wife offered. "We have nothing else to allay her discomfort and anxiety. I have seen it work many times with young women laboring with a first child."

The midwives agreed to follow this suggestion, encouraging the Queen to imbibe liberally between each contraction. The Queen's bizarre behavior entertained them until she delivered a male infant twelve hours later. Unfortunately, the infant also received a substantial dose of alcohol while awaiting delivery from his mother's contracting womb.

"He is floppy and blue!" exclaimed one midwife.

"He doesn't cry like a newborn. He behaves like his inebriated mother!" another mocked.

No one laughed.

"He isn't breathing. We must stimulate him—his death may cost us our lives!" insisted a third terrified midwife.

The midwives felt the infant would not survive but they repeatedly pinched and slapped him. They dressed him warmly, holding him close while stimulating him. These adjustments helped him endure the critical hours after birth. Finally, effects of the alcohol abated and the infant's condition dramatically improved. Midwives returned him to his mother six hours later. The Queen rejoiced upon receiving a newborn son, despite her weariness.

"I shall name him, Tammuz," she declared.

Semiramis convalesced for several weeks until she strengthened enough to govern the Empire. She then summoned the artisans.

"I have recovered sufficiently to pose with my son for several portraits. I will choose the best for display in the Tower of Babel."

Word traveled throughout the Empire that Semiramis had delivered a male child. Citizens rejoiced and many sent gifts to the Queen's newborn son. The infant was actually quite healthy following the dangerous hours after birth. He nursed well, gaining weight and noticeably growing in the first month of life. Tammuz was a normal-sized infant, lacking the ebony skin of his father. No one dared mention these obvious facts. The King and Queen decided to dedicate their son at his one-month birthday. The Monarchs assigned the priests to perform the dedication before the entire population of Babel.

"Allow the people a day from their labor. Invite them to witness the dedication and participate in the celebration that follows," Nimrod instructed the city leaders. "Give the slaves a day of rest because the taskmasters will be free from duty that day. Make attendance to this magnificent event mandatory for all citizens of Babel."

"Restrict the slaves to their quarters, but invite a select few to the dedication of my son," Nimrod ordered the commanders. "Allow Shem, Shelah, and Seth to attend the event. Work productivity has significantly improved, and no slaves have escaped since Shem's arrival."

Nimrod decided this was because the slaves finally accepted their destiny in the Empire, but he also realized Shem's presence likely contributed to the improvement.

"Reward the slaves who have performed an exemplary service to this city by permitting them to attend, as well."

* * * * * * * * *

The appointed day arrived. Tammuz was the first child born to the first Monarchs of the Empire.

Nimrod's warriors assembled the citizens in the City Square to witness the gala. More than forty thousand attended this momentous affair. Several elite warriors guarded the few slaves that attended. These warriors were high in the military ranks, and therefore received special seating close to the platform. They positioned the slaves nearby and the highest ranked commander forewarned them:

"You will behave or face the blade of the executioner."

The dedication began early in the afternoon. Carpenters had erected a large wooden platform before the Tower of Babel. They constructed a roof over it to protect the infant from the intense afternoon sun. The Monarchs sat on thrones in the center of the platform and Semiramis held Tammuz in her lap. A delicate golden circlet crowned her head, symbolizing her conception by a golden sunbeam from the king of gods. Nimrod wore his usual crown of bullhorns, symbolic of his authority in the Empire.

The high priest of Babel began the infant's dedication with a cultic religious ceremony, commemorating the conception of the Queen. He performed a loathsome act with a young virgin, selected from the adolescents of Babel. The priest carried out the spectacle before thousands gathered to view the dedication. Multitudes cheered wildly during the sordid event. Shem thought this contemptible affair demonstrated the depravity of mankind. He considered it an abomination before God and bowed his head to pray for the people and the innocent young girl. The other slaves prayed with him.

Other priests waved large bowls of burning incense. One priest sacrificed a pig on the altar. He removed the liver and examined it in the sunlight, declaring it free of defects, and then he forecasted good omens for the Empire.

Diviners invoked the gods' blessings for the infant and citizens of the Empire. Priests prayed the Tower of Babel would soon become the house of gods. All this occurred simultaneous with the despicable act performed by the high priest.

Shem and the other slaves did not raise their heads until the blasphemous service was over. Memories of similar perversions in the Old World flooded into Shem's consciousness. He imagined how these perversions must grieve a holy God. Shem knew God's judgment would soon come to this wicked world.

* * * * * * * * *

Nimrod was expecting Shem's presence at the dedication. It did not take him long to locate Shem and the other slaves. Nimrod was impressed they had choice seating so close to the platform. He smiled while observing those stubborn Shemites. Their obvious discomfort delighted him. They either sat in their chairs with heads bowed or stood with their eyes riveted to the ground. Nimrod hoped someday even Shem would bow before the dark lord. Then they would enjoy real worship! Nimrod would take pleasure in executing Shem if he refused to embrace the mystery religion of Babylon. He would personally make an example of the old man before his followers.

* * * * * * * * *

When the priests finished the religious ceremony Nimrod rose to address the people. All the people stood and politely applauded the King. The crowd was scattered on three sides of the platform. The gigantic Tower of Babel occupied the remaining side.

Nimrod's booming voice projected to the masses gathered in the City Square.

"Citizens of Babel and the unified Empire... I am honored by your presence at the dedication of our infant. The Queen and I greet you on this wonderful day the gods have made. Seated around this platform are priests, astrologers, artisans, and diviners. These men commune with the gods to determine their desires for this great city. Each performs special duties during construction of the Tower of Babel. They are the elite in their professions and will continue their religious functions after the tower is built. I have assigned them to make the mystery religion of Babylon uniform throughout the Empire. They currently train many in their skills and will one day send them to cities throughout the Empire to unify our religion."

Cheers and applause erupted from the crowd.

"This Empire is strong because you—its citizens—are committed to the vision of a one world government. Consequently, the Empire grows daily in area and population. The Empire will continue to grow until it encompasses everyone in the New World. The Queen and I desire to make your lives happy and secure. Babel is 'the Jewel of the Empire,' and you make it sparkle before the gods!"

He continued: "The gods have given us this day to dedicate our infant son, who will someday inherit the throne. The dark lord will never leave this throne empty in future generations!"

Applause erupted spontaneously. Nimrod permitted the noise to abate before continuing.

"And now... I present Queen Semiramis, and her son, Tammuz."

People jumped to their feet cheering wildly as the Queen rose from the throne. She initially supported Tammuz on her right hip, and then she lifted him high to face the people.

Multitudes chanted in rhythm, "T-A-M-M-U-Z...T-A-M-M-U-Z." The noise increased ten decibels and continued several minutes.

"Surely this deafening chant stirs the gods," Nimrod murmured silently.

He eventually raised his hands for silence. When the clamor finally abated, Semiramis stepped to the podium and addressed the crowd.

"Honorable citizens of this invincible city... I am proud to stand before you with my son at my side. Indeed, the gods have blessed me. The dark lord brought my son and me into this New World for a designated purpose. He granted us the privilege of serving the citizens of this wondrous Empire, and I am committed to successfully accomplish that duty!"

Semiramis had previously determined to disclose the secret she and her husband shared. She would reveal the origin of the infant (not the real origin, of course). Semiramis intended the people of future generations to worship her. She felt certain this divine mystery would bring that desire to fruition.

"My people, I stand before you to proclaim good news about my infant, Tammuz. He is special and unique among all infants of the world."

The crowd became extremely quiet, trying to hear every word.

"I am the mother of Tammuz, but the King is not his father."

She paused momentarily, allowing this revelation to impact the minds of the people. Moans and gasps escaped from the crowd.

"The dark lord fathered Tammuz. He visited me while the King was busy conquering the northern lands. The infant was conceived that very night. My lord chose me as his humble handmaid and blessed me with the seed that fathered this child. Tammuz is not only heir to the throne, but he has also inherited divinity from the dark lord!"

Semiramis held the infant high once again, but no applause followed that statement. Several gasps were audible, but an eerie stillness pervaded the astonished crowd. They never imagined such a thing could occur. Many now apprehended the significance of the preceding service.

* * * * * * * * *

Shem had heard enough of this foolishness. He felt the Lord prompting him to respond to this blasphemy.

"That is a lie from the dark lord, who is none other than Satan—enemy of the One True God. There is no other god! Satan cannot create life. He only creates lies. He is the author of lies! A god did not father this infant. There is no other god! Your Queen's adulterous affair produced

Tammuz—another man fathered him. Do not believe her lie! Tammuz is a normal child—not a god to be worshipped. Only Satan and the Queen would concoct this preposterous tale!"

More gasps, moans, and some laughter escaped from the crowd. Did this revelation come from Shem—the man of God who Nimrod enslaved? Is he not the man whose reputation is built upon sharing Truth?

* * * * * * * * * *

Semiramis was speechless. Nimrod rose from his throne, prepared to execute Shem on the spot. He reached to draw his sword but could not pull it from the sheath. He had no words for the moment and slumped back onto the throne, dismayed at this sudden turn of events.

The high priest stepped forward and pointed his right index finger at Shem.

"This man blasphemes the dark lord! He makes a mockery of our Queen, deceiving men and opposing the gods. Shem is the foremost enemy of this Empire! His own words condemn him, and he deserves to die!"

Nimrod's men grabbed Shem and tied his hands behind him. They quickly pushed him through the crowd, along with the other slaves. The warriors hurried Shem to a small building, where he would be held in solitary confinement until the King determined his fate. They returned the remaining slaves to their quarters. Commanders doubled the guards at each slave residence. Nimrod assigned six of his fiercest warriors to guard the building where Shem was imprisoned.

The dedication continued but the crowd's enthusiasm had dampened considerably. Many left before the ceremony ended. The Monarchs felt unable to address the people. Priests completed the formalities, and then the celebration began. Beer and food were provided in abundance to all participants. Debauchery of all sorts ruled the city that night.

Nimrod could not find a moment's rest for his weary soul. He did not speak with the Queen or share her room. Nimrod was furious with Shem for humiliating his wife before the citizens of Babel. He was outraged the dedication of Tammuz had become a mockery of the Monarchs. Nimrod would not tolerate the blasphemy of this man and determined to eliminate him. Thoughts churned in his mind that night, depriving him of sleep for endless hours. As much as Nimrod hated his great uncle, he knew of Shem's sterling reputation. No one had ever accused him of lying. Surely he would not compromise the testimony of his God—especially before such a large crowd. Nimrod decided he would have another discussion with the dark lord before facing his wife. He would then rehash these suspicions with Semiramis if the dark lord permitted.

Chapter 19

Judgment in the New World

"I worry about the condition of Shem, Shelah, and Seth," Milcah told Eber one day. "They left nearly six months ago and still have not returned."

"We are all concerned," stated Eber. "Rumors have circulated that Nimrod's warriors have captured them. I have not shared this with you until now because I knew the news would consume your thoughts."

"Eber, I fear for their welfare because I personally experienced slavery in that wicked city. Nimrod would jump at an opportunity to execute Shem and the others, as well."

"Some of our brethren traveling from the south have informed me Shem was imprisoned. Others have conveyed word Shem, Shelah, and Seth are working as slaves. All the messengers agree that Shem still lives but his condition is unknown."

"We must pray ceaselessly for God's protection, Eber. Terrible forces of evil reign in that city."

"I have been praying day and night that God will encompass them with an army of angels," Eber replied.

Jared and his mother lived with Eber's family. Earth-shaking events also occurred in Eber's home shortly thereafter.

Leah's labor suddenly began in earnest. Milcah sensed God's protective hand throughout the labor and delivery. Leah safely delivered two infant boys after laboring ten hours, and all present praised God for His new gifts to the family.

"The name of our first born son is Peleg, according to God's command. We shall call the other son, Joktan," declared Eber.

"I eagerly await God's intervention in the affairs of mankind. I am weary of this wicked world and I yearn to see His glorious City," Milcah remarked.

Nimrod's army encroached further into rural areas of the northern lands. They encountered peaceful resistance from families of believers. Most refused to resettle in the cities. Warriors severely persecuted them for resisting the policies of the Empire, and Asshur did not restrict this treatment. Many Shemites died and thousands were enslaved, but none took up arms. Asshur did not support his family despite their faithful stand. His relatives grieved and prayed daily for him, but Asshur chose his destiny. The true believers feared that Asshur's wide path would one day open into the fires of God's eternal judgment.

Tentacles of the evil Empire had nearly reached all people of the New World.

* * * * * * * * *

Shem remained in solitary confinement, restricted from contact with any slaves. Six warriors patrolled the prison continuously, and two additional guards stayed inside, watching his every move. This did not disturb Shem. He adjusted to life behind prison walls, continually looking to God for guidance. Two guards curiously observed Shem, marveling that he never complained despite his circumstances. One day they questioned him about the source of his strength.

"My flesh is weak but God's strength sustains me. I confess I do not comprehend the workings of our amazing Lord," Shem explained. "God embodies pure holiness and infinite love. Sin that commonly besets mankind cannot possibly taint Him. I cannot imagine how an awesome, holy God can tolerate the wickedness that fills this world. Yet He does so because of His incredible love. These traits are perfectly balanced in His character."

"Tell us more about God's love," requested one of the guards.

"His love is greater than human language can describe. God waited so long to destroy the Old World because of His unfathomable love. He endured utter wickedness and human depravity for several millennia. Of all people living in the last century of the Old World, only Noah sought God and lived righteously. We emulated Noah's godly example. Our father's faith in the presence of incredible persecution motivated Ham, Japheth, and me. The trials I face do not compare with my father's suffering in the Old World. God can easily destroy this entire world with a single word, yet His heart melts at the simple faith of a wicked man—like an ant moving a mountain. I have difficulty comprehending these things but they have significantly stirred my soul. Your great, great grandfather, Ham, has also witnessed God's tender love and His awesome wrath. Ham grieves when his children align with false gods. My brother and the angels in heaven rejoice when one of his descendants submit to the True God. Perhaps you will meet the God of creation today."

Shem felt God's Spirit working in the hearts of these young men.

"I am prepared to meet Him this very moment!" exclaimed the taller guard.

"My tender heart is also ripe for His healing touch," the smaller guard acknowledged as large tears of conviction rolled down his dark angular face.

"Then we shall meet the God of heaven and earth on our knees."

He dropped to a kneeling position with the very guards charged to prevent his escape. They were among the first of Ham's descendants to know God.

"Visit your great, great grandfather when you complete your work in this city. Joy will overflow his heart when he hears of your new commitment."

"I do not feel right about keeping you in this wicked place. We will assist you to leave this city, my lord," the smaller guard offered.

"I am your brother," Shem corrected. "There is only one Lord, and we must obey His will. I appreciate your concern but God desires me to stay here for now. If He chooses, He can provide a way for me to leave. I will not endanger your lives by escaping this prison. I am content to sit patiently, waiting on God to direct my life. Perhaps He will bring other men with tender hearts, desiring to know Him. I shall be grateful if He does."

These two men continued to guard Shem in shifts, rotating with other warriors from Babel. Shem instructed them about God during those times. Their work became joyous fellowship, which they enjoyed more than life's other pleasures. Shem ministered to many of Nimrod's men. Most rejected a personal relationship with God, but this faithful old man profoundly affected their lives.

Shem's life in prison became a constant prayer to the Lord. He did not bring self-centered supplications before God's throne. He prayed for the welfare of slaves and the salvation of their guards. He petitioned God for people of the New World, relentlessly exposed to evil from high places. Shem beseeched the Lord for the safety of Leah and her twins. He begged God to destroy fortresses of wickedness, spiritual authorities, and powers of darkness in the New World. He even prayed for Nimrod and Semiramis—that their hearts would soften and minds open to God's Truth. The Creator of heaven and earth heard Shem's prayers and answered each of them according to His perfect will.

* * * * * * * * *

Nimrod prayed to his lord the night following the dedication. A lone candle illuminated the room.

"I need your guidance, my lord. Reassure me about Tammuz. Have you fathered him or does he belong to another man?"

Silence reigned for several minutes, and then the candlelight flickered and bent to one side as if blown by a steady, soft breeze. Once again, that eerie voice filled the room.

"Do you doubt my previous answer, Nimrod?"

"I do not doubt you, my lord, but Shem does not lie."

"Do you believe the supreme god, or would you prefer to trust in words of a mere man—one who has even admitted being my enemy?"

"You are my lord and I have placed my trust in you."

"Then you know my answer to that question. Now, what other concerns do you bring before me?"

Nimrod had only one other question. He hesitated, fearing the answer he might receive.

"What must I do with Shem? He has caused many problems for the Queen and me, and he continues to oppose the Empire."

"Shem resists your goals for this world and he defies me also. He is a man of faith, but his faith offends me. You will not alter his allegiance. He hinders the progress of the Empire by his teaching, as you have personally witnessed. Therefore, you will execute Shem as an example for his followers. They must understand no one can rebel against the authority of Nimrod and his lord."

"I shall carry out your command."

Nimrod had serious reservations about this assignment. Shem was his grandfather's brother and father's uncle. Nimrod knew many in his family would oppose the execution of this world-famous man. He must eliminate Shem without announcing his intentions beforehand. Nimrod felt uneasy. Something had always restrained him from harming Shem, and that dreadful sickness invariably occurred. Surely this frail old man wouldn't pose a problem for the mighty Nimrod. The dark lord would grant the power to fulfill this duty of darkness. As an extra precaution he determined to wear the fleece 'anointed' with 'Divine power' from Adam's God.

* * * * * * * * * *

The following morning all citizens of Babel returned to work. Commanders manned their posts and slaves busily hauled clay and bricks. People united with zeal to finish the magnificent tower. Then they would construct Babel—and what a splendid city it would be! Yesterday's dedication had unified them in this one purpose. The Monarchs and their new infant had pleased the gods. After all, the dark lord had fathered Tammuz. Surely the infant's existence demonstrated the dark lord's confidence in people of this important city. They boasted of their citizenship in the Empire. The gods were satisfied with Sumerian accomplishments. Soon they would shower rich rewards, enabling even more extraordinary achievements.

Workers neared completion of the tower, which almost reached the clouds. Sixty- thousand workers had incorporated millions of bricks into this enormous edifice. They had erected six layers of the tower, and only the seventh and final layer remained unfinished. Nimrod and the architects had designed this top layer to contain the thrones of the most important gods. Artisans would portray remarkable works there. Priests eagerly waited to practice secret cultic rituals of the mystery religion in the pinnacle of the tower. Everyone desired to finish the work, but no one was more anxious than Nimrod.

* * * * * * * * *

The day was unlike any other in the history of mankind. Slaves, brick masons, and their commanders were hard at work shortly after sunrise. Nimrod and Semiramis stood nearby, watching the priests invoke the gods' blessings at the commencement of work on the pinnacle of the great tower. Priests had bound animals and several children next to the altar for sacrificial use in the ceremony.

A large black cloud gathered directly over the Tower of Babel before the ceremony began. Without warning, a huge bolt of lightning divided the cloud and descended on the unfinished tower. A terrifying rumble in the heavens followed. The earth shook violently for less than a minute. Thousands of bricks fell from the highest parts of the tower, and large cracks appeared in the uppermost layers. Nimrod and Semiramis witnessed the events. In fact, the shaking earth knocked them to their knees. Damage to the tower dismayed them because they knew its completion would be significantly delayed.

The black cloud vanished along with the terrifying lightning and thunder. The earth instantly stopped seizing. Nimrod was amazed at the suddenness of it all, and now a blue sky framed the tower. He realized work could continue for many more hours that day.

"Repair the damage promptly so we can press on to complete this project!"

Bewildered commanders only stared at him. Nimrod was furious, and his booming voice bellowed ten decibels louder.

"I command you to begin work immediately, or you will

face the terrible consequences of my wrath!"

Many commanders responded simultaneously, but Nimrod could not understand them. Strange sounds spewed from their lips. Grunts, guttural sounds, high pitched babble—none of it made any sense. How could this be?

Nimrod and Semiramis watched the commanders trying to communicate with one another. They could not understand each other at all! Several appeared to give orders to masons, who stood with puzzled expressions, unable to comprehend their superiors. One mason threw bricks from the tower instead of laying them. Another appeared to request bricks, but the slave handed him a pot filled with mortar. Slaves could not grasp instructions to transport clay to the brick makers. Workers could not even agree how to fire-up the large ovens. All communication in the city came to a screeching halt.

Chaos reigned in Babel as all semblance of order was instantly destroyed. Fights erupted due to the communication problems. Looting, vandalism, and other criminal activity ravaged the city in the absence of effective police authority.

* * * * * * * * * *

Pandemonium reigned in the Empire. Business and commerce abruptly halted in every city. Farming, trading, shipping, and building ceased immediately. Attendance in the temples declined to a trickle of worshippers. People could not understand the priests, so religious services offered no benefits.

The well-organized city of Kish now appeared in disarray. People no longer enjoyed the convenience and security of city life. Vandalism quickly destroyed the most powerful city of the Empire. Elders could not counsel the King, and Canaan could not advise the priests. Canaan could not even understand Cush, and neither could understand their brothers, Mizraim and Put. In fact, all members of Ham's large family were unable to communicate with one another.

Families of Japheth and Shem struggled with similar problems in the northern lands. The tongue divided families everywhere—even the believers of Shem's family. However, believers discerned the reason for the many languages. God had dramatically fulfilled His prophecy by intervening in the affairs of men. Once again, God had meted out His judgment to mankind. Shem's descendants now understood Eber's angelic visitation. The birth of Peleg heralded God's division of the world's people by many languages.

At least seventy new languages suddenly appeared in the New World. Those who spoke a common language congregated together. These groups began to move from their home cities within several months.

Anguish and frustration hounded Cush daily because of his inability to govern the city of Kish. He realized it would be simpler to move from Kish and start his life over again. He gathered those few individuals speaking his language and moved south to the continent of Africa. He founded a large country there and named it after himself.

The brothers of Cush also moved from Kish. Mizriam and Put moved to Africa and started two additional nations.[55]

Canaan, the youngest of Ham's sons, felt compelled to move from Kish. He and most of his children moved far west of Mesopotamia to the land of Palestine.[56] He named it Canaan—after himself, of course. Ham had directed Canaan to move elsewhere, but Canaan rarely heeded the advice of his father. Ham warned Canaan his descendants would later regret this impetuous decision. More languages divided the large family of Canaan than any of Ham's other sons.

Sons of Japheth moved far north and west of the Mesopotamian Valley, settling many new countries[57]—each with a different language.

Two of Shem's five sons stayed in the general region of Mesopotamia after God's judgment. Asshur stayed in the area north of Akkad and founded the mighty Assyrian Empire.

Arphaxad, Shem's godliest son, settled north of the Persian Gulf.[58] Shem had predicted God's prophesied Seed would come through the lineage of Arphaxad, Shelah, Eber, and Peleg.

Chapter 20

The Final Showdown

Chaos reigned more in Babel than any city of the New World. Sixty thousand laborers building the Tower of Babel suddenly found themselves unemployed. Planning and construction on all city projects ceased immediately. The inability to communicate became everyone's overriding concern.

Nimrod desperately tried to regain control of the populace but his attempts were futile. Commanders, warriors, priests, farmers, businessmen, and common laborers quickly left the city in small groups to settle elsewhere. Nimrod retained a remnant of people speaking his language and amassed a small army from that group. The number of people remaining in Babel was woefully inadequate to resume building the city and its enormous tower. Nimrod knew he must repopulate the city to finish these projects. Some groups did not move far from Babel, intending to start independent communities near their original home. However, Nimrod would not permit these settlements. He pursued the settlers, attempting to coerce them to return to Babel. He persecuted and killed those who refused to cooperate. Nimrod busily hunted people for his city, but the expeditions usually ended in failure. These pursuits added little to the dwindling population. Many fled to distant lands, fearing his wrath. Some families even lived in caves for years until lands became safer to settle. Nomadic families arose who feared staying in one spot. Nimrod considered all of them disobedient renegades and traitors to the Empire.

Babel quickly became a shadow of its former self. The small number of people remaining could not sustain the city with vital agriculture and commerce. Religious worship ceased because the majority of priests fled the city.

Nimrod became a frustrated tyrant as the Empire slipped rapidly from his control. Every city he had previously conquered refused to recognize his authority. The population of each city dramatically decreased. Languages of the remaining city leaders differed from Nimrod's. He hunted and terrorized residents of these cities, trying to coerce them into submission—but he only chased the wind.

* * * * * * * * * *

Most Shemitic slaves escaped their captors during the confusion following God's judgment. They fled north and then dispersed with their clans to distant lands. However, Nimrod did not let Shem escape. He even increased the number of guards surrounding the small prison. Shelah and Seth chose to stay with Shem despite the likelihood of execution. God graciously allowed them to retain their original language, but no one remaining in Babel could communicate with them—including Nimrod. The King had other concerns occupying his time, and Shem's punishment did not rank high on the priority list.

Shem and his companions were imprisoned for six long months while Nimrod tried unsuccessfully to repopulate Babel. Shem continued to mentor his grandchildren each day of the confinement.

"Do you think Leah has safely delivered twins, Grandfather?" Shelah asked one morning while they languished in prison.

"Leah has delivered two sons and I am certain they are healthy."

"How do you know that?" inquired Seth.

"I know because God's judgment has come, and He has divided the world with languages. The population of Babel has dwindled to a handful of people. Those remaining cannot communicate with us. Even our brethren have escaped the city. God has shown mercy, my sons."

"Did you anticipate His judgment would be more severe?" asked Seth.

"I expected Him to eliminate all people from the earth."

Shem pondered why he answered the question in that manner.

"You must understand I lived through another of God's terrible worldwide judgments. I will never forget those horrible memories. God destroyed mankind as well as animals and plants living in the Old World. He only allowed my father and our immediate family to escape, because we entered the covering of His ark by faith. God's judgment eliminated the appalling wickedness of the Old World—Satan being the only exception. God's present judgment did not eliminate him either, unfortunately. Satan's punishment will occur at a later time, as I have taught. Evil quickly returned in the New World because of Satan's deception. Satan used Nimrod to propagate his wickedness."

Shem paused a moment to collect his thoughts.

"The second worldwide intervention of God—the languages—was just as calamitous as the flood. However, this time our merciful God chose to preserve mankind, despite the presence of rampant sin in the world. God protected His Seed and our remnant of believers through this gracious intervention. Languages are His gift to us. They are like the ark, which transported our family through the deadly flood-waters enveloping the world. God used both as vehicles for deliverance."

"How has God purged wickedness through this act?" asked Shelah.

Shem appreciated these wise questions. He knew someday Shelah and Seth would apprehend God's greater plan for mankind.

"God has not eliminated wickedness, my son. He has only frustrated Satan's plan for a season. Man will now obey God's command to spread over the face of the earth. Indeed, Nimrod unwittingly accomplishes God's command by pursuing people to faraway lands. Nimrod and the dark lord will not achieve their Empire, but Satan will continue striving for it. He lusts for the dominion of God's throne. Complete control of the human race is a stepping-stone towards this goal. He will step on that stone until the Lord removes him altogether."

"When will that occur, Grandfather," asked Seth.

"It will occur when God's prophesied Seed delivers the mortal wound to Satan. Until that time Satan will sow his evil seeds in this world. The promise of God's Seed has been recorded in the Holy Scriptures. His Seed has passed through the generations from Adam to Noah. Transmission will continue through future generations of believers in the New World until the Hope of His coming is finally realized."

* * * * * * * * *

Anger and depression became Nimrod's constant companions. He rarely conversed with the Queen, but one day they communed over breakfast. Semiramis had resorted to cooking because all her servants had fled the city. Nimrod knew she was unhappy because she detested the menial chores of a housewife. He appreciated her sacrifice for him.

"I cannot understand how the Empire completely unraveled in several weeks. I nearly controlled the entire world, yet it slipped so easily from my grasp. The mighty one-world government became impotent in one day! How has this happened?" Nimrod asked incredulously.

"Perhaps your dark lord does not wield the authority you thought he did," Semiramis answered sarcastically. "I would rather manage my tavern than sit in the dust of this empty city."

"The power of the tongue has rendered the magnificent Empire meaningless to people of the New World. My dominion is less than ever before."

"You certainly have not hunted many citizens for this city. In fact, I believe you have lost your hunting skills altogether," she accused.

Nimrod detected more scorn in those green eyes than in her words. He had no appetite to respond, however.

* * * * * * * * *

Nimrod's headaches and dizziness recurred with increasing frequency. His head throbbed intensely one night as he contemplated the dissolution of the Empire. He reclined on the bed, gazing at plain brick walls. Suddenly a thick oppressive blackness obliterated everything in view. Was the darkness associated with the headache, or was it caused by a spiritual phenomenon? A familiar throaty voice answered the question, pressing in from all sides and pinning him to the bed.

"Nimrod, why have you avoided your lord these many months? Have you rejected guidance from your source of strength?"

Nimrod felt the dark lord's anger.

"I have failed to accomplish your vision for the Empire. I could not finish the Tower of Babel—your dwelling on this earth. The workers had begun the pinnacle of the tower, and your throne room was just weeks from completion. However, an earthquake and a lightning strike damaged the fifth and sixth layers, eliminating any hope of finishing the project according to plan. The World Empire was within my grasp, but it slipped through my fingers like water poured into my hand."

"You have failed me, Nimrod... However, my foremost enemy in the spirit realm caused this catastrophe. He is the only One who threatens my authority in this world. Someday I shall defeat Him and render Him impotent. Then He will never intervene in my affairs again. You have not finished the work, my son. We shall build this Empire once again."

"What do you desire of me now, my lord?"

"You have bungled your previous instructions! I ordered you to eliminate Shem months ago, but you disobeyed!"

"I lost control of the Empire with the confusion of languages. Citizens of Babel rapidly moved away. Since that terrible event I have spent all my waking hours trying to regain control of this city. Prison walls have silenced Shem. He has not bothered me, and I have not had time to deal with him. I have not forgotten your instructions, and I intend to eliminate him when time permits."

"When my command reaches your ears, I expect you to give it the highest priority! Too much time has already passed since I issued that order. I will not tolerate further delay!"

"How can the execution of an old man exceed the importance of rebuilding your Empire?"

"Do you question my judgment?" demanded the dark lord.

"I do not question your wisdom, but I cannot comprehend it. I thought you would prefer to salvage what remains of the Empire. I considered it a higher priority to get a crew of workers back on the tower."

"Indeed, these are important works, but my command exceeds their importance! You have yet to learn your work proceeds more efficiently when you obey my orders. Shem is our chief enemy in this world because he petitions his God to sabotage my plans. Shem's powerful prayers greatly influence his God. Shem's elimination would strengthen my hand in the world. My archenemy has predicted His Seed will someday destroy me. That Seed has come from the Old World through the lineage of Noah and Shem. If we destroy the lineage of God's Seed, then He can never defeat me again. Do you understand the significance of this?"

Nimrod pondered the explanation.

"Yes, my lord. The logic clearly supports your order. I shall execute this enemy in the morning without further delay. A defeat of Shem and his God will substantially advance our control over this world."

"I shall richly bless your work, my son. You will have greater authority in this world than ever before—as long as obedience is your chief priority."

Absolute darkness lifted from the room, and Nimrod's headache improved. He began to plan his next course of action, preparing to eliminate Shem in the morning. A restless sleep finally overcame him.

* * * * * * * * *

Morning arrived quickly but Nimrod slept well beyond sunrise. He dressed in the special garment made by God and wore armor on top of the extraordinary fleece. He then summoned the remaining warriors.

"I shall return Shem and his cronies to the dust of the earth by noon today!"

The warriors armed themselves maximally, and then they all proceeded to the small brick prison housing the enemies of the Empire. Six warriors guarded the entrance to the prison.

"I command you to bring Shem and his associates at once!"

"Yes sir!" several guards replied simultaneously.

The guards entered the building to find the prisoners.

Shem and his grandsons often slept late each morning. No windows existed to break the monotony of brick walls. Oil lamps provided the only light illuminating the interior of the prison. Guards extinguished them at night, and it remained quite dark until late morning when they lit the lamps once again. It took the guards several minutes to waken the prisoners and bring them before Nimrod—bound in chains.

"Shem appears as old and frail as any man in the New World. I shall accomplish this work without difficulty," Nimrod muttered quietly.

"Well Shem...many months have passed since our last encounter. I remember that event as if it occurred yesterday. In fact, the memory is ever-present in my mind. Your sharp tongue achieved its intended purpose—to insult the Queen and me. I come to receive your apology."

Nimrod knew Shem would not apologize for his statements. Furthermore, he felt certain Shem would not even understand him because of the language barrier. But to Nimrod's amazement, Shem understood perfectly.

"I will never apologize for speaking the truth, because a man of truth honors God." Shem replied with clearly understandable words that strangely did not appear to match his lip movements.

"If you refuse to apologize, I must proceed to the next order of business," Nimrod threatened. "You have strongly resisted the Empire since its inception. You have vocally opposed the magnificent tower I dedicated to the gods. You have even assailed my marriage, trying to drive a wedge between the Queen and me."

"Once again, I maintain I have always spoken the truth God has provided."

Shem did not appear intimidated in the least. He continued his response.

"If you have interpreted Truth as obstruction, then it is as you say. However, if the Truth opposes you, deception and lies have clearly won your heart. I would suggest a change of direction would better serve you and your Empire!"

"How dare you criticize the direction I choose to take this Empire! For such insolence my lord requires your life this very day, and I shall gladly give it to him!"

Shelah and Seth stood nearby, fearfully watching the scene unfold. They were also miraculously able to comprehend the entire conversation.

"I do not have the privilege to judge your works, Nimrod, but God will burn them all to ashes in the fire of His wrath!"

"This frail old man seems to be growing stronger," thought Nimrod.

Suddenly Nimrod saw thousands of bright streaking lights surrounding Shem. "That wretched headache is returning again," muttered Nimrod, with dismay.

Shem suddenly received a word from the Lord and did not hesitate to proclaim it.

"The Lord God says to Nimrod,

> **'I am the Lord**; that is My name!
> I will not give My glory to another or My praise to idols!'[59]
> 'My servants will sing out of the joy of their hearts, but you will cry out from anguish of heart and wail in brokenness of spirit. You will leave your name to my chosen ones as a curse.' 'My Sovereign Lord will put you to death.'[60]

We shall no longer be slaves to Nimrod – the rebel who set his plans against God!"

"I have heard more words from your twisted mouth than I care to hear. The time has come for me to silence you!" Nimrod roared in anger, grabbing a dagger in his left hand and a sword in his right hand.

He advanced towards the enemy, looking at Shem one last time to identify target points for dagger and sword thrusts. The streaking lights Nimrod had seen now clearly became a thousand warriors with white robes and brilliant swords flashing with fire. Nimrod's men also saw these fearsome warriors and immediately fell to their knees. Seth and Shelah lifted their hands to glorify the God of creation.

Nimrod clutched his spinning head and fell instantly to the ground. The severe throbbing earthquake in his head caused extreme pain—worse than ever before. He could see nothing but brilliant flashing lights spinning wildly before him.

"Your warriors cannot harm me!" Nimrod declared defiantly between waves of nausea. "I wear the 'anointed' fleece your God made for Adam. I am invincible!"

"You certainly don't look invincible, lying there in a puddle of vomit. The garment you wear is merely an animal skin to God. It has no special powers as you claim and is no idol for worship. Your sin-stained heart glares as a crimson sunset beneath that fleece. The eyes of God have focused only on that sinful heart. God is prepared to execute His Holy Justice!"

How the oppressor has come to an end! How his fury has ended! The Lord has broken the rod of the wicked, the scepter of the rulers which in anger struck down peoples with unceasing blows, and in fury subdued nations with relentless aggression.[61]

But you are brought down to the grave, to the depths of the pit. Those who see you stare at you, they ponder your fate: 'Is this the man who shook the earth and made kingdoms tremble, the man who made the world a desert, and overthrew its cities and would not let his captives go home?'[62] The grave below is all astir to meet you at your coming; it rouses the spirits of the departed to greet you—all those who were leaders in the world; it makes them rise from their thrones... They will all respond and they will say to you, 'You have become weak, as we are; you have become like us. All your pomp has been brought down to the grave, along with the noise of your harps; maggots are spread out beneath you and worms cover you.'[63]

Shem completed the message God had given him but added a few last comments.

"You are but a small frail man to the One True God. Your bravado is mere chirping of birds to Him. Pride has been your weakness, Nimrod. Rebellion against the One and only God has become your downfall. Your allegiance with the enemy of God has also made you the enemy of God. For all these things God requires your soul this very moment!"

Nimrod rolled on the ground in intense pain—beyond imagination. He could see the bright fire of God's judgment behind closed eyelids. He moaned and cried in agony. Suddenly Nimrod's writhing stopped and his breaths became shallow and labored. After several minutes the respirations also ceased, but the pain and agony continued as his soul entered the fire of God's eternal judgment.

* * * * * * * * * *

"Remove these chains from my hands and feet! God has freed us from the bondage of this wicked man," Shem ordered.

The guards complied immediately, and they also removed the bonds of Shelah and Seth. Thereafter, they bowed before Shem.

"I am only a man like you. Rise to your feet! You must bow only before God. Now observe what I am going to do."

Shem dropped down beside Nimrod's corpse. He removed the armor, and then peeled off the garment that God had intended only for Adam. He handed it to Shelah.

"Remember Shelah, this fleece has no power in itself. God did not create it for us to worship. He fashioned it because of his love and mercy—to cover the sin of Adam. It has served its purpose in this world and must be destroyed. We shall soon dispose of it when we leave this wicked city."

Shem hoped those words had penetrated the hearts of everyone there that morning.

"The God of creation has prompted me to do something that will seem strange to all witnessing this event."

Shem took Nimrod's sword, raised it high, and then let it fall quickly upon Nimrod's neck, severing the head in one swift blow. He removed the dagger from Nimrod's left hand and deftly severed hands and feet from the extremities. He then cut the arms and legs from the trunk. Finally, he divided the trunk into three pieces with Nimrod's sword.

"This carcass is nothing more than a piece of meat. It no longer houses the wicked soul that once inhabited it. The magnitude of this man's offense and the scope of his rebellion do not permit an honorable burial in the eyes of God. Come before me at once!" Shem commanded Nimrod's warriors, who had observed the entire grotesque scene.

The warriors instantly obeyed, terrified of this man whose God had made such short work of their commander. Even though they spoke another language, they clearly understood Shem just as they previously apprehended his words.

Shem separated twelve warriors from the group and addressed them: "I command you to carry these portions of Nimrod's carcass to different regions of his fallen Empire. Some of you will carry this flesh to cities of the northern lands. Others will carry it to cities in the south and east. Your duty before the Holy God is to transport this carcass to all parts of Nimrod's wicked Empire.[64] God will pour out His wrath on the disobedient, just as He did with Nimrod. Do you understand?"

The warriors vigorously nodded their heads.

"Proclaim this message to all people as you deliver the carcass. 'Mighty Nimrod has fallen. The Holy God of Shem has conquered him. The soul of this wicked man will never rest from the fire of God's eternal judgment. Nimrod is an example to all who rebel against God. The One True God— the God of Noah and Shem—will have no other gods before Him. Indeed, there are no other gods! God has demonstrated He can and will intervene in the affairs of men. He is a Holy God and expects the allegiance of every man!'"

Shem handed a portion of Nimrod's carcass to each of the twelve warriors. He then divided the warriors into twelve equal groups. Shem charged each group to escort one of the twelve warriors assigned to carry a piece of Nimrod's flesh.

"Lay down your weapons before me at once! God does not need the weapons of men to do His work. Go in humility before God. Ask His forgiveness for the sins you have committed. You have murdered many innocent people and have actively participated in this terrible rebellion against the God of creation. God is Holy. Pray He might have mercy upon your souls!"

The warriors promptly threw down swords, daggers, and spears at Shem's feet, as he issued his last orders.

"Our Lord requires the obedience of His children. Now

go and do this good work He demands of you!"

The men left immediately, without hesitation.

Shem then turned to the prison guards: "Throw your weapons onto this pile before me!"

They promptly complied. Shem pulled one guard from the group and addressed him before the others.

"Our Lord detests weapons of warfare. They are repugnant in His sight! I command you to take these weapons and melt them down. Make plows and other farm implements with them. Do you understand?"

The prison guard nodded. Then Shem spoke to the entire group of guards.

"I charge you to help your partner in this important task. God considers this one deed more important than all the works you have done up to this day. Now go without delay and demonstrate your obedience to the One True God. Know that His eyes go everywhere and they see all you do. They see the thoughts in your mind—even before you think them."

The group of six men left quickly, each carrying a full load of weapons. Shem observed the fear of God in the eyes of each man. Not a sound came from their lips as they left to accomplish the assignment.

Shem, Shelah, and Seth stood alone watching the men depart. Seth prayed aloud that God would personally deal with each man's heart.

Shelah petitioned God: "Father in heaven, please allow the events of this fateful day be a testimony of Your awesome power. Enable the inhabitants of this world to clearly comprehend Your purpose for every living soul."

"I suppose we are free from this prison of men," Shem declared, as he turned to his companions and smiled lovingly. "Let's go home. We have fulfilled our duties here."

The three men embraced one another and praised God for the powerful work He had performed.

They joyously left the prison and walked through the city of Babel. They passed through the wicked city one last time before departing to the northern lands. Empty homes lined the streets, and no children played in the deserted city. Large building projects remained unfinished—beginning to deteriorate. The most obvious of these was the great Tower of Babel, which stood as a monumental eyesore on the horizon. Shem thankfully noticed no workers on the tower and no slaves trudging up steps with armloads of bricks. Priests were conspicuously absent. This once magnificent tower seemed trivial compared with the works of an awesome God, Shem thought. Bricks had fallen from the walls, and large portions of the fifth and sixth layers seemed precariously close to toppling. Several prominent cracks extended through the top layers, and the pinnacle of the great tower remained notably absent

"The throne of the dark lord is only a fantasy in minds of evil men," Shem declared.

The three walked past the unfinished tower, noticing the partially completed palace across the City Square. The magnificent palace of the Monarchs actually seemed unimpressive, Shem mused. He knew it would also remain unfinished. Soldiers stood guard in front of it. Warriors who had witnessed the sudden demise of their King had already spread the news. All remaining in the city knew how easily Shem's God had defeated this terrifying man. Palace guards did not impede the movements of Shem and his companions. They gave him a wide berth to travel the streets of Babel. Shem noticed the Queen emerging from the front entrance, carrying Tammuz on her hip. He also observed she immediately recognized him, and he literally felt her vengeful spirit.

The Queen walked right up to Shem and demanded: "How do you walk freely on the streets of this city?"

Shem smiled at Semiramis and responded: "The One

and only God has freed us from the prison of men! I credit Him for this miraculous deed!"

The Queen looked directly into Shem's eyes—her green eyes burning with hatred.

"You are still a prisoner of the Empire! I order you back to prison!"

"Apprehend Shem and these worthless men at once!" she commanded the warriors. "They are not worthy to walk the streets of our city!"

These guards feared the fury of Semiramis, but the wrath of Shem's God terrified them even more. No one moved to obey the Queen. Not one of them would dare lay a hand on Shem or his companions.

The furious Queen screamed at the guards, "Do you not know I can have you executed for such disobedience!"

The sentries winced but did not budge from their frozen stance.

"Your guards stand like stone statues," Shem remarked.

Shem looked at the Queen and smiled once again before addressing her.

"I am not here to bring harm to you or your son. We both know the truth about this child. His father is merely a man. You have paraded this lie about his paternity to the people of this city, foolishly assuming you can deceive God. He knows your heart even better than you do, Semiramis. We cannot hide our sins from Him, however small and insignificant they might seem."

Semiramis glared at him, and Shem detected the rage boiling in her soul.

"I should cut you down myself! My son would enjoy seeing your head mounted on the spear of my husband!"

"You may do with me as you wish, my lady. Your husband had similar intentions. Now the pieces of his carcass are traveling all over the crumbling Empire. God could not ignore the stench of his numerous sins. That putrid flesh is now being carried to men and women of this world. The stench will reveal his wickedness to the people of your Empire. I carry no weapons of men, as you can see. I do not battle in the flesh, but I wage war in the power of God's Spirit. God reigns in His creation, and His purpose will not be thwarted. Threats of men and women are mere foolishness to Him. You are like a tiny mouse strutting up to a giant cat in the wilderness, threatening to wrest the territory from his control. Will the cat not make a quick meal of that mouse, who cannot see beyond his own arrogance? I say, my lady, you are like that tiny mouse before our omnipotent God. Will you dare stand before His judgment?"

This frail old man would not undo Semiramis.

"You may walk from this city, but someday I will hunt you and your descendants even as my husband once did!"

Shem received a word from the Lord, and felt compelled to share it:

> Go down, sit in the dust, Virgin daughter of Babylon; sit on the ground without a throne, Daughter of the Babylonians. No more will you be called tender or delicate. Take millstones and grind flower; take off your veil. Lift up your skirts, bare your legs, and wade through the streams.
> Your nakedness will be exposed and your shame uncovered.
> I will take vengeance; I will spare no one.[65]
> Sit in silence, go into darkness, Daughter of the Babylonians; no more will you be called Queen of kingdoms.[66]
> You said, "I will continue forever—the eternal Queen!"
> But you did not consider these things or reflect on what might happen. Now then, listen, you wanton creature, lounging in your security and saying to

yourself, "I am, and there is none besides me.
I will never be a widow or suffer the loss of children."
Both of these will overtake you in a moment, on a single day: loss of children and widowhood. They will come upon you in full measure, in spite of your many sorceries and all your potent spells.
You have trusted in your wickedness and have said, "No one sees me."
Your wisdom and knowledge mislead you when you say to yourself, "I am, and there is none besides me."
Disaster will come upon you, and you will not know how to conjure it away. A calamity will fall upon you that you cannot ward off with a ransom; a catastrophe you cannot foresee will suddenly come upon you... All the counsel you have received has only worn you out! Let your astrologers come forward, those stargazers who make predictions month by month, let them save you from what is coming upon you. Surely they are like stubble; the fire will burn them up. They cannot even save themselves from the power of the flame. Here are no coals to warm anyone; here is no fire to sit by. That is all they can do for you— these you have labored with and trafficked with since childhood.
Each of them goes on in his error; there is not one that can save you.[67]

"God's word to you, my lady," Shem smiled politely.

Shem knew Semiramis had closed her ears to God's Word.

"We shall see whose god prevails! At this moment my son and I are happy to see you walk out of our lives!"

The Queen turned and ascended the steps to the palace entrance. Tammuz wailed in her arms... but suddenly the infant became silent—his crying and breathing instantly ceased. Semiramis noticed the peculiar stillness of the child, so she looked down into his blue face. She gasped in horror as the revelation of his sudden death struck her with full force. Semiramis turned one last time to face Shem. Those brilliant green eyes no longer burned with anger. Now they revealed the pain of a mother's greatest loss. The Queen could find no words for the moment. She clutched the dead infant and ran quickly into the palace.

Shem turned to the palace guards, addressing them with a clear voice, "I hope you have a good and godly day. For what value is a good day if one does not recognize the God of creation as the Author of all blessings?"

Shem smiled at the palace guards. He knew they would remember that smile for years to come. Then Shem, Shelah, and Seth walked slowly from the city of Babel. They had a long journey before them and would not wear themselves out prematurely. The Lord would lead them home in His time. God had other human hearts to touch with His Truth before He would permit Shem and his companions to return to the northern lands.

* * * * * * * * *

The few warriors left in Babel closely watched the departure of these three men who had made a lasting impression on all remaining in that city. Shem carried the fleece, which still radiated its golden color in the morning sun. However, the warriors were even more impressed with the white robes worn by Shem and his companions. These robes were so brilliant in the morning sun that human eyes could not linger on them for more than several seconds.... and then the glory disappeared from their lives...forever.

Endnotes

1 Isaiah 14:12-14; "The Bible"
2 Isaiah 44:14-20; "The Bible"
3 Genesis 4:20-22; "The Bible"
4 Genesis 6:7; "The Bible"
5 Genesis 6:1-4; "The Bible"
6 2 Peter 2:4; "The Bible"
7 Epic of Gilgamesh; This documents that the Sumerians were the first known people to learn the art of distillery and brewing beer. http://www.eat-online.net/english/habits/beer_in_ancient_times.htm
8 www.home.cfl.rr.com/crossland/AncientCivilizations/Middle_East_ Civilizat.../sumerians.htm; pg 4
9 Alexander Hislop; "The Two Babylons;" pg 32-37
10 ibid; pg 87
11 Genesis 8:10-11; "The Bible"
12 Alexander Hislop; "The Two Babylons;" pg 79
13 2 Peter 3:8; "The Bible"
14 Psalm 119:105; "The Bible"
15 Genesis 3:15; "The Bible"
16 1 Corinthians 15:53-56; "The Bible"
17 Genesis 9:1; "The Bible"
18 Isaiah 2:12, 17-18; "The Bible"
19 Isaiah 2:22; "The Bible"
20 Isaiah 5:20-21; "The Bible"
21 Isaiah 44:24-26; "The Bible"
22 Isaiah 57:13; "The Bible"
23 Samuel Noah Kramer; "History Begins at Sumer"
24 http://home.achilles.net/~sal/uruk.html; "City of Uruk" Christopher Siren; "Sumerian Mythology" FAQ(version 2.0html); pg 9
25 Genesis 11:3-4; "The Bible"

[26] http://www.bible-history.com/babylonia/BabyloniaThe Ziggurat.htm; pg 3

[27] S.H. Hooke; "Middle Eastern Mythology"

[28] Pritchard J.B.; "Ancient Near Eastern Texts Relating to the Old Testament" Hooke, S.H.; "Middle Eastern Mythology"

[29] Samuel Kramer and John Maier; "Myths of Enki, the Crafty God"

[30] Genesis 1:14-15; "The Bible"

[31] 1 Corinthians 15:54-56; "The Bible"

[32] Genesis 3:15; "The Bible"

[33] Psalm 147:4; "The Bible"

[34] E. W. Bullinger; "The Witness of the Stars" Joseph Seiss; "The Gospel in the Stars of Primeval Astronomy" - both of these books offer an excellent discussion of the signs of the zodiac, according to the original intentions of God and the pre- Flood patriarchs.

[35] Joshua 1:5; "The Bible" Psalm 118:6; "The Bible" Hebrews 13:5-6; "The Bible"

[36] Psalm 118:24; "The Bible"

[37] Genesis 10:25; "The Bible"

[38] Genesis 3:14-19; "The Bible"

[39] Hebrews 6:19; "The Bible"

[40] Romans 8:22-24; "The Bible"

[41] Jeremiah 6:16-19; Proverbs 15:24; Matthew 7:13-14; "The Bible"

[42] John 15:13; Romans 5:7-8; "The Bible"

[43] Genesis 9:25-27; "The Bible"

[44] Genesis 10-11; "The Bible"

[45] Job 39:7; "The Bible"

[46] Job 39:27-29; "The Bible"

[47] Proverbs 15:8b; James 5:16b; "The Bible"

[48] Isaiah 1:18-20; "The Bible"

[49] Isaiah 42:8-9; "The Bible"

[50] Isaiah 43:10b-13; "The Bible"

[51] Ezekiel 28:2b; "The Bible"

[52] Isaiah 40:6-8; "The Bible"

[53] Titus 1:2; "The Bible"

[54] Hebrews 6:19; "The Bible"

[55] Henry Morris; "The Genesis Record;" pg 250

[56] ibid; pg 254-256

[57] ibid; pg 246-249

[58] Henry Morris; "The Genesis Record;" pg 259

[59] Isaiah 42:8; "The Bible"

[60] Isaiah 65:14-15; "The Bible"

61 Isaiah 14:4-6; "The Bible"

62 Isaiah 14:15-17; "The Bible"

63 Isaiah 14:9-11; "The Bible"

64 Diodorus; lib. 1; pg 58 Alexander Hislop; "The Two Babylons;" pg 63-66

65 Isaiah 47:1-3; "The Bible"

66 Isaiah 47:5; "The Bible"

67 Isaiah 47:7-15; "The Bible"

PART II

Chapter 1

The Support for
Nimrod in History

Hereafter, a discussion of the historical evidence for
Nimrod and his associates will ensue. The names
given for most of the people in this novel are historically
accurate. Biblical and extra-Biblical sources have confirmed
the existence of these individuals. Determining the precise
time frame for their lives, however, is much more difficult.
The plot development and character selection of this novel
depends upon which time frame is selected.

* * * * * * * * * *

Theologians do not agree on the timing of the worldwide
flood. One could easily date the life of Nimrod if the time of
the flood was conclusively established. Historians have proposed various dates for Nimrod's reign between 3000 and
1200 BC.[1] A recognized authority on biblical lands and
archeology, E.A. Spieser, has proposed that Tukulti-Ninurta

I (1246-1206 B.C.) was the Biblical Nimrod.[2]

Some suggest King Sargon of Akkad was Nimrod, because he ruled a region extending beyond the borders of the Mesopotamian Valley.[3] Sargon reigned between the years 2334-2279 BC. He ruled his kingdom from Akkad, but his kingship originated in Kish. However, the ancestors of Sargon are not precisely known with certainty. Many have suggested his origin was Shemitic because of his subsequent rule from Akkad. Most archeologists believe Akkadians were of Shemitic origin. Nimrod descended from the lineage of Ham.[4] Legend suggests Sargon's mother placed him in a waterproof basket after giving birth to him, and then floated it in the Euphrates River (similar to the Biblical story of the infant Moses).[5] A man named Aggi saved Sargon from the river and raised him until adulthood, teaching him the profession of farming.[6] Sargon began his political career as a gardener of the King of Kish.[7] The King later promoted him to the position of cupbearer. Finally, Sargon incited a successful rebellion against the King and usurped control of the throne. Sargon amassed a military force and overthrew the mighty King of Uruk—the most powerful King of Mesopotamia at that time. He then extended his kingdom north and south of these cities.[8]

Many historians place Nimrod's reign somewhat later than Sargon, between 2194 -2094 BC, because this corresponds to the Egyptian history of the Dynasty of Thinis I. The time frame of that reign likely includes the reign of his wife, Semiramis, who assumed the throne after Nimrod's execution. Abraham could have executed Nimrod if this time frame were accurate, because it correlates well with the dating of Abraham's life. "The Book of Jasher," "Antiquities of the Jews," and "The Legends of the Jews" all identify Abraham as the one who executed Nimrod. These writings suggest Nimrod and King Amraphel of Shinar are the same person.[9]

Amraphel, King of Shinar, accompanied Kederlaomer, King of Elam, and several other kings to invade Palestine. Kederlaomer commanded these invading kings. Invading armies came from the northeast, initially conquering many villages in northern Palestine. They completed their conquest south of the Dead Sea in a region encompassing the cities of Sodom and Gomorrah. Kings of these cities fought invading armies in the Valley of Siddim—south of the Dead Sea. The Kings of Sodom and Gomorrah lost the battle, and the invaders pillaged their cities. Abraham's nephew, Lot, was one of many taken captive. Abraham subsequently pursued the enemy with three hundred eighteen men. He finally chased them down between northern Israel and Damascus. Abraham totally defeated the armies there and King Amraphel was slain. This story is recorded in Genesis10 and further highlighted in "The Book of Jasher," "Antiquities of the Jews," and "The Legends of the Jews." [10]

Another group of historians place Nimrod's lifespan much earlier and the Bible also seems to support this. No centralized government ruled in Mesopotamia prior to 3000 BC. Historians agree the city of Kish was one of the first cities to develop in the Sumerian civilization. Archeological finds have established its presence in 2850 BC. Biblical records identify Nimrod as the son of Cush and grandson of Ham. [11] Nimrod's father, Cush probably founded the city of Kish (Kush) and named it after himself. Timing of his life cannot be precisely determined, but there is one likely possibility. Many historians place the reign of King Etana between the years 3000-2750 BC. Ancient historical records designate Etana as the first King of Kish [12]—the most powerful city in the Mesopotamian Valley at that time. Because this author believes King Etana was the Biblical Nimrod, the events of this novel are portrayed in his time frame. Ample evidence for this assertion is available and some of that will briefly be presented.

The Book of Genesis describes eight cities Nimrod either conquered or founded.[13] Eusebius records Ninus (another name of Nimrod) as the first king to rule in Assyria.[14] The prophet Micah referred to Assyria as the land of Nimrod,[15] suggesting Nimrod's previous control of this land. The first prominent King of Kish, Etana, was the first to conquer the large cities of Mesopotamia and place them under his rule.[16] The exploits of King Etana, noted in extra-Biblical history, approximate those attributed to the Biblical Nimrod, and therefore may indicate these men are one and the same.[17]

Many extra-Biblical sources credit Nimrod as the first man to develop weapons of warfare. The Jerusalem Targum notes the following about this man: "He was powerful in hunting and in wickedness before the Lord, for he was a hunter of the sons of men, and he said to them, 'Depart from the judgment of the Lord, and adhere to the judgment of Nimrod!' Therefore is it said...'As Nimrod [is] the strong one, strong in hunting, and in wickedness before the Lord.'"[18]

Nimrod is noted as the first to assemble armies for conquest in the post-flood world.[19] He was the first King to conquer the ancient world. "Nimrod was the first who carried on war against his neighbors and he conquered all nations from Assyria to Lybia, as they were yet unacquainted with the arts of war."[20] All sources describe Nimrod as having an insatiable lust for power and dominion over people. He conquered many large cities and placed them all under his authority. The Greek historian Diodorus lived as a contemporary of Julius Caesar. His record states Ninus (Nimrod) built the great city of Nineveh and gave it his name. Diodorus also recorded Ninus as a great warrior who subdued Asia.[21] Josephus, a Jewish historian, noted Nimrod was a tyrant, demanding complete control of his people. He brought people into complete dependence upon him.[22] The

Roman historian Justin stated the following about Nimrod: "Ninus strengthened the greatness of his acquired dominion by continued possession. Having subdued, therefore, his neighbors...he went forth against other tribes and every new victory paved the way for another. He subdued all peoples of the east." [23]

Numerous extra-Biblical sources describe wars and conquests occurring in the 300-500 year period preceding Abraham. If they are accurate, and if Nimrod introduced warfare in the post-flood world, he likely existed well before the time of Abraham. The genealogy of Abraham listed in the Book of Genesis places the birth of Nimrod approximately 335 years prior to the encounter of Abraham with Amraphel. [24]

The Bible curiously portrays Kedorlaomer—King of Elam—as leader of the kings who attacked Sodom and Gomorrah. [25] Amraphel did not command these invading armies. This information also suggests Nimrod and Amraphel were not the same individual. Nimrod was in complete control of his Empire. However, during Abraham's life other competing kings rivaled and surpassed Ampraphel's dominion.

Nowhere is it suggested Nimrod enjoyed the longevity of his Uncle Shem (600 years). [26] Shelah, son of Arphaxad, was a contemporary of Nimrod. Both were born at approximately the same time. Shelah lived 403 years, making it conceivable Nimrod *could* have lived to the time period of Abraham, provided his life did not end prematurely. However, Peleg was born when Shelah (his grandfather) was 64 years old. Peleg lived to an age of 209 years. The Bible clearly states, "in his time the earth was divided." [27] God's judgment at the Tower of Babel occurred during the life of Peleg, who lived generations before Abraham. If Nimrod lived to the end of Peleg's life, he would have been approximately 273 years old (209[age of Peleg at his death] +

64[age of Shelah and Nimrod at Peleg's birth] = 273 years). God's judgment could have occurred anytime in the 209 years prior to Peleg's death, between Nimrod's ages 64-273. This information further supports Nimrod's reign at an earlier time period.

Shem was Nimrod's great uncle, according to the Bible.[28] Alexander Hislop's classic text, "The Two Babylons," provides compelling evidence to support the contention that Shem was involved in the execution of Nimrod, and that Nimrod's body was subsequently cut into pieces.[29] Ancient Egyptian mythology describes the fate of their god Osiris, who was none other than a deified Nimrod.[30] The Egyptian god Hercules executed Osiris for 'very serious transgressions.' Seventy-two leading men of Egypt agreed upon the punishment of execution according to this legend. Egyptian law specified seventy-two judges were required to determine the punishment of one having committed such a severe offense. Thirty judges had the authority to determine life or death for the offender. Forty-two additional judges determined whether the body should be buried after execution. Burial was the honorable way to dispose of the deceased. In the case of Osiris, the severity of the offense caused the judges to render a decision not to bury the body after execution. The body of Osiris (Nimrod) was cut into pieces. The severed parts were sent to all cities of the Empire with a message denoting the seriousness of his transgression. According to Alexander Hislop, Hercules was the historical, Biblical Shem—son of Noah. Osiris was a very important Egyptian god. Egyptian mythology also records Hercules as the archenemy of Osiris. Hercules (Shem) convinced seventy-two judges of Osiris's (Nimrod) enormous transgression.[31]

Similar legends existed in the ancient cultures of Greece, India, Mexico, and Scandinavia. Maimonides, in "The Teaching of the Chaldeans," gives the following account of the death of Tammuz (also Nimrod): "When the false prophet Tammuz preached to a certain King that he should worship the stars and the twelve signs of the zodiac, the King ordered him to be put to a certain death."[32] That King was Shem.

The hideous death and dismemberment of Nimrod likely caused his followers to fear Shem and his Holy God. Therefore, one might reasonably assume the false religion of Babylon went underground at that time. It became known as the mystery religion of Babylon, because its adherents practiced it in secret.[33] The tongues of seventy different languages disseminated this mystery religion throughout the entire world following God's judgment at Babel. Indeed, it became the foundation for all religions and philosophies that have fiercely opposed the One True God.

* * * * * * * * *

Nimrod is famous in the Middle East—even to this day. The city of Calah (founded by Nimrod)[34] exists today as the city of Nimrud in Iraq. Other sites of interest in this region of the Middle East are also named after this man. Arabs from this area revere his name.

Some have written Nimrod was a giant black nephilim, and they have hypothesized his enormous size was the result of genetic characteristics he inherited from his grandmother.[35] The wife of Ham purportedly descended from Cain[36]—the first son of Adam, who murdered his younger brother Abel. God banished Cain from the presence of his family as punishment for that crime. The Bible records that Cain subsequently founded the first city of history and named it after his son, Enoch.[37] Genesis, Chapter 6, describes the bizarre corruption of Cain's lineage by demonic angels. The resulting giant progeny were called nephilim, and they were infamous for their wickedness in the antediluvian world.[38] The Sumerians worshipped them as gods.[39]

The Bible states Nimrod was a mighty hunter before the Lord.[40] Extra-Biblical sources also affirm Nimrod hunted fearsome animals in his younger years.[41] These animals threatened people living in the wilderness. Nimrod probably developed an early reputation by eliminating some of these animals from the Mesopotamian Valley. He possibly hunted dinosaurs living at that time. The Book of Job, written later than Nimrod's life, suggests the existence of these huge reptiles.[42] Perhaps recurring images of Nimrod with dragons and serpents in the artwork of antiquity memorialized these remarkable exploits. However, these portrayals also represented another more sinister association, which will be discussed in a later section.

Nimrod tamed a leopard, according to legend. The leopard supposedly accompanied him on hunting expeditions.[43] The Babylonian name for leopard is Nimr, and Rod means, 'to subdue.' Nimrod is often depicted wearing a garment of leopard skin in the artwork of antiquity.[44]

The Hebrew word Nimrod means, 'to rebel,' or 'to revolt.' That definition illustrates the story of this man's life. He was the chief instigator of the rebellion against God and is credited for building the Tower of Babel.

* * * * * * * * *

Tammuz and Nimrod are names for the same person.[45] Even though Tammuz was the illegitimate son of Semiramis in this novel, legend suggests he was Nimrod. Myths from civilizations of antiquity describe the sun god (deified Nimrod) fathered Tammuz using a sunbeam to impregnate the maiden Semiramis. The result was a re-incarnated Nimrod. Mythology portrays Semiramis as married to god and mother of that same god.[46] Sumerians and subsequent world civilizations worshipped her in that way. Extra-Biblical legends about Tammuz are plentiful. Sumerians called him Dumuzi. He was allegedly a shepherd king of Uruk during his lifetime. Dumuzi (Nimrod) married Inanna (Semiramis). The gods granted him divine power over the fertility of plants and animals following the consummation of their marriage.[47] According to legend, Dumuzi gave his life as a ransom for Inanna after the goddess of the underworld captured her.[48] Demons from the underworld slayed Dumuzi after Inanna was released, and they took his spirit to their domain. Satan, trying to save face, probably used this legend to explain the reason for the trial and execution of Nimrod. Dumuzi was later freed from the underworld for half the year while his sister, Geshtinanna (goddess of wine), served out his term.[49] The gods permitted this rotational arrangement because Inanna mourned ceaselessly before the gods.[50]

Rotation of Dumuzi with his sister in the underworld represented the change of seasons. Dumuzi and Inanna were lovers prior to their life in the underworld. Sumerian mythology describes them continuing their intimate relationship for six months out of every year, beginning each spring. The goddess of the underworld released Dumuzi when his sister arrived to replace him. An intimate reunion of Dumuzi and Inanna recurred each spring and lasted throughout the growing season. Their reunion enabled a bountiful season of crops and vegetables for the Sumerians.[51] Babylonian priests and temple prostitutes openly reenacted the reunion each spring in pagan temples of worship.[52] The death of Dumuzi recurred at harvest time, when he returned to the underworld for another six-month cycle.[53] This sordid affair mimicked the resurrection of the true Son of God in a twisted sort of way.

* * * * * * * * *

Historical records of those ruling after Nimrod are somewhat confusing, but there is general agreement between them. Confusion arises because different names were attributed to the same kings by different civilizations. This confusion is easily understood in light of the various languages and civilizations that arose following the human dispersion from Babel.

Gilgamesh of Mesopotamia was likely the real son of Semiramis. His Egyptian name was Thus Horus. Gilgamesh and Thus Horus are both described similarly in legends of antiquity. Each claimed legitimate inheritance to the emperor's throne, and legends describe the Queen of heaven birthing each of them—Isis in Egypt and Ishtar in Babylon. Mythology describes a spirit god fathered both of them. The Epic of Gilgamesh is a famous legend describing the life and travels of this man. Archeologists have discovered this Babylonian legend in written form, and it is available in many public libraries. Feats reportedly performed by this man are well beyond the abilities of mere mortals. When Gilgamesh died, his wife and servants were also sacrificed as offerings to deities of the underworld.[54] Archeologists have unearthed at least one such massive gravesite of a Sumerian king (which might be that of Gilgamesh) buried simultaneously with family, servants, animals, and valuable belongings. Gilgamesh was deified after his death as a lesser god of the underworld.[55]

Ur-Lugal succeeded Gilgamesh as King of the Mesopotamian cities, according to the historical listing of Kings of Erech (Uruk). The name, Ur-lugal, means 'Great King.' Uruk dominated all cities of Mesopotamia during his lifetime, and it supplanted the powerful city of Kish. Its King, Ur-lugal, was probably the Biblical Amraphel of Abraham's time.

Chapter 2

The Historical Support
for Semiramis

S everal different legends describe events leading to the infamous marriage of Nimrod and Semiramis. One legend, recorded by Diodorus Siculus, claims a lake goddess gave birth to Semiramis.[56] The lake goddess allegedly had sexual relations with a man and became pregnant with Semiramis. The guilt-ridden goddess killed the father and abandoned the child. A flock of doves found the infant and cared for her by stealing milk and cheese from nearby shepherds. The shepherds later discovered the infant and brought her to their chief, who raised her as his child. He gave her the name Semiramis, which in Syrian means, 'the one who comes from the doves.' When she grew to adulthood, one of the King's generals (Onnes) noticed her beauty and married her in Nineveh. King Ninus had engaged neighboring Bactria in a war at that time. Nimrod recruited the aid of Onnes for the battle. Onnes missed his new wife and summoned her to join him on the battlefront. After arriving there, she observed the battle against Bactria. Ninus (Nimrod) had lost many men early in the battle and was precariously close to losing the war altogether. Semiramis supposedly provided critical advice, ultimately enabling Ninus to conquer Bactria. Thereafter, Ninus fell in love with Semiramis and demanded her as his wife. He commanded Onnes to release her from the marriage contract, but Onnes resisted. When Nimrod threatened to gouge out his eyes, Onnes reluctantly capitulated to Nimrod's demand. Onnes then committed suicide.

A more believable legend (at least for this author) describes Nimrod meeting Semiramis while she was a brothel owner in Uruk.[57] This likely occurred when Nimrod was consolidating control over that city. The history of a Queen/goddess as prostitute/ brothel owner is not the material of good legends. Therefore, more acceptable legends describing the origin of this woman arose. These portray her as a mythic-goddess figure rather than a brothel owner. This power-hungry woman would surely have chosen to be memorialized as a goddess rather than a prostitute. One woman, Ku-Baba, became a ruler after rising from the lowly position of tavern owner.[58] Early Sumerian myths portray a mother goddess as the central figure of creation.[59] Innana (Ishtar, Aphrodite) is the goddess of sex and prostitutes.[60] Herodotus, writing about Babylon in the fifth century BC, stated that "every woman once in her life had to go to the temple of 'Aphrodite' (Ishtar), and sit there waiting until a stranger cast a coin in her lap as the price of her favors. Then she was obliged to go with him outside the temple and have intercourse, to render her duty to the goddess." [61]

Semiramis became a powerful ruler in Mesopotamia following the death of Nimrod. Legends record Semiramis as a Queen who led her warriors in battle. Purportedly, she was seriously wounded in one battle, but survived her injuries.[62] At least one revolt attempted to displace her from the throne, but she maintained authority by force.

This Queen was fond of building projects.[63] She is credited with building an immense wall surrounding Uruk, which contained guard towers spaced at regular intervals. She constructed it to defend the city against enemies desiring her overthrow. Semiramis wore a crown symbolizing the turreted wall—the first known monarch to wear such a crown. She erected a majestic mausoleum in Nineveh to honor Ninus, according to historians Pyramus and Herodotus. She allegedly directed construction of a 900-meter bridge spanning the Euphrates River. A fortified castle was located on each side of that bridge. She supposedly built splendid monuments, parks, and other structures in the Mesopotamian Valley. Some even attribute the famous 'Hanging Gardens of Babylon' to Semiramis. This author doubts the validity of most of these accomplishments. Her enthusiastic adherents likely exaggerated the legends over the generations. Nevertheless, many amazing feats are attributed to this infamous woman of antiquity.

The Sumerian name Sammur-amat was the original name of this woman.[64] The name is translated 'Gift of the Sea.' The first part of this name, Sammur, becomes Shinar when translated into Hebrew. The land of Shinar is the Biblical name for the region of southern Mesopotamia. People of this land were called Sumerians—a name also derived from Sammur. Both the Sumerians and their land of Shinar (Sumer) were named after this notorious woman! This also supports an earlier time period for Nimrod and Semiramis. The Sumerians were the first to develop cities in this present world. Most anthropologists credit them with beginning human civilization.

Semiramis ruled for more than forty years after Nimrod's death.[65] Her son was most likely Gilgamesh, as discussed earlier. She was permitted to rule in place of her son until he reached an age when he could responsibly assume authority of the throne. However, when he reached that age, she managed to continue her reign by deceit for many more years. Semiramis suddenly disappeared from history at the age of sixty years. Some have written her son executed her when he assumed the throne, but the exact fate of this woman is not known with certainty. Mythology portrays her ascending to heaven as a dove, where she became the goddess Inanna.[66]

The most important celebration of the ancient Sumerian civilization occurred at the beginning of the Babylonian New Year, when King Dumuzi married the goddess Inanna, the goddess of life and love. The Sumerians believed this ritualistic celebration would make the New Year prosperous and fruitful.[67]

Chapter 3

The Dispersion of Mankind Following God's Judgment of Tongues at Babel

G enesis, Chapter 10 of The Bible is often called the Table of Nations. This chapter delineates the children, grandchildren, and great grandchildren of Noah. Most theologians credit Shem as the one who recorded the genealogy of Noah's family. Moses later incorporated it into the Book of Genesis. God gave all the individuals mentioned distinct languages and dispersed them from Mesopotamia to begin new nations in different regions of the New World.

Cush gathered those few individuals speaking his language and moved south to the continent of Africa, following God's judgment at Babel. He founded a large country there and named it after himself.[68] Hundreds of years later his descendants renamed it Ethiopia.

The brothers of Cush also moved from Mesopotamia. Each moved with his family and those sharing a common language. Mizraim moved south to a very large area of land surrounding the Nile River delta, in northern Africa. He named the country after himself.[69] Generations later its residents renamed it, Egypt. Put also moved to Africa. He founded the country of Put,[70] renamed Libya millennia later.

Canaan was the youngest of Ham's sons. He and most of his children moved far west of the Mesopotamian Valley to the land of Palestine. He named that land Canaan—after himself, of course. More languages divided Canaan's large family than any of Ham's other sons. Each of his eleven sons spoke a unique language. Most accompanied Canaan to Palestine, but several moved to lands east of Mesopotamia. These sons likely founded the great civilizations in the Far East, which ultimately gave rise to Japan and China.[71]

The sons of Japheth moved north and west of the Mesopotamian Valley. They settled lands stretching across Europe and Asia, from the Black and Caspian Seas all the way to Spain. Japheth's sons and grandsons founded many ancient countries—each with a different language. His descendants founded all the countries of Europe.[72]

Shem had five sons. Of all Shem's sons, Asshur enjoyed the most fame and fortune at that time. He and Nimrod founded the cities north of the Mesopotamian Valley. The city of Asshur was named after him. Asshur stayed in this area after God bestowed the languages. His descendants established the mighty Assyrian Empire, and they named it after him.[73] Nineveh (previously named after Nimrod) became its capital.

Shem's son, Aram, moved northwest of the Mesopotamian Valley. He founded the country of Aram.[74] Thousands of years later this country was renamed Syria, but prior to that a virgin woman from a small village in northern Israel (Nazareth) gave birth to God's Seed (Jesus). He spoke Aramaic—a language derived from the original tongue of Aram.

Shem's son, Elam, fathered the Elamites, who later combined with descendants of Japheth's son, Madai, to establish the vast Medo-Persian Empire.[75] It subsequently conquered the powerful Babylonian Empire. Thousands of years later, descendants of the Medo-Persian Empire comprised a country named Iran.

Shem's son, Lud, settled in Asia Minor and became the ancestor of the Lydians.[76]

Arphaxad was the godliest of Shem's sons. The Seed of the woman came through the lineage of Arphaxad, Shelah, Eber, and Peleg. God promised Adam and Eve His Seed would inflict a mortal wound to Satan's head.[77] God's Seed is His incarnate Son, destined to restore the fallen creation to its original state of perfection. One day He will place the infamous enemy of God in eternal punishment, rendering him forever powerless in the affairs of men.

Many famous men of God descended from Arphaxad. These famous men of faith included Abraham, Isaac, Jacob, Joseph, Moses, Aaron, David, Solomon, Isaiah, Jeremiah, Ezekiel, and Daniel. The entire Jewish nation descended from Arphaxad. He settled north of the Persian Gulf and became the ancestor of the Chaldeans.[78] These people were world-renowned for their mastery of mathematics, magic, and astrology. Three wise men from their ranks traveled hundreds of miles westward to witness the incarnation of that promised Seed in the world of mankind.[79]

Theologians have written prolifically about the genealogies of Noah's sons, the origin of languages, and the establishment of nations in the post-flood world. This information is beyond the scope of this book, but several helpful sources are listed in the Bibliography for the interested reader.

Chapter 4

People of History Become the Gods of Mythology

The mystery religion of Babylon probably originated in the evil mind of Semiramis.[80] Nimrod and Cush also contributed significantly to its development. Many learned individuals have taught polytheism was the evolutionary forerunner of monotheism. They have described polytheism as a primitive form of religion. However, polytheism began in the minds of Nimrod and Semiramis. They heavily suffused the mystery religion of Babylon with human deification.

Euhemerus was an ancient Greek mythographer who lived around 300 BC. He wrote that gods and their associated legends arose from the deification of dead human heroes. Corruption of earlier historical events of these individuals became the origin of myths surrounding their deification. Euhemerus claimed to have discovered ancient inscriptions that recorded events in the lives of Zeus, Ouranus, and Kronos during a time when they had all been men of significant importance.[81]

Nimrod forced his subjects to worship him as a military

and political hero. He proclaimed himself high priest of the mystery religion.[82] Semiramis deified Nimrod after his death.[83] Archeologists have found written accounts of the Sumerian kings from the time period 2900-2370 BC. Mythic tales developed describing the lives of several of these kings and they were subsequently deified.[84] It is interesting the Babylonians believed their ancient King Etana (mentioned previously as a possibility for the person of Nimrod) rode to heaven on the back of a giant eagle so he could receive the 'plant of birth' from Ishtar (Inanna) and produce an heir for his throne.[85]

Nimrod's Babylonian followers revered him as Marduk, and he quickly ascended to the pinnacle of Babylonian and Assyrian gods.[86] Marduk was the god of war and fortresses. The Sumerians built the ziggurat of Etemenanki to honor their supreme god Marduk.[87] Many believe this ziggurat was the Tower of Babel.[88]

His name was altered by various civilizations of the world due to the many languages given at the Tower of Babel. His Akkadian name was Amarutuk.[89] Egyptians called him Osiris,[90] and in Egyptian artwork he is often portrayed wearing a leopard skin (Nimrod was known and named as the one who subdued the leopard).[91] The Phonecians referred to him as Tammuz.[92] Nimrod was the same god, named differently in each civilization.

Nimrod became the Canaanite god, Molech—god of fire.[93] Canaanite parents often sacrificed their first born to this god by placing the child in the outstretched hands of a large statue of Molech, while a blazing fire raged beneath. Infants were considered the most acceptable offerings at altars of Molech and Baal. This horrible form of idol worship incited God's judgment upon the Canaanite people. God had previously warned the Israelites and pagans in that land.

Say to the Israelites: Any Israelite or any alien living in Israel who gives any of his children to Molech must be put to death.[94]
Has Israel no sons? Has she no heirs? Why then has Molech taken possession of Gad? Why do his people live in its towns?[95]
The prophet Jeremiah pronounced this Word of the Lord to the Israelites:
They turned their backs to me and not their faces; though I taught them again and again, they would not listen or respond to discipline. They set up their abominable idols in the house that bears my Name and defiled it. They built high places for Baal in the Valley of Ben Hinnom to sacrifice their sons and daughters to Molech, though I never commanded, nor did it enter my mind that they should do such a detestable thing and so make Judah sin.[96]

Should people of this present time be concerned that God might judge a world of people who have murdered millions of their children on the altar of abortion? Indeed, clear scriptural references suggest the detestable practice of child sacrifice incited God's terrible wrath on multiple occasions. God often judged His own people, the Israelites, more severely than the pagans adhering to these practices.

Nimrod became the Roman god, Bacchus.[97] This name means 'the son of Cush.' Bacchus was god of wine and revelry. Marduk was the Roman god Kronos, whose name means, 'the horned one.'[98] Artists often depicted Nimrod wearing a crown of bullhorns. Kronos was also the Roman god Saturn, who devoured his own sons as soon as they were born.[99] Eusebius recorded, "the Phoenicians every year sacrificed their beloved and only begotten children to Kronos, or Saturn; and the Rhodesians often did the same."[100]

Romans celebrated the birth of Saturn by orgies, drunkenness and debauchery in the famous Roman festival, Saturnalia. Egyptians celebrated the birth of their god Osiris (son of the goddess Isis—Semiramis) on that very same day each year. That day was December 25th—Christmas day.[101] The Roman Emperor Constantine later changed the festival of Saturnalia to commemorate the birthday of Jesus Christ. Constantine had an honorable motive for this action. He desired citizens of the Roman Empire to adopt Christianity as their personal religion. He established it as the national religion. Previous Roman Emperors had severely persecuted Christian believers for their faith. Nevertheless, no historical or Biblical evidence exists that supports December 25th as the true birthday of Jesus. This author does not advocate cessation of the Christmas celebration, but people should understand the origin of this holiday.

Nimrod's followers assigned him many mythical names that implicate works achieved only by the true Son of God, Jesus Christ. These counterfeit names deceptively attracted multitudes to worship Nimrod. People north of Mesopotamia commonly knew him as Ninus, 'the son'—even before his deification.[102] Nimrod was called Zoraster, which means 'the seed of Aster' (Ishtar—Semiramis). People revered Zoraster through the generations as the promised seed of the woman, destined to bruise the head of the serpent.[103] Zorastrianism rests on this foundational doctrine. The Greeks deified Nimrod as the god, Adonis.[104] Adonai means 'The Lord.' They also knew Nimrod as Dionysus, 'the sin bearer.'[105] The Greeks gave homage to him as Zeus, 'the Savior,'[106] and Mithras—'the mediator.'[107] The Babylonians worshipped Nimrod as El-Bar, or 'god, the son.'[108] Archeologists in the ancient city of Nineveh have unearthed sculptures inscribed with this name.

People of ancient civilizations worshipped deified Nimrod in conjunction with snakes, serpents, and dragons.

Nimrod appropriated the dragon and the snake as his personal emblems, and from this association various myths about gods and serpents originated in antiquity.[109] These likely symbolize his satanic connection. Many Scriptures in the Bible identify Satan as the great serpent. Greek and Roman mythology abound with serpent lore, and their artisans frequently sculpted popular gods with serpent representations. Many Hamitic civilizations (i.e. Ethiopians, Hittites, Chinese, Japanese, and American Indians) have favorably portrayed dragons and serpents.

The Egyptians depicted their sun god, Osiris, as the sun surrounded by a serpent.[110] Sun worship and serpent worship began simultaneously in antiquity.[111] Artists generally painted dragons and serpents a fiery red color to suggest their association with the sun. The Canaanites clearly understood the connection between their god of fire, Molech, and the serpent.[112] Roman mythology repeatedly illustrates an affiliation between a serpent and the fire god—often the Romans worshipped them together.

The Apostle Paul wrote in the Epistle of the Romans:

> For although they knew God, they neither glorified Him as God, nor gave thanks to Him; but their thinking became futile, and their foolish hearts were darkened. Although they claimed to be wise, they became fools, and exchanged the glory of the immortal God for images made to look like mortal man, and birds, and animals, and creeping things.[113]

Perhaps the 'creeping things' refers to the worship of serpents.

A very interesting Biblical reference describing a dragon is located in the prophetic New Testament Book of Revelation.

A great and wondrous sign appeared in heaven: a
woman clothed with the sun, with the moon under
her feet and a crown of twelve stars on her head.
She was pregnant and cried out in pain as she was
about to give birth. Then another sign appeared in
heaven: an enormous red dragon with seven heads
and ten horns and seven crowns on his heads. His
tail swept a third of the stars out of the sky and
flung them to the earth. The dragon stood in front
of the woman who was about to give birth, so that
he might devour her child the moment it was born.
She gave birth to a son, a male child, who will rule
all the nations with an iron scepter. And her child
was snatched up to God and to His throne.[114]

The pregnant woman described in this passage is God's
chosen nation, Israel. The infant represents the Seed of the
woman, prophesied thousands of years earlier in Genesis
3:15. The child awaits delivery by the laboring woman
(Israel). She is God's chosen nation through which His
Seed—the Son of God—would come. The fearsome red
dragon depicted here is the same fiery red dragon portrayed
with the sun god in the mystery religion of Babylon. The
dragon is none other than Satan, himself. He is portrayed
here, eagerly awaiting the birth of the prophesied Seed so he
can devour Him. Satan has feared the prophesied Seed since
God pronounced the curse in the Garden of Eden. God has
provided clues throughout Biblical history suggesting the
lineage of His Seed. From the beginning of time Satan has
done everything in his power to destroy that lineage. Old
Testament Scriptures record the history of this momentous
conflict over the millennia preceding the incarnation of
Jesus Christ. Satan's multiple attempts to destroy the Seed
are chronicled in the pages of God's Word. A thorough discussion of these attempts is not within the scope of this

book. Nevertheless, the dragon did await the birth of that infant (Jesus). When the woman (Israel) bore the child, the fiery serpent finally had an opportunity to devour her Seed. Herod's massacre of infants in the city of Bethlehem was a horrific attempt to accomplish that goal. Satan ultimately attempted to destroy God's promised Seed by crucifying the Christ. The crucifixion initially appeared to accomplish his goal, but Satan failed that attempt also—fortunately for mankind. He had not anticipated the resurrection of God's Son.[115] Thereafter, Satan realized his time was short, for the Son's destiny is to terminate Satan's reign over the world of mankind.

The seed of a plant illustrates the miracle of God's Seed. A plant dies but its seed springs forth into new life. Cycles of life and death in God's creation are examples He has provided to understand the birth, death, and resurrection of God's Seed. God has created these examples to help a finite human mind grasp an infinite Truth—that eternal life exists beyond the realm of our present experience. Life cycles bear witness to the reality of God's purpose, but the reality transcends its earthly portrayal. God's Seed springs into Life for eternity. He will never die! His wound was not mortal! Christ was the first fruit of those destined for resurrection.[116] His followers will experience the indescribable joy of eternity in His presence. God's enemies will suffer the unfathomable horror of eternity in Satan's presence.

The previous verse from the Book of Revelation explains the Child was taken up to God's throne. The resurrected Seed ascended to sit at God's right hand. The Seed of God lives today, and one day He will deliver the mortal blow to the dragon. That Seed is the Son of God, Jesus Christ, who will rule the nations with an iron scepter, as illustrated in this same verse.

Nimrod worship was scattered over the entire world by the dispersion of humanity from Babel. The dragon used this opportunity to spread his venom throughout the world. The mystery religion of Babylon survived through the generations in new civilizations that subsequently arose.

* * * * * * * * *

Deified Cush was revered as several gods of ancient mythology. Canaanites worshipped him as Bel or Baal, and he was their most important God.[117] Baal worship was an abomination to God and a major factor provoking His judgment on the Canaanites and Israelites. The prophet, Jeremiah, spoke the Word of God to Israelites who had participated in this Baal worship:

> Listen! I am going to bring a disaster on this place that will make the ears of everyone who hears of it tingle. For they have forsaken me and made this a place of foreign gods; they have burned sacrifices in it to gods that neither they nor their fathers nor the kings of Judah ever knew, and they have filled this place with the blood of the innocent. They have built the high places of Baal to burn their sons in the fire as offerings to Baal—something I did not command or mention, nor did it enter my mind.[118]

God executed that judgment shortly thereafter, when King Nebuchadnezzar's Babylonian army destroyed Jerusalem. Many Jews surviving the onslaught were taken to Babylon to live the rest of their lives in slavery.

Babel means 'the gate of god,' but it can also mean 'son of Bel.' Perhaps Nimrod named the city after himself, as the son of Bel.

The Egyptians commemorated Cush as the god Hermes, whose name means 'son of Ham.'[119] Hermes was recognized as the author of religious rites and the interpreter of the gods. Hermeneutics is the study of interpretation of the Scriptures. The word is derived from the Egyptian god, Hermes. Ancient mythology describes Hermes as the interpreter of languages. Mercury was another name for the god Hermes.[120] Mercury purportedly divided the speech of men. The name, Bel, also means 'the Confounder.'[121] Cush likely assisted in the planning and building of the Tower of Babel. He initiated the rebellion against God. Indeed, he named his first son Nimrod, which means, 'to rebel.' The mythological names of Cush suggest his sin was an inciting cause for God's worldwide judgment—the confusion of languages. Cush was known as the ancient god Janus, and all gods supposedly originated from him.[122] People of antiquity recorded a statement Janus reportedly made about himself: "The ancients.... called me Chaos."[123] Chaos is the 'god of confusion.' Chaos is derived from the name Cush. The symbol of Janus is a club, and its Babylonian name means 'to break in pieces', or 'to scatter abroad.' The sin of Cush broke the one language of mankind and caused the chaos of languages that scattered men abroad. Janus and Vulcan are names for the same god. Vulcan broke and divided the world with a stroke of his well-known hammer.[124]

* * * * * * * * *

All attempts to trace the origin of goddess worship lead ultimately to one single woman of ancient history—Semiramis.[125] She promoted deification of Nimrod and herself after his death. She contributed substantially to the mystery religion of Babylon. God's judgment and Nimrod's execution forced the mystery religion underground. Its adherents realized the danger of practicing their religion in the public domain. Hence, the name 'mystery religion of Babylon' refers to its secretive nature. During her lifetime,

Semiramis commanded total authority over her subjects and clandestinely indoctrinated the priesthood with this mystery religion.[126] Priests and astrologers obeyed her commands, aggressively marketing the mystery religion.

Ancient Sumerians knew Semiramis as the goddess Inanna.[127] People adored her, especially in the city of Uruk—her home city. They erected many temples to commemorate her. Inanna's son was Tammuz, the sun god. Sumerians worshiped the mother/son duo. Mother/son worship was incorporated into most civilizations of antiquity following God's judgment and dispersion of mankind. Babylonians knew Inanna as Ishtar.[128] Unfortunately, the name for our holiday, Easter, originated from Ishtar of the Babylonians.[129] The date of the resurrection of Jesus Christ is historically valid, but a more appropriate name for this momentous day could have been selected.

Egyptians worshipped the mother/son duo as Isis and Osiris. There is an inscription engraved in an Egyptian temple of Isis that reads: "I am all that has been, or that is, or that shall be. No mortal has removed my veil. The fruit which I have brought forth is the sun."[130] The sun was Osiris—deified Nimrod.

The Egyptians identified their god, Osiris, as both son and husband of the goddess Isis, as Tammuz (Nimrod) was son and husband of Ishtar (Semiramis) in Babylonia.[131] Indians worshipped them as Isi and Iswara.[132] Romans exalted them as Venus and Cupid.[133] People venerated them in Asia as Rhea (or Cybele) and Deoius.[134] Cybele was the wife of Kronos (Saturn). Greeks knew them as the goddess Irene and her son Plutus.[135] Even ancient civilizations of Tibet, China, and Japan worshipped the mother goddess and her son.[136]

The Babylonian goddess, Ishtar, was named Shing Moo in China. The Greeks recognized her as Aphrodite. The Ephesians gave her two names—Dianna and Artemis.[137]

They built an elaborate temple for the goddess, Dianna. People of antiquity considered it one of the Seven Wonders of the World, and thousands worshipped in her temple during the lifetime of the Apostle Paul.[138] A giant statue of Dianna filled the main temple. A turreted crown adorned her head, depicting her as goddess of fortifications. Canaanites worshipped her in high places as Ashteroth, 'the woman who made the encompassing wall.'[139] This goddess surely refers to Semiramis, who built a huge wall around Babylon, according to legends.

Once again, Jeremiah prophesied about the worship of this goddess:

> The women added, 'When we burned incense to the Queen of Heaven and poured out drink offerings to her, did not our husbands know that we were making cakes like her image and pouring out drink offerings to her?' Then Jeremiah said to all the people, both men and women, who were answering him, 'Did not the Lord remember and think about the incense burned in the towns of Judah and the streets of Jerusalem by you and your fathers, your kings and your officials and the people of the land? When the Lord could no longer endure your wicked actions and the detestable things you did, your land became an object of cursing and a desolate waste without inhabitants, as it is today. Because you have burned incense and have sinned against the Lord and have not obeyed Him or followed His law or His decrees or His stipulations, this disaster has come upon you, as you now see.'[140]

Sumerians and Babylonians identified Inanna (Ishtar) as the goddess of sexual love and fertility. This description of her mythical duties is likely an exaggeration of her true life as a prostitute. The truth of history often grows to superhuman feats in mythology.

A dove often symbolizes the deified Queen in the artwork of antiquity. The mystery religion of Babylon commonly portrays the dove with an olive branch in its beak.[141] This represented the work attributed to the goddess in the worldwide flood—providing safe passage for mankind into the New World. The Righteous Branch in the Bible refers to the Son of God—the prophesied King who will rule the world. He came from the root of Jesse and lineage of King David.[142] This partially fulfilled prophecy will come to fruition when He assumes the authority of His throne in this world. The olive tree symbolizes the nation of Israel in Old Testament Scripture. The olive branch represents the son (Nimrod) of the goddess of heaven (Semiramis) in the mystery religion of Babylon.[143] The prince of darkness has repeatedly corrupted God's symbols in Scripture to claim God's works for himself.

Golden discs crowning the heads of the goddess and her son in the artwork of ancient civilizations represent golden sunrays and symbolize her conception by the sun god.[144]

The world of antiquity deified Semiramis as Queen of Heaven and Queen of the gods. Goddess worship became wildly popular wherever it was introduced. Its adherents enthusiastically embraced the mystery religion of Babylon. Nations became intoxicated with worship of this woman.[145]

* * * * * * * * * *

The mystery religion of Babylon incorporated human deification, Satan worship, and astrology in cultic religious services. Astrologers corrupted the signs of the zodiac to authenticate their new religion.

God provided the antediluvian patriarchs with visual

pictures of constellations as a story of His intervention in the history of mankind. Constellations are a testimony of God's work in the world. They portray the heavenly testimony of God's promise for the coming Seed and Savior of mankind.[146] Scriptures in Genesis reveal God created the heavenly bodies to divide the night from day, to give light to the earth, and for SIGNS and for SEASONS.[147] He designed the constellations to portray the rebellion of Satan, his deception of mankind, and the original sin of Adam and Eve. God pictures His virgin-born Seed as the Lion who will return to restore the creation from its curse. God's Son will deliver man from the curse of sin by defeating Satan—the great serpent. The rightful owner of the creation will then resume His reign on the earth. God illustrates all this by His artwork in the heavens. His celestial testimony serves as a perpetual reminder of man's fall and God's promise of a Redeemer. This was the Gospel—the good news—to people of the ancient world. God originally intended signs of the zodiac to testify of the work He has performed and will accomplish in the world of mankind. The Apostle Paul has recorded the following in the Book of Romans:

> For since the creation of the world God's invisible qualities—His eternal power and divine nature—have been clearly seen, being understood from what has been made, so that men are without excuse.[148]
> God's testimony in the heavens was given to mankind before He provided the witness of His Word and His Son. It was well known to the ante-diluvian patriarchs. Books written by Bullinger and Seiss describe God's testimony in the constellations.[149]

Semiramis and her astrologers corrupted the original

intent of God's work in the heavens by creating their own constellations of the zodiac.[150] They retooled the zodiac to illustrate myths of the mystery religion of Babylon. The dragon was portrayed as rightful lord of the universe who created man in his present fallen state. The serpent promised a divine mother would one-day give birth to a divine child, who would ultimately become a god and return dominion of the universe to Satan. Semiramis had astrologers portray her as Queen of Heaven in the constellation Cassiopeia. Nimrod was pictured in the heavens as the constellation Orion.

The Tower of Babel was most likely intended to have an astrological observatory in the pinnacle of the ziggurat, where astrologers would study stars, planets, and constellations.[151] Astrologers preferred to study the heavens from high places. Astrologers depicted Nimrod as god of the planets Mars and Saturn. In fact, they named these planets after him. Mars was named after the god, Marduk.[152] The Romans christened the planet, Saturn, after their god with the same name.[153] The planet, Mercury, memorializes the legacy of Nimrod's deified father, Cush.[154] The goddess, Venus, was none other than deified Semiramis, and the planet, Venus, commemorates her.[155] Ancient astrologers avidly studied the sun, moon, planets, and stars. In fact, ancient Chaldeans (Babylonians) are credited as the founders of astrology and the science of astronomy.

The mystery religion of Babylon was replete with cultic rituals of prostitution, idol worship, child sacrifice, magic, divination, and animal sacrifice. Priests, diviners, magicians, and prostitutes all participated regularly in these cultic rituals. The Bible is filled with examples of mediums, astrologers, diviners, temple prostitutes, and child sacrifice, which were all associated with this religion in various civilizations of the ancient world. These Biblical examples bear testimony of an apostate religion that was detestable to the Holy God—but there was one notable exception...

Three wise men traveling from the east (probably Babylon) followed the star of God. They had set out to find the promised Seed—the legitimate Son of God, born of a truly virgin woman. These men were schooled in the astrology of the Chaldeans, but it is probable a famous Jewish prophet had taught their ancestors. This Jew had ascended the hierarchy of ruling elite in Babylon hundreds of years before. His name was Daniel—the same prophet who wrote the Old Testament book bearing his name. Daniel likely knew God's message of truth in the constellations. His parents probably instructed him about these heavenly signs. Daniel understood God's promise to provide the Seed who would one day redeem mankind. His own prophecies describe this God/Man as Redeemer of the Jewish nation. Daniel presumably imparted his knowledge to astrologers during his lifetime in Babylon. After all, Daniel saved the lives of these men by describing, then interpreting a dream of King Nebuchadnezzar![156] Daniel's God must have significantly impressed these counselors of the King. Perhaps they listened intently as Daniel taught them about the Seed of God who would someday come into the world of mankind. These men likely passed down Daniel's prophetic wisdom through subsequent generations. When God's Son was born in humble circumstances over four-hundred years later, three wise men of Babylon apprehended the heavenly 'signs' the Lord provided them. They followed a star to the ultimate place of worship—a stable, where the Son of God lay in a lonely manger. The promised Seed was virtually unnoticed by the rest of the world. In that unlikely place, three wise men (astrologers) met the One True God and Redeemer of mankind.

* * * * * * * * *

The mystery religion of Babylon has remained an

abomination to God since its inception. Most false religions practiced by people of this world originated from the mystery religion of Babylon. This mystery religion is destined for a final judgment by fire. The God of the universe will someday destroy it along with those who have propagated it through the millennia. Prophetic writers of the Old and New Testaments had much to say about this coming judgment. The last book of the Bible spends two entire chapters discussing this subject. The author will highlight several verses from these chapters to demonstrate this fact:

> One of the seven angels who had the seven bowls came and said to me, 'Come, I will show you the punishment of the great prostitute, who sits on many waters. With her the kings of the earth committed adultery and the inhabitants of the earth were intoxicated with the wine of her adulteries.'
> Then the angel carried me away in the Spirit into a desert. There I saw a woman sitting on a scarlet beast that was covered with blasphemous names and had seven heads and ten horns. The woman was dressed in purple and scarlet, and was glittering with gold, precious stones and pearls. She held a golden cup in her hand, filled with abominable things and the filth of her adulteries. This title was written on her forehead: 'Mystery Babylon the Great The Mother of Prostitutes and of the Abominations of the Earth.'
> I saw that the woman was drunk with the blood of the saints, the blood of those who bore testimony to Jesus. When I saw her, I was greatly astonished. Then the angel said to me, 'The waters you saw, where the prostitute sits, are the peoples, multitudes, nations and languages. The beast and the ten horns you saw will hate the prostitute. They

will bring her to ruin and leave her naked; they will eat her flesh and burn her with fire. For God has put it into their hearts to accomplish His purpose by agreeing to give the beast their power to rule, until God's words are fulfilled. The woman you saw is the great city that rules over the kings of the earth.'[157]

The woman portrayed in these prophecies is the mystery religion of Babylon, and she is destined for the fire of God's wrath. Remarkably, she is a prostitute—like Semiramis, the founder of this wicked religion. This Scripture portrays her committing adulteries with kings and multitudes from various nationalities and *languages*. She holds a *golden cup* in her hand, filled with the abominable filth of her adulteries. Artwork of antiquity also depicts the goddess of heaven (Semiramis) holding a golden cup in her hand.[158] The prostitute in this prophecy has adorned herself with enticing things of this world—gold, precious jewels, and an alluring appearance. Likewise, the adulterous mystery religion seduces people from all nations and languages into its far-reaching tentacles. A wicked prostitute, Semiramis, seduced and deceived people of the New World to follow her in a momentous rebellion against the True God of the universe. Indeed, she is not the Goddess of Heaven! Semiramis is the prostitute of hell! Unfortunately, she will drag countless souls into the fiery cauldron of God's judgment!

Chapter 5

Discussion of the History of the Post-Flood Civilization

The Bible says little about people of the immediate post-flood era, except for Nimrod's conquests and God's judgment of languages at Babel. However, extra-Biblical records describe these civilizations in great detail. One can glean information about the post-flood world by studying archeological evidence from that period.

The Book of Genesis records post-flood civilization began where Noah's ark landed on Mount Ararat, which lies between the Black Sea and Caspian Sea—in present day Georgia, Armenia, or Turkey. Within several decades, most of Ham's family moved southward into the Mesopotamian Valley. This move likely occurred following the time when Ham saw his father lying drunk and naked in his tent.[159] Considerable speculation persists regarding the exact nature of that sin. Theologians will continue to debate those possibilities. However, interesting information in The Book of Jasher (extra-Biblical document) claims Ham stole Noah's garment while he lay drunk in his tent. The Book of Jasher also indicates this was the original garment God made for

Adam shortly before he was banished from the Garden of Eden. Other sources also make this claim.[160] The eminent Jewish rabbi, Eleazer, and other reputable rabbis believed the Hebrew word for nakedness in Genesis 9:22 more accurately refers to loss of skin covering. They also agree that Ham took the garment God had made for Adam. They postulated Ham took the garment as an attempt to steal the spiritual inheritance from his father. When Noah awoke he cursed Ham's son, Canaan. Noah subsequently recognized the priesthood of his older son, Shem. Ham later gave the garment to his oldest son, Cush, who ultimately conferred it to *his* elder son, Nimrod. According to the Jewish Talmud, Nimrod's hunting success resulted from wearing the coat of skin God made for Adam.[161] This amazing tale is somewhat difficult to believe, but it makes for interesting novel material! Ham and his family moved south into Mesopotamia following that sordid event.

Many other descendants of Noah subsequently followed Ham's family into this new land. They were attracted to the warm climate and fertile soil. In fact, the majority of the earth's population resided in the Mesopotamian Valley several hundred years after the flood. Most archeologists agree the first civilization of mankind began in this immense valley—the Sumerian civilization.

Archeological evidence for ancient civilization in Mesopotamia is nothing less than astounding! Scientists cannot explain the sudden appearance of a highly advanced culture in the Mesopotamian Valley. The abrupt appearance of similar civilizations in other parts of the world far removed from Mesopotamia has further perplexed archeologists. These civilizations appeared simultaneously within several hundred years after the remarkable Sumerian civilization. They arose as well-advanced societies from Egypt all the way to South America. All had technological advances similar to the Sumerians—huge pyramids, an advanced understanding of mathematics and astronomy, and agriculture. They tracked time and seasons with calendars. Scientists have never adequately accounted for this amazing phenomenon. However, God's Word satisfactorily explains this incredible occurrence. The Bible states God dispersed people with many languages from Babel over the entire world. People quickly left the Mesopotamian Valley following God's judgment. They took their knowledge from the Sumerian civilization to new lands. Some groups traveled thousands of miles to settle new continents.

* * * * * * * * *

Sumerians were Hamitic people—a homogeneous race, for the most part. For a period of time (decades or longer), Sumerian people dwelled with their extended families in small clannish units. The population of Mesopotamia grew quickly. The clans moved together in larger units—villages, and then these coalesced to form cities. Several factors accounted for this migration into cities: safety from predatory animals, recurrent flooding of the great rivers, increased agricultural productivity, and protection against starvation.

Technology advanced rapidly as larger cities developed. The proliferation of inventions within this civilization has amazed scientists. Sumerians invented the wheel, and shortly thereafter, they built carts for hauling goods throughout Mesopotamia. Sumerians invented the pottery wheel, which enabled mass production of high quality pottery. Convincing evidence suggests writing and the recording of business transactions began in the Sumerian culture.[162] The earliest known description of paradise has been found in the form of a poem inscribed on a clay tablet from ancient Sumeria.[163] It describes a past in which people lived in a god-created paradise, where no animals threatened humanity and conflicts did not exist among people. The poem suggests that the

Sumerian god Enki found some inappropriate behavior among humans and subsequently judged mankind with conflict, wars, and the confusion of languages.[164] Another surviving clay tablet from Sumerian excavations has a poem describing the great flood and the man who survived it on a great boat, carrying with him vegetation and the 'seed of mankind.'[165]

The Sumerians developed an extensive commerce by land and sea, building ships and importing items from afar made from wood, stone, tin and copper. Archeologists have found goods from Egypt and India in the rubble of Sumerian cities.[166]

Government quickly evolved in each Sumerian city.[167] Schooling in early Sumerian civilization was associated with the priesthood and took place in the temples.[168]

Sumerians developed mathematics and astronomy.[169] They accurately tracked the time and seasons. In addition, Sumerians excelled in agriculture, engineering, masonry, animal husbandry and even metallurgy. They drained swampy, mosquito-infested lands adjacent to the large rivers by digging irrigation canals into parched farmlands.[170] They even discovered how to brew beer.[171] They also distilled wine but clearly derived that skill from their ancestor, Noah.

Substantial archeological evidence reveals the Sumerians as the inventors of many war implements.[172] Chariots, spears, swords, bows, arrows, and helmets have all been unearthed in archeological digs of that civilization. The Sumerians also introduced slavery in the post-flood world.[173] They enslaved fellow Sumerians and people beyond the borders of Sumer they had captured in various wars.

Sumerians initially made farm and war implements from copper, but soon learned to smelt tin and copper together to make bronze. Bronze was harder and more durable than copper. Deposits of copper and tin were not present in the Mesopotamian Valley. Sumerians traveled great distances to obtain these materials. Copper deposits were found in mountains north of Mesopotamia, but deposits of tin were unknown in the Middle East. These people may have journeyed as far as the British Isles, or even North and South America, to obtain tin.[174] Furthermore, these metals were not found as surface materials. They had to be mined in sophisticated ways. An interesting article appeared in a 1975 Time magazine. The following quotation was obtained from that article.

> Archeologists once thought that Bronze Age people got their metals largely by chipping away at surface rocks; at most, they would tunnel only a few dozen feet. The newly discovered mine shows that the Bronze Age miners were far more skilled and adventurous than that. Located at the base of towering 2,200-foot red sandstone cliffs, the mine contains a complex, multilevel network of some 200 shafts and galleries.... Bronze Age miners were able to produce 22 pound copper ingots that were 97% to 98% pure, a degree of purity not exceeded until modern times.[175]

Archeologists have excavated many bronze farm and war implements from Sumerian ruins.

How did this civilization advance so rapidly? Anthropologists do not have good answers to this question. Perhaps the Sumerians used technologies that existed at an earlier time. The Holy Scriptures affirmatively support this hypothesis. Several archeological finds also corroborate this. The Book of Genesis describes the lineage of Cain (the first son of Adam, who killed his brother). His descendants rapidly made technological advances in the antediluvian world. The Scriptures record a descendant six generations from Cain invented music. The Bible lists another as the founder of animal husbandry, and a seventh generation descendant of Cain, Tubal-Cain, forged all kinds of tools from bronze and iron.[176] The knowledge for these technologies probably traveled with Noah and his sons on the ark. When conditions became ripe for introducing them into the New World, these new inventions suddenly appeared. Indeed, conditions did become suitable in the Mesopotamian Valley—in Sumerian cities. Archeologists have also found implements of iron and bronze in excavations of the ancient Egyptian civilization. They have unearthed musical instruments from ancient Sumerian and Egyptian cultures, as well.

People have unearthed some amazing artifacts, which suggest extraordinary intelligence of our antediluvian ancestors. Archeologists excavated the ruins of Kish between 1923 and 1933. Digging to virgin soil, 60 feet below the top of the mound, the expedition found remains of several ancient cultures. A band of alluvial soil about 40 feet below the surface indicated that Kish had been flooded in about 3200 BC. Many take this to be evidence of the great Biblical flood. Most astounding was the discovery, below the flood stratum of a four-wheeled chariot, the earliest known wheeled vehicle.[177]

A rock hound found a geode in the Cosa Mountains of California. When he split the geode in half, he found an ancient electrical device of some sort: Sliced in two, the object showed a hexagonal part, a porcelain or ceramic insulator with a central metallic shaft, and the remains of a corroded piece of metal with threads. The overall impression is that the object in the geode was man-made and not a bizarre trick of nature. It appeared to be some kind of electrical device—specifically, a spark plug.[178] People have discovered other unusual artifacts at random locations throughout the world. These may point to the existence of a very advanced civilization prior to the flood. Very little record of that civilization remains, due to the cataclysmic change that occurred in the surface of the earth during the worldwide flood. Donald Chittick has provided a more detailed discussion about advanced technologies of ancient cultures.[179]

The Bible is strangely silent about numerous inventions and technologies that developed in the time of Nimrod. Advances of the antediluvian world are only briefly mentioned in the pages of Scripture. However, God had much to say about the wicked lineage of Cain. Many great Empires existed prior to the life of Christ. They and their leaders are mentioned by name in Scripture, but the Bible records virtually nothing about their amazing achievements.

Men are quick to record their new inventions and technologies. However, it appears God is not as impressed with these human accomplishments. The Apostle Paul exhorts the Corinthians with the following advice: "the foolishness of God is wiser than man's wisdom, and the weakness of God is stronger than man's strength."[180]

Civilizations demonstrating man's greatest achievements are frequently associated with enormous spiritual depravity. Biblical records suggest God intervenes with His judgment during times when men favorably record their own history. This is because moral depravity and wickedness simultaneously occur at these times. He judged mankind by the cataclysmic worldwide flood, which destroyed the entire human race—Noah's family being the exception. God's next global intervention occurred at the Tower of Babel, where He gave the tongues of many languages to mankind. God previously commanded the human race to disperse over the entire earth. Nimrod and most people of the post-flood world rebelled against God's command, refusing to leave their cities. The confusion of one universal language accomplished God's goal. His judgment at Babel also preserved the human lineage carrying His prophesied Seed. God's judgment has subsequently fallen upon many advanced empires of history. These powerful empires often ended abruptly after facing God's wrath.

Biblical Scriptures clearly prophesy a future worldwide intervention of God. These prophetic Scriptures describe God's terrible wrath meted out to the world's inhabitants. God will wrest dominion of this world from His archenemy once and for all. His judgment of eternal fire is reserved for Satan and the souls of men who have followed the mystery religion of Babylon throughout the ages. All God's enemies, including Nimrod, are destined for this horrific judgment.

* * * * * * * * * *

Some people in this present world live in cultures less advanced than the ancient Sumerian civilization, which flourished 5,000 years ago! In fact, citizens of many countries currently endure more primitive living conditions than existed in the antediluvian world, 6,000 years ago! Yet, what appears advanced to man is foolishness to God.

Americans once lived in quite archaic conditions. Nimrod and his cronies would not have enjoyed that environment. American pioneers had no brick masons to build their homes. They did not pave streets with bricks, nor build defensive walls around their cities. Dangers of the American wilderness possibly surpassed those facing the Sumerians. However, our forefathers zealously followed God, founding this great nation upon Judeo-Christian principles. It has rapidly advanced over the past 250 years because God rewarded their faithfulness. These men and women established the spiritual foundation of our remarkable nation. Today, Americans reap the rewards of their sacrifices.

Citizens of western civilization live in a precarious time—much like the days of Nimrod. Once again, man's technology has rapidly advanced. Most people enjoy the benefits of television, computers, impressive health care, and space exploration. Mankind has learned to clone life—even human life. Scientists have mapped the human genome. Soon man will create bacterial life in test tubes. What marvelous accomplishments! What good history this will make! But that history will not find its way into God's record book. God will not bother to note these accomplishments. They are mere foolishness to Him. He will record the spiritual depravity, which has entered the lives of our people. He will chronicle the violence and sexual immorality that have rapidly exploded in present times. He has counted each of the millions of infants sacrificed on the altar of abortion and stem cell research. God has already documented all this in His record, as He did in the days of Nimrod. Once again, He is poised to intervene in the history of mankind.....

Bibliography

The Bible - New International Version.
The Book of Jasher
The Jerusalem Targum
Adam, Ben. *The Origin of Heathendom*. Minneapolis;
  Bethany Fellowship, 1963.
Algaze, Guillermo. *The Uruk Expansion*. **Current
  Anthropology**. December, 1989.
Black, Jeremy and Green, Anthony. *Gods, Demons and
  Symbols of Ancient Mesopotamia: An Illustrated
Dictionary*. University of Texas Press; Austin, 1992.
Bullinger, E.W. *Appendixes to the Companion Bible.*
Bullinger, E.W. *The Witness of the Stars*. Kregel, 1893.
Bury, J.B., Cook, S.A., Adcock, M.A., *The Cambridge
  Ancient History*. Cambridge Univ. Press, 1965.
Camping, Harold. *The Biblical Calendar of History*.
  Family Stations, Inc.; Oakland, Calif., 1999
Chittick, Donald. *The Puzzle of Ancient Man*. Creation
  Compass, 1997.
Cooper, B.A. *After the Flood*. New Wine Press, 1995.
Corliss, William. *Ancient Man: A Handbook of Puzzling
  Artifacts*. The Sourcebook Project, 1978.
Crawford, Harriet. *Sumer and the Sumerians*. Cambridge
  University Press; Cambridge, 1991.
Custance, Arthur. *Noah's Three Sons.* Zondervan
  Publishing House; Grand Rapids, 1975.

Diodorus Siculus. *Antiquities of Asia, Book II of the Library of History*. Transaction Publishers, 1989.

Diodorus Siculus. *Library of History, Books I-VI*. Translated by C.H. Oldfather. Harvard University Press; Cambridge, Mass., 1937.

Ginzberg, Louis. *The Legends of the Jews*. The Johns Hopkins University Press, 1937,

Hislop, Alexander. *The Two Babylons*. Loizeaux Brothers; Neptune, New Jersey, 1959.

The History of Herodotus. *Grolier Classics*. Translated by George Rawlinson. Grolier Inc., 1956. pg 185-208

Hooke, S.H. *Middle Eastern Mythology*. Penguin Books; New York, 1963.

Jacobsen, Thorkild. *The Treasures of Darkness*. Yale University Press; New Haven, 1976.

Josephus, Flavius. *Antiquities of the Jews*.

Kramer, S.N. *History Begins at Sumer*. University of Pennsylvania Press; Philadelphia, 1981.

Kramer, S.N. and Maier, John. *Myths of Enki, the Crafty God*. Oxford Univ. Press; New York, 1989.

Kramer, S.N. *The Sumerians*. The University of Chicago Press; Chicago, 1963.

Kramer, S.N. *Sumerian Mythology*. Harper & Brothers; New York, 1961.

Leupold, Herbert. *Exposition of Genesis*. Baker Book House; Grand Rapids, 1949.

Morris, Henry. *The Genesis Record*. Baker Book House, 1976.

Nibley, Hugh. *Collected Works of Hugh Nibley*. Volume 5, Part 2.

Patton, Robert. *OOPARTS*. Omni; September, 1982.

Pritchard, J.B. *Ancient Near Eastern Texts Relating to the Old Testament*. Princeton, 1955.

Roux, Georges. *Ancient Iraq*. Penguin Books, 1992.

Rowton, M.B. *The Cambridge Ancient History*. Cambridge University Press, 1964.

Seiss, Joseph. *The Gospel in the Stars of Primevil Astronomy*. Kregel, 1884.

Smith, W. Robertson. *Ctesias and the Semiramis Legend*. English Historical Review.

Speiser, E.A. *In Search of Nimrod*. Eretz_Israel, Mazar Volume, 1958.

Stedman, Ray. *The Beginnings*. Word Books, 1978.

Steiger, Brad. *Were Ancient Scientists Really Tuned to Today?* Parade; March, 1979.

Siseman, P.J. *New Discoveries in Babylonia about Genesis*. Marshall, Morgan, and Scott, 1946.

Whyfe-Melville, G.J. *Sarchedon: A Legend of the Great Queen*

Whiston, William. *Josephus: Complete Works*. Pickering & Inglis; London, 1981.

Whitlock, R. *Here be Dragons*. George Allen & Unwin; Boston, 1983.

Wolkstein, Diane and Kramer, S.N. *Inanna: Queen of Heaven and Earth*. Harper & Row; NY., 1983

Wooley, Sir Leonard. *The Beginings of Civilization*. The New York American Library, 1965

Endnotes

1 http://www.1dolphin.org/Nimrod.html; G. Edward Foryan—author

2 E.A. Speiser; **"In Search of the Biblical Nimrod"**

3 http://www.mazzaroth.com/ChapterFour/SargonDidHeExist.htm

4 Genesis 10:6-8; **"The Bible"**

5 http://www.fordham.edu/halsall/ancient/2300sargon1.html

6 http://members.tripod.com/historel/orient/01mesop.htm

7 http://www.mazzaroth.com/ChapterFour/SargonDidHexist.htm

8 ibid

9 William Whiston; **Josephus, Complete Works**. Louis Ginzberg; "**The Legends of the Jews;**" Volume 1; pg 177-234 "**The Book of Jasher**"

10 Ibid
Genesis 14:1-17; "**The Bible**"

11 Genesis 10:8-12; **"The Bible"**

12 http://www.crystalinks.com/sumerhistory.html

13 Genesis 10:6-12; **"The Bible"**

14 Alexander Hislop; **"The Two Babylons;"** pg 28

15 Micah 5:6; **"The Bible"**

16 M.B. Rowton; **"The Cambridge Ancient History."** Samuel Noah Kramer; **"History Begins at Sumer. "** http://www.crystalinks.com/sumerhistory.html http://members.tripod.com/histororel/orient/01mesop.hem

17 http://www.assyriansocietycanada.org/legend_of_semiramis.htm http://www.cwd.co.uk/babel/nimrod.htm

18 http://www.levendwater.org/companion/append28.html

19 **The Book of Jasher 7:44-45**

20 Justin's Trogus Pompeius; "History Rom. Script;" vol 2; pg 615

21 Diodorus Siculus; **"Library of History"**

22 Flavius Josephus; **"Antiquities of the Jews"**

23 Justin; **"Histori Romani Scriptorium"**

24 Genesis 11:10-32; **"The Bible"**

25 Genesis 14:1-17; **"The Bible"**

26 Genesis 11:10-11; **"The Bible"**

27 Genesis 10:25; **"The Bible"**

28 Genesis 10:1-8; **"The Bible"**

29 Alexander Hislop; **"The Two Babylons;"** pgs 55-56, 63-66 Apollodorus; Bibliotheca,lib. i. cap. 4 and 7; pg 17

30 Alexander Hislop; **"The Two Babylons;"** pgs 55-56, 63-66

31 ibid

32 ibid; pg 62

33 ibid; pg 66-67

34 Genesis 10:11; **"The Bible"**

35 http://www.assyriansocietycanada.org/legend_of_semiramis.htm
http://www.ldolphin.org/Nimrod.html; G. Edward Foryan – author
Alexander Hislop; **"The Two Babylons;"** pg 34, 43-44, 63

36 http://www.onesimus@ix.netcom.com; Bryce Self—author of article on Semiramis

37 Genesis 4:1-17; **"The Bible"**

38 Genesis 6:1-5; **"The Bible"**

39 http://www.mazzaroth.com/ChapterThree/BiblicalinfoOfGiants.htm

40 Genesis 10:9; **"The Bible"**

41 Alexander Hislop; **"The Two Babylons;"** pg 44-46, et al

42 Job 40:15- 41:34; **"The Bible"**

43 Alexander Hislop; **"The Two Babylons;"** pg 44-46
http://www.cwd.co.uk/babel/nimrod.htm

44 Alexander Hislop; **"The Two Babylons;"** pg 44-46

45 Alexander Hislop; **"The Two Babylons;"** pg 56, 62, 68-70, et al

46 Alexander Hislop; **"The Two Babylons;"** pg 22, 43, 86-88,162, et al

47 http://www.fsmitha.com/h1/ch01.htm
http://www.mystae.com/restricted/streams/scripts/ishtar.html

48 Diane Wolkstein and Samuel Kramer; **"Inanna: Queen of Heaven and Earth."** Samuel Noah Kramer; **"Sumerian Mythology."**

http://www.members.bellatlantic.net/~vze33gpz/sumer-faq.html; pg 9-10

49 http://www.crystalinks.com/sumergods2.html

50 Diane Wolkstein and Samuel Kramer; "**Inanna: Queen of Heaven and Earth.**" Samuel Noah Kramer; "**Sumerian Mythology.**"

51 Sir James George Frazer; "**The Illustrated Golden Bough**"

52 http://www.mystae.com/restricted/streams/scripts/ishtar.html

53 Diane Wolkstein and Samuel Kramer; "**Inanna: Queen of Heaven and Earth.** Samuel Noah Kramer; "**Sumerian Mythology.**" Thorkild Jacobsen; "**The Treasures of Darkness**"

54 http://www.members.bellatlantic.net/~vze33gpz/sumer-faq.html; pg 14-16

55 ibid

56 http://www.assyriansocietycanada.org/legend_of_semiramis.htm

57 http://www.onesimus@ix.netcom.com; Bryce Self—author of article on Semiramis

58 ibid

59 http://home.cfl.rr.com/crossland/AncientCivilizations/Middle_East_Civilizat.../sumerians.htm

60 http://www.mystae.com/restricted/streams/scripts/ishtar.html

61 Black and Green; "Gods, Demons and Symbols of Ancient Mesopotamia" http://www.mystae.com/restricted/streams/scripts/ishtar.html

62 http://www.assyriansocietycanada.org/legend_of_semiramis.htm

63 ibid

64 ibid
http://www.onesimus@ix.netcom.com; Bryce Self—author of article on Semiramis

65 ibid

66 ibid

67 http://home.cfl.rr.com/crossland/AncientCivilizations/Middle_East_Civilizat.../sumerians.htm

68 Henry Morris; "The Genesis Record;" pg 250

69 ibid

70 Henry Morris; "The Genesis Record;" pg 250

71 ibid; pg 254-256

72 ibid; pg 246-249

73 ibid; pg 259

74 ibid; pg 259

75 Henry Morris; "The Genesis Record;" pg 258

76 Henry Morris; "The Genesis Record;" pg 259 Genesis 10:21-32; "**The Bible**"

77 Genesis 3:15; "**The Bible**"

78 Henry Morris; "The Genesis Record;" pg 259-260 Genesis 11:10-26; Matthew 1:1-6; Luke 3:23-36; "**The Bible**"

79 Matthew 2:1-12; "**The Bible**"

80 Alexander Hislop; "**The Two Babylons;**" pg 5, 69-70 http://www.cwd.co.uk/babel/nimrod.htm

81 Diodorus of Sicily; "**The Library of History;**" **Book VI**

82 Henry Morris; "**The Genesis Record;**" pg 265

83 Alexander Hislop; "**The Two Babylons;**" pg 5, 69-70, et al

84 http://www.members.bellatlantic.net/~vze33gpz/sumer-faq.html; pg 3

85 http://www.crystalinks.com/sumerhistory.html http://www.members.bellatlantic.net/~vze33gpz/sumer-faq.html; pg 3

86 Alexander Hislop; "**The Two Babylons;**" pg 44, 246, et al Henry Morris; "**The Genesis Record;**" pg 264

87 ibid

88 http://www.ldolphin.org/Nimrod.html; G. Edward Foryan – author http://www.mazzaroth.com/ChapterThree/SumerianInfoOfAnnunaki-Anakim.htm

89 http://www.onesimus@ix.netcom.com; Bryce Self—author of article on Nimrod

90 Alexander Hislop; "**The Two Babylons;**" pg 20-22, 31, 43-46, 50-56, 63-66, 101-105, et al

91 Alexander Hislop; "**The Two Babylons;**" pg 44-46

92 ibid; pg 62, 113-114, et al

93 ibid; pg 229, 231, 315, et al

94 Leviticus 20:2; "**The Bible**"

95 Jeremiah 49:1; "**The Bible**"

96 Jeremiah 32:33-35; "**The Bible**"

97 Alexander Hislop; "**The Two Babylons;**" pg 22, 33, 46-49

98 Alexander Hislop; "**The Two Babylons;**" pg 31-35; 42-43; 97-98

99 Alexander Hislop; "**The Two Babylons;**" pg 231

100 Eusebius; "**De Laud. Constantini**;" chap. 13; pg 267

101 Alexander Hislop; "**The Two Babylons**;" pg 93-96

102 Alexander Hislop; "**The Two Babylons**;" pg 23-25

103 ibid; pg 59, 61-67, 71, 120-121,170, 180, et al

104 Alexander Hislop; "**The Two Babylons**;" pg 70

105 ibid; pg 71-72

106 ibid; pg 72

107 ibid; pg 70

108 ibid; pg 73

109 http//www.ldolphin.org/Nimrod.html; Bryce Self—author

110 Alexander Hislop; "**The Two Babylons**;" pg 227

111 Alexander Hislop; "**The Two Babylons**;" pg 98, 227-228

112 ibid; pg 228-232

113 Romans 1:21-23; "**The Bible**"

114 Revelation 12:1-5; "**The Bible**"

115 1 Corinthians 2:8; "**The Bible**"

116 1Corinthians 15:23; "**The Bible**"

117 Alexander Hislop; "**The Two Babylons**;" pg 25

118 Jeremiah 19:3-5; "**The Bible**"

119 Alexander Hislop; "**The Two Babylons**;" pg 25

120 ibid; pg 25-26

121 ibid; pg 26

122 ibid; pg 26

123 ibid

124 Alexander Hislop; "**The Two Babylons**;" pg 26-28

125 ibid; pg 5, 20-21, 30-31, 74-75, 141
http://www.assyriansocietycanada.org/legend_of_semiramis.htm

126 ibid

127 http://www.mystae.com/restricted/streams/scripts/ishtar.html

128 ibid

129 Alexander Hislop; "**The Two Babylons**;" pg 103-113

130 Alexander Hislop; "**The Two Babylons**;" pg 77

131 Alexander Hislop; "**The Two Babylons**;" pg 20

132 ibid

133 ibid

134 ibid

135 Alexander Hislop; **"The Two Babylons;"** pg 20

136 ibid

137 ibid; pg 20, 30

138 Acts 19:23-41; **"The Bible"**

139 Alexander Hislop; **"The Two Babylons;"** pg 308

140 Jeremiah 44:19-23; **"The Bible"**

141 Alexander Hislop; **"The Two Babylons;"** pg 78-79

142 Jeremiah 23:5; 33:15; Isaiah 4:2; **"The Bible"**

143 Alexander Hislop; **"The Two Babylons;"** pg 78-79

144 Alexander Hislop; **"The Two Babylons;"** pg 74-75; 87-88; 160

145 Revelation 17:2; **"The Bible"**

146 E.W. Bullinger; **"Appendixes to the Companion Bible"** Joseph Augustus Seiss; **"The Gospel in the Stars of Primeval Astronomy"** http://www.levendwater.org/companion/append12.html Henry Morris; "The Genesis Record;" pg 265

147 Genesis 1:14-17; **"The Bible"**

148 Romans 1:20; **"The Bible"**

149 E.W. Bullinger; **"Appendixes to the Companion Bible"** Joseph Augustus Seiss; **"The Gospel in the Stars of Primeval Astronomy"** http://www.levendwater.org/companion/append12.html

150 Henry Morris; **"The Genesis Record;"** pg 265

151 ibid

152 http//www.ldolphin.org/Nimrod.html

153 Alexander Hislop; **"The Two Babylons;"** pg 31-35; 41-5; 78, 93-97; et al

154 ibid; pg 25-26

155 Alexander Hislop; **"The Two Babylons;"** pg 5, 13, 40, 56, 74-80, 85

156 Daniel 2:24-45; **"The Bible"**

157 Rev 17:1-6; 15-18; **"The Bible"**

158 Alexander Hislop; **"The Two Babylons;"** pg 4-5

159 Gen 9:21-27; **"The Bible"**

160 **Collected Works of Hugh Nibley**; Vol. 5; Part 2; Ch. 1, pp. 169-171

161 **Collected Works of Hugh Nibley**; Vol. 5; Part 2; Ch. 1, pp. 169-171

162 http://www.fsmitha.com/h1/ch01.htm http://www.bibleandscience.com/Sumerians.htm

163 http://www.fsmitha.com/h1/ch01.htm

164 ibid

165 ibid

166 http://home.cfl.rr.com/crossland/AncientCivilizations/Middle_East
_Civilizat.../sumerians.htm

167 ibid

168 http://www.fsmitha.com/h1/ch01.htm

169 http://www.fsmitha.com/h1/ch01.htm
http://home.cfl.rr.com/crossland/AncientCivilizations/Middle_East
_Civilizat.../sumerians.htm

170 http://homepage.ntlworld.com/giza.necropolis/development/
Vanessa/civ3.htm

171 http://www.fsmitha.com/h1/ch01.htm
http://www.eat-online.net/english/habits/beer_in_ancient_times.htm

172 http://www.inisfail.com/~ancients/sumerians.html

173 http://www.fsmitha.com/h1/ch01.htm

174 Donald E. Chittick; "**The Puzzle of Ancient Man.**"

175 "**The Oldest Mine?**" Time, January 13, 1975, pg. 65

176 Genesis 4:20-22; "**The Bible**"

177 http://www.crystalinks.com/sumerhistory.html

178 Brad Steiger; "**Were Ancient Scientists Really Tuned to Today?**"
Parade; March 4, 1979; pg 10

179 Donald E. Chittick; " **The Puzzle of Ancient Man**"

180 1 Corinthians; 1:25; "**The Bible**"

Printed in the United States
27255LVS00009B/187-327

9 781594 678431